Parenting Dyslexia

Parenting Dyslexia

A Comprehensive Guide to Helping
Kids Combat Shame, Build Confidence,
and Achieve Their True Potential

Lisa Rappaport, PhD,
and Jody Lyons, MEd

NEW YORK BOSTON

Note: The information in this book is true and complete to the best of our knowledge. This book is intended only as an informative guide for those wishing to know more about health issues. In no way is this book intended to replace, countermand, or conflict with the advice given to you by your own physician. The ultimate decision concerning care should be made between you and your doctor. We strongly recommend you follow their advice. Information in this book is general and is offered with no guarantees on the part of the authors or Balance. The authors and publisher disclaim all liability in connection with the use of this book.

Copyright © 2025 by Lisa Rappaport and Jody Lyons

Cover design by YY Liak. Cover illustration © Tannikart/Shutterstock. Cover copyright © 2025 by Hachette Book Group, Inc.

Hachette Book Group supports the right to free expression and the value of copyright. The purpose of copyright is to encourage writers and artists to produce the creative works that enrich our culture.

The scanning, uploading, and distribution of this book without permission is a theft of the author's intellectual property. If you would like permission to use material from the book (other than for review purposes), please contact permissions@hbgusa.com. Thank you for your support of the author's rights.

Balance
Hachette Book Group
1290 Avenue of the Americas
New York, NY 10104
GCP-Balance.com
@GCPBalance

First Edition: April 2025

Balance is an imprint of Grand Central Publishing. The Balance name and logo are registered trademarks of Hachette Book Group, Inc.

The publisher is not responsible for websites (or their content) that are not owned by the publisher.

The Hachette Speakers Bureau provides a wide range of authors for speaking events. To find out more, go to hachettespeakersbureau.com or email HachetteSpeakers@hbgusa.com.

Balance books may be purchased in bulk for business, educational, or promotional use. For information, please contact your local bookseller or the Hachette Book Group Special Markets Department at special.markets@hbgusa.com.

Print book interior design by Sheryl Kober.

Library of Congress Control Number: 2024951433

ISBNs: 978-0-306-83458-5 (paperback); 978-0-306-83459-2 (ebook)

Printed in the United States of America

LSC-C

Printing 1, 2025

This book is dedicated to my mom, who saw my potential and never gave up on me, no matter how bad things got. You continue to be my unrelenting champion and my best friend. Words can't express how much I love you.—Lisa

To my cousin Adam and the legions of bright neurodiverse thinkers like him, whose lives were forever impacted at a delicate age by self-doubt and self-judgment.—Jody

Dyslexics think differently. They are intuitive and excel at problem solving, seeing the big picture, and simplifying. They feast on visualizing, abstract thinking, and thinking out of the box.... Adult dyslexics are tough: Having struggled, they are used to adversity; hard work and perseverance now come naturally. Having experienced failure, they are fearless, undaunted by setbacks. Repetition and practice are a way of life. Each person I've focused on was rescued by a special person—a parent or a teacher—who saw the raw talent and nurtured it in the midst of all the naysayers. Yes, the symptoms of dyslexia persist, but they needn't interfere with success.

—SALLY SHAYWITZ, MD, AND JONATHAN SHAYWITZ, MD,
OVERCOMING DYSLEXIA

Shame hates it when we reach out and tell our story. It hates having words wrapped around it—it can't survive being shared. Shame loves secrecy.

—BRENÉ BROWN, THE GIFTS OF IMPERFECTION

Contents

Foreword ix
Introduction xi

Part 1: The World of Dyslexia

CHAPTER 1: Understanding Dyslexia 3
CHAPTER 2: Diagnosing Dyslexia 23
CHAPTER 3: Moving Forward After a Diagnosis 41
CHAPTER 4: Enhancing Skills from Home 55

Part 2: Adapting to Dyslexia's Challenges

CHAPTER 5: Building the Foundation for Your Family Team 79
CHAPTER 6: Promoting the Best Study Skills and Habits 99
CHAPTER 7: Practices to Bolster Self-Esteem 119

Part 3: Navigating Challenges in School

CHAPTER 8: Skill Building in Elementary School 147
CHAPTER 9: Adapting to Middle School 157
CHAPTER 10: Thriving in High School 181
CHAPTER 11: The Path to Higher Education 203
CHAPTER 12: Life After College 217

Part 4: Making Peace with Dyslexia

CHAPTER 13: A Bright Future 225
AFTERWORD: More Dyslexia Confessions 229

Resources 237
Glossary 243
Notes 251
Bibliography 255
Acknowledgments 259
Index 265

Foreword

Raising children is a journey filled with moments of joy, discovery, and, sometimes, unexpected challenges. As parents, we want nothing more than to watch our kids thrive. But when a child is diagnosed with dyslexia, it can feel as though the path we've been following has suddenly veered into a shadowy and unfamiliar forest. The once-straightforward route to learning now demands that we quickly acquire new knowledge to understand and advocate for our child's academic needs.

Parenting Dyslexia is an illuminating, practical guide for parents suddenly navigating an unfamiliar world. It offers a roadmap to understanding dyslexia and to embracing it as part of your child's unique learning profile. With warmth, compassion, and a wealth of practical advice, Lisa Rappaport, PhD, and Jody Lyons, MEd, demystify the complexities of dyslexia and provide clear, actionable steps so that you can support your child every step of the way.

Dr. Rappaport brings an unparalleled depth of knowledge to this book. As both a professional in the field and someone who has experienced dyslexia firsthand, she offers insights that extend beyond academic theory. Her training, combined with her personal experience, allows her to understand the particular challenges children with dyslexia face, both in the classroom and in everyday life. She bridges the gap between clinical knowledge and lived experience, providing tools grounded in both science and compassion.

Foreword

One of the most powerful aspects of this book is how it addresses not just the academic difficulties children with dyslexia face but also the emotional toll a diagnosis can take. Dr. Rappaport and Ms. Lyons understand that dyslexia can bring feelings of frustration, self-doubt, and anxiety, and offer strategies to help you nurture your child's confidence and emotional well-being. Their advice is designed to ensure that your child feels supported, understood, and capable, even as they make their way along the sometimes-bumpy road to learning.

But this book does far more than help parents support their children. It provides adults with exactly the reinforcement they need as well. Of course, a child's dyslexia diagnosis can come as a relief when it provides a helpful explanation for why a child has been struggling at school. At the same time, a dyslexia diagnosis can leave parents feeling isolated and unsure or, even worse, feeling ashamed of themselves or their child. In *Parenting Dyslexia* adults will find exactly the companion they need—one that truly understands the trials and triumphs of raising a child with a learning difference. It will leave you not only informed but inspired, inviting you into a community of parents learning, growing, and championing their children's unique abilities every step of the way.

Ultimately, *Parenting Dyslexia* is more than a guide to addressing learning challenges—it is a resource for building stronger, more powerful relationships between parents and their children. By following the advice in these pages, you won't just be helping your child overcome obstacles in reading or writing; you'll be cultivating a deeper bond, one rooted in understanding, empathy, and shared determination. This book will leave you better equipped to support your child in every way: emotionally, academically, and personally.

Parenting Dyslexia is a gift to families everywhere. I feel profoundly grateful to Lisa and Jody for writing it.

Lisa Damour, PhD
October 24, 2024

Introduction

From the time I was a baby, my mother dressed me up in Penn State T-shirts and talked about how one day I would go to college where she did. As the years passed and despite being a bright kid, by high school, my academics had become such a struggle that Penn State was no longer mentioned. "I believe Miami University has basket weaving," my mother would offer without irony.

Later, she dialed back her pleas further to just get through high school: "At the very minimum, every entry level job requires a high school diploma," she implored. Finally, by my junior year, the conversations at home had devolved further still after nightly bouts with my mother heroically trying to help me with my homework. "Quit," she finally pleaded. "I can't take it anymore. You are sixteen. You can legally quit, so do it. Maybe one day you can get a high-school equivalency diploma, but I am done forcing you."

Those were the words that changed everything for me. In the throes of an all-night crying jag after my independent high school's dean had implied I was "stupid" hours prior, I thought long and hard about whether or not to keep battling on and about the pain I was experiencing daily in school and inflicting upon my family. Now my parents were at the end of their rope as well. I realized that I had hit rock bottom and had nothing left to lose—and it finally dawned upon me: I had nowhere else to go but up.

Yet my first reflex was to consider if my dean might have actually been correct. Those early self-esteem lapses remain as unforgettable for me as my accomplishment in graduating high school. More astonishing, years later, was my acceptance to, and graduation from, the University of Pennsylvania, and then, eventually, getting my PhD from Fordham University.

It was as fortunate as it felt unlikely, that my challenging high school experience pushed me to recognize that my dream career was attainable if I continued to work hard. Without the benefit of the accommodations that are now more customarily in place for dyslexic learners, I struggled to keep up with my classmates, overwhelmed daily by the volume of work and pressure to perform as rapidly as my peers on exams. Yet despite all of my struggles, somehow, I knew that I was not at all "stupid"—which helped fuel my desire to become a psychologist and work with children with learning differences to achieve their full potential. This life's purpose gave me something to aspire to beyond myself and corralled me to move through my fears of failure. I became determined to help others avoid the humiliation I had experienced getting through my education.

So, unexpectedly, even to myself, I gathered the grit and perseverance that I had been unaware I had been cultivating throughout school, and applied myself as never before. I vowed that I would return to my dean one day with a PhD and the word "Doctor" before my name, to show her that I wasn't "stupid" after all.

What I've learned since that joyful high school graduation day, that my family and I had feared might never happen, is that my journey has not been more extreme nor dramatic than those of millions like me all over the world. I regularly meet dyslexic adults, regardless of their education level or economic standing, who have survived heart-wrenching humiliations during their education, and many of them had much less support at home than I did.

The common thread for so many of us is the self-consciousness, shame, and embarrassment that seeps in as we watch ourselves separate, inch by inch, from our classmates, during our earliest experiences of learning to read in school. Interpersonally we may feel very much like our peers, but when confronted in a classroom with teaching styles that don't jibe with our brains' wiring, we take on a predictable and deep-seated shame; the nagging fear that there is something wrong with us; an understandable conclusion drawn from a deluge of subtle and sometimes not so subtle messages delivered daily and sometimes hourly during school and beyond.

This very human and reflexive self-attack is part of what I hope to chip away at with the methods outlined in these pages. The academic tools discussed will also provide straightforward strategies to help your child with their schoolwork. My approach is to comprehensively explain the many challenges dyslexia presents as well as manageable ways to address them at home. Ultimately, my goal is to reassure parents (and indirectly their dyslexic children) that not only can they make a measurable difference for their child, but that there is so much room for optimism.

Fortunately, with the increased awareness of learning differences, early interventions, more effective remediations, psychosocial practices (like those we discuss at great length in this book), and more universally accessible technologies, a parent should not have to spend endless hours helping their child at home like my mom did.

My family relied upon an unconventional lifestyle, with late nights of studying that often ended with fun and laughter. Humor, it turns out, was and continues to be one of the greatest coping mechanisms and stress relievers—and we used it often. It lightened the mood after some trying days and no doubt helped keep us together. The challenge of my being a different learner, in the end, actually made our family bond especially close; it created a tightly knit team.

Despite having grown up when there were fewer supportive technologies and less scientific understanding of dyslexia, many of my family's creative strategies are just as relevant, if not more so, today. My parents' approach to helping me learn was built upon a multitude of practical ways to motivate, teach, and cajole me into pushing forward with my studies. Having had the benefit of their recollections, I have gained insight into how dyslexia can impact family members differently. My hope is that these insights and approaches will not only help remediate and emotionally support your child but will also galvanize and strengthen your own family team.

The writing of this book is in many ways the culmination of that high school dream—and it dredged up some raw and painful memories. An early draft sat in my computer for decades partially because throughout my career, I have hidden my dyslexia from my coworkers. Apparently, I am still not immune to the self-esteem hurdles of growing up severely dyslexic.

I feel fortunate that my training, as well as my insight into what I was experiencing as a child, affords me an understanding of the neuropsychological issues at play for my patients and gives me a unique perch from which to help guide others through what can be a long journey. During my career as a licensed psychologist, with a specialty in the area of neuropsychological disorders (including dyslexia, attention deficit disorder, and pervasive developmental disorders), I have often reflected back on my own formative experiences with dyslexia and feel grateful that I can reassure parents that there really is hope for their children.

Of course, there are varying kinds and degrees of dyslexia, and your child's strengths and weaknesses will surely be somewhat unique since each individual is so different. But regardless of specific deficits or the progress made in the field, one message to parents is still clear: you must be alert and follow your instincts if you sense that your child is struggling to learn. Early intervention remains one of the keys to success.

An in-depth neuropsychological evaluation along with recommendations for proper remediations and accommodations are the next steps to put in place for a dyslexic learner. Once you are armed with a professional assessment of your child's strengths and weaknesses, my suggestions can help you and your child navigate through the many aspects of dyslexia that often don't get discussed. In particular, it can be easy, amidst academic struggles, to overlook the self-esteem toll that nascent learners often suffer during the scramble to catch up with their peers academically. My hope is that this step-by-step guide for parents will demystify the process of helping a child through phases of their academic hurdles as well as the psychoemotional aspects of their education that are so often overlooked.

Parents will find that, as with any child, there are issues in both realms that you'll likely need to continually be working on with your dyslexic child. These themes present themselves repeatedly throughout this book, including building up organizational, time-management, and study skills while developing the ethos of hard work, reframing failures as opportunities to pivot, building confidence by fostering independence, and promoting exposure to and mastery of a variety of skills. Advocating for gratitude practices, creating a safe family space, and infusing humor about one's shortcomings can all add a counterbalance to the challenges dyslexic students face daily, as well.

The many gifts that accompany neurological differences were certainly invisible to me as a child. My own special skill set flew under the radar until early adulthood. But research in recent years has revealed new insights into the hidden strengths that dyslexia can bring.[1] We now know that the alternate cognitive pathways dyslexic learners use can facilitate highly dynamic and complex abilities, which respected authors Dr. Fernette Eide and Dr. Brock Eide call the "dyslexic advantage." These are skills that may not shine through in elementary school or even middle school, but when more developed, often in high school and adulthood, can lead to great creativity, new perspectives, and sophisticated approaches to problem-solving.[2] Therefore, educating young dyslexic learners early about their different wiring, exposing them not only to the challenges they may confront but also to the many real advantages that their learning processes may bring, is an essential pivot for today's generation of dyslexic children.

Keeping these strengths and advantages front of mind for your child can reposition dyslexia more appropriately as simply a difference devoid of any notion of stigma or shame. The goal is that if we can get to a child early enough, reframing and grounding their thought patterns in disciplined practices and perspectives, they can build lasting self-esteem and come to fully appreciate the value of what they bring to the table. The earlier the intervention, the more likely it can empower a child to feel less alone and left behind. Along the way, the gifts of humility, humor, and tenacity are all there for the taking.

My many years of working with individuals like myself have shown me that a parent's support can make a significant difference for their dyslexic child in so many ways—*if* the parent has the right tools. Therefore, the multitiered psychosocial practices I offer here are meant to refocus a child's perspective and build their resilience to avoid the pitfalls of experiencing themselves as "less than." The idea is to accept the feeling of being "different than," as we all must ultimately work to do—and learn early on how to work hard, capitalize on their own unique strengths, and think of challenges less as barriers and more as indicators to find a better tack. Adapting good work-arounds and learning strategies tailored to an individual's strengths can help a child emerge to be less anxious and more resilient, and build real confidence.

Fortunately, students today have many tools in their arsenal to support their academics in taking on dyslexia's challenges thanks to ever-evolving technologies and the better understanding of dyslexia. Still, your child's gains are not likely to build passively. They will likely need your involvement to reframe what "dyslexia" means for them, to pursue and commit to activities that excite them and that they excel at, as well as to remediate classic weaknesses with effective skill-building techniques.

These practices can mean many long hours and possible added financial strain and may not be particularly convenient. Engaging your family to be part of your dyslexic learner's team will, no doubt, be an adjustment for everybody, as well—but it can also appropriately align you all to adjust your focus towards supporting each other. This was a seismic shift for my family, which continues to bestow benefits to this day.

Putting together all of these pieces is manageable and doesn't need to be overwhelming. Understanding what steps your child will need to take as well as ways you can help nurture their progress is the true purpose of this book. My hope is to reassure and bolster parents: to remind them that they can get through this with their child very much intact and primed for success—and that they are far from alone.

I have written this book for you and your child, for educators and tutors. It is the one that I wished my parents had available to them when they were confronted with my dyslexia diagnosis years ago. *Parenting Dyslexia* is the collection of information that I've longed to consolidate and offer to the parents of my dyslexic patients for years—a resource to empower with practical and accessible suggestions, along with a strong dose of optimism to encourage dyslexic children to realize their full potential.

So, I hope you are ready to roll up your sleeves with your child and bring along your patience. Be prepared to work hard and energize your whole family; I promise it will be the most worthwhile investment of time and energy you can imagine.

How to Use This Book

Parenting Dyslexia is designed to provide you with a clear and deep understanding of how you can most effectively support your child through the challenges and opportunities dyslexia can present. Part 1 begins by laying out the basics of the processes you and your child will encounter along the way to getting a diagnosis. Part 2 delves into supportive emotional and academic practices for dyslexic learners. Part 3 provides tips on how to facilitate the developmental tasks your child may require for each level of their schooling. Finally, in Part 4, I bring perspective to what it can mean to live life as a dyslexic person.

Where it is warranted, I include toolboxes, which summarize a chapter's actionable ideas and suggestions to make them as accessible as possible for busy parents. Since some of the specific terminology may be new to you, important vocabulary is defined throughout the book as well as in the Glossary.

Building Skill Sets Matched to Your Child's Needs

I wrote this book to help you support your dyslexic child both academically and social-emotionally, fostering the best outcome possible for them by arming you with very approachable guiding principles to ease their path forward at each stage of their development.

With the hope that you will refer to it throughout your child's educational journey, *Parenting Dyslexia* is meant to be used alongside a thorough psychoeducational evaluation. By partnering with their school and getting the proper interventions and accommodations in place to bolster their progress early on, my suggestions will offer you further insight into how to best help your child at home.

Towards this end, I will discuss enhancing relevant academic topics, such as reading, writing, and study skills, as well as their underlying neurodevelopmental issues, like phonemic awareness, temporal sequencing, time management, and spatial orientation. All are building blocks that can be greatly improved and remediated by using approachable, targeted practices.

Specifically, Chapter 4 will be a quick dive into casual but effective exercises to try with your child. These can reveal some basic gaps in their abilities and show you how to begin to bridge them. Unexpected disparities in their abilities are not uncommon, and as mentioned previously, this gets to the very core of dyslexia. But when your child *can* accomplish the suggested tasks with relative ease, there is no need to revisit those specific exercises.

Helpful Definitions

Phonemic Awareness: The ability to hear, identify, and manipulate individual sounds in spoken words. Developing phonemic awareness helps with articulation (the ability to pronounce words correctly).

Temporal Sequencing: The chronological ordering of when things happen in time.

Spatial Orientation: Simply put, where your body is in space in relation to other things. Dyslexic children may experience difficulty with spatial orientation. This can describe a young child who may appear physically clumsy, bumps into things, or hits their head when getting out from under a table, or an older child who may have particular difficulties in sports that require eye-hand coordination.

Equally, I will offer ways to help you prepare your child to navigate some of the most emotionally tricky parts of growing up as a dyslexic learner. These include making the best use of your family team as well as a multitude of self-esteem practices. My hope is to support you and your family to help your child in a fun and engaging manner.

It makes sense that the more you understand the underpinnings of the remediation strategies recommended for your child, the better you can support them in confronting their challenges. Again, since each child's strengths and weaknesses will vary, if some suggestions prove not to be relevant for your child, I wholeheartedly encourage you to move past them. Being selective for these reasons will allow you more time to focus on their individual needs.

PART 1

The World of Dyslexia

CHAPTER 1

Understanding Dyslexia

Welcome to the world of parenting a child with dyslexia! If you are new to this sphere, you may not be aware that dyslexia is now the most common learning difference, encompassing a full fifth of the world's population. If you haven't heard much about it previously, it may be because dyslexia can hide in plain sight, most often causing bright students to have learning challenges in great contrast to their other abilities and aptitudes. In fact, the confusing disconnect between a child's marked intelligence and their surprising weaknesses in certain areas can be a key indicator of the presence of dyslexia.

The fascinating nature of dyslexia, in conjunction with the way individual brains develop, is part of what makes its effects so contradictory at times. Both clinicians and parents can be surprised, for example, by how a verbal and bright child may have difficulty sounding out seemingly simple words, rhyming, learning to tell time, or writing a sentence, among countless other confounding possibilities.

The reason for this disparity in learning relates to alternate wiring of the brain. The relatively recent introduction of fMRI (functional magnetic resonance imaging) technology has allowed researchers to quite literally *see* why it is that dyslexic learners have apparent struggles relative to more neurotypical learners; their more indirect neural connections shed light on the fascinating phenomenon that has smart and inquisitive children suddenly hitting a wall, for example, when initially attempting to read.

Alternatively, a child who struggles to quickly process receptive (hearing) and/or expressive (speaking) language may have processing lags that require them to need more time to be able to take part in class discussions to express their thoughts. They may have a lot to add to a conversation, but by the time they have formulated their thoughts, the class has moved on—causing a dyslexic student to become frustrated and potentially withdraw emotionally in the classroom.

Fortunately, the impressive aspect of these often-gifted learners is that they are usually more than capable of adapting work-arounds and finding clever compensatory skills to cover their shortcomings—at least for a time. Many even manage to mask their deficits for years without being diagnosed.

Once their dyslexia is detected, they can not only learn to work through these weaknesses, they can also eventually evolve into resilient, original thinkers and high achievers. Yet they will first, likely, need to accept the reality of working longer hours throughout their education, with the possibility of delayed academic success along the way. They may also need to develop humility to work harder for lower grades while they put in the extra time to catch up to their age-mates.

Defining Dyslexia

Since dyslexia encompasses a wide range of symptoms, it's important to be as clear as possible in establishing an understanding of its meaning. I will exclusively discuss dyslexic learners as a broad, well-defined group, diagnosed by established, neuropsychological evaluations performed by trained psychologists. This science-based diagnostic process, made after the administration of a wide-ranging battery of tests, is the best way to fully and clearly diagnose the many tentacles that signify dyslexia, as well as prescribe the relevant remediations needed.

For the purposes of this book, my definition of dyslexia is as follows:

> **Dyslexia:** A language disorder that can affect reading fluency and reading comprehension as well as spelling, writing, and math that is not primarily due to any developmental disability; emotional disturbance; or environmental, cultural, or economic disadvantage. It may appear as a struggle to listen, speak, read, write, spell, or do mathematical calculations. Perceptual, spatial skills, and sequencing skills may also be hindered, but intelligence is not affected. The condition varies with individuals and affects people differently, on a continuum.

Dyslexia and the Controversy over Subgroups

The welcome increase in exposure that dyslexia has been enjoying today has had a positive impact in moving the cultural needle forward towards normalizing neurodiversity. Along with the extra attention, however, has come a large proliferation of "information" on the internet, which may or may not be based on rigorous scientific research.

One burgeoning area in particular is the vast array of subcategories or subtypes of dyslexia. While different professionals may have diverging opinions about these delineations within the diagnosis of dyslexia, it is important to note that most of these subtypes are not universally agreed upon in the community of learning specialists, nor currently mentioned by the most respected dyslexia organizations, including the International Dyslexia Association (IDA) or Learning Disabilities Association of America (LDA), nor necessarily by well-established researchers.

Some parents and educators may find specific subgroups clarifying or helpful in some ways, but I prefer to address a general discussion of dyslexia, viewing it more as an umbrella term describing a constellation of connected issues, as opposed to discussing the many controversies that exist within this realm.

The two subgroups that I *will* include are that of dysgraphia (difficulty forming letters, writing neatly, spacing them appropriately or in a straight line, as well as difficulty with grammar and composition) and dyscalculia (challenges with processing numbers and mathematical functions including addition, subtraction, multiplication, or understanding numbers). These are long established and distinct subgroups that I will call out in relation to skills or technologies that have particular relevance to these specific learners.

It may seem counterintuitive to choose to use a more *general* concept of dyslexia rather than breaking it down into subcategories of symptoms, but with so many possible permutations and variations of how different brain wiring can affect acquiring specific and varied skills, parsing into subcategories can sometimes lead to overlooking significant deficits for individuals.

Even the *Diagnostic and Statistical Manual of Mental Disorders*, Fifth Edition (DSM-5)—the diagnostic tool published by the American Psychiatric Association to be used as a reference for mental health and brain-related conditions and disorders—has adapted their terminology in the latest edition by removing the term "dyslexia" and replacing it with "Specific Learning Disorder with impairment in reading, written expression, or mathematics."

The DSM-5's replacement with the broader "specific learning disorder" indicates the diagnostic importance of a description that allows for a *wide* breadth of learning variables and alludes to the variety of impacts that this alternate wiring in the brain may cause.

What I think is most important to note is that the existence of subcategories is not universally agreed upon and may fail to comprehensively capture the many issues that individuals experience. So, while I will mostly bypass naming subgroups in this book, I *will* address the majority of issues that dyslexic learners encounter and discuss means to remediate them.

That being said, if you have previously found comfort and clarity in a specific subgroup label that seems to accurately describe the challenges your dyslexic child is confronting, and that label has been substantiated by a professional you trust, by all means use it. The fact is that there is often significant overlap in addressing related challenges for dyslexia—and regardless, this book will present you with lots of effective tips and suggestions that provide pertinent information.

The Importance of Terminology

As someone who may be new to the world of dyslexia, you will note that there has been much consideration given to selecting appropriate terminology in these pages, with respect to sensitivity to neural differences. The specific wording in these labels can have great significance, not only for your child, but also for legal and diagnostic purposes. These distinctions are also meaningful to those of us who are dyslexic and can directly impact how others regard our differences and, perhaps more importantly, how we see ourselves.

Thankfully, as our culture evolves and familiarity with dyslexia increases, so has compassion and understanding. Because of this enhanced awareness, I prefer, whenever possible, to avoid using vague terms like "different learners" or "neurodiversity" while *distinctly discussing dyslexic learners*, so as to avoid misinterpretation. My preference is to use the term "dyslexia," which, as previously stated, describes a broad array of connected symptoms.

I believe that being specific in this way provides a much more meaningful description of the population I am addressing (myself included) and conveys the most precise and straightforward representation of the differences between dyslexic and standard learners. At the same time, when describing the broad range of ways individuals learn, I appreciate the term "different learners" because it both acknowledges and accurately describes the vast variability in how human brains acquire knowledge.

Detecting Dyslexia—Early Signs Are Often Missed

Because of the sneaky and evasive ways that children (and sometimes even adults) can adapt and compensate for different wiring, it is not uncommon that dyslexic learners go undiagnosed for years and sometimes decades. If you wish you or a professional had picked up on your child's learning issues earlier than they did, you can join the legions of parents before you who have blamed themselves for not recognizing sooner what in retrospect can seem to have been obvious signs. The fact is that the average age children are diagnosed varies greatly, occurring as late as middle school and beyond, often eluding detection by experienced educators.

Just as when your child goes through many phases throughout infancy, with no two children behaving identically, the complex system of connectivity in varied regions of the brain develops and manifests itself in so many ways that it can hide early warning signs. Moreover, since dyslexia so often occurs in children who are above average in intelligence, delays can be even more unexpected to discover. Bright children are likely to adapt quickly and develop clever compensatory skills that mask a variety of language processing issues, making detecting dyslexia even more elusive.

In my practice, I've seen plenty of patients who landed in my office, having gone undiagnosed for dyslexia as late as adulthood. One such individual managed to compensate for his struggles all the way through an Ivy League graduate program despite being a slow reader. But for most children, the risk of falling behind increases the longer they evade diagnosis[1]—and more insidiously, likely so does their risk of internalizing more years of shame from negative self-comparisons to their peers.

Hence, the challenge for early educators is to try to identify learning struggles as soon as they are detectable. *Ideally*, that would mean in kindergarten or even before. But for now, realistically, we are catching children significantly later. Compounding the problem, sadly, is that not all teachers are trained to catch signs of learning differences like dyslexia.

As awareness and more screening tests proliferate and improve, my hope is that we can lower the age of diagnosis, to avoid cases such as those I've mentioned. The good news is that a trained professional psychologist, well versed in the evaluation process, can generally make a conclusive diagnosis, which can then set in motion the delivery of solid interventions and accommodations to improve a child's ability to keep pace with their classmates. Once they understand the extra effort needed academically, and gain insight into all they are capable of, they will have a solid foundation to enable them to avoid feeling shame from their learning difference.

The Genetic Component

It's worth mentioning that researchers have long noted a substantial hereditary component for dyslexia. Statistics show that approximately 40 percent of dyslexic children have a dyslexic parent or close relative. If you (or an immediate family member) are dyslexic, it makes sense to keep a keen eye out for symptoms and signs that can indicate your child's learning difference.

Subtle "Soft Signs" of Trouble

When a child starts to show some "soft signs" of a learning difference (indicators of a developmental lag, but not yet clear markers of an issue), parents can feel unsure of how to proceed. Dr. Spock, the renowned American pediatrician who wrote the best-selling manual *Baby and Child Care*, famously opened his book by telling parents to trust themselves: "You know more than you think you do."[2]

I'll share the same advice with you. As a parent of a child with learning differences, you may sense a discrepancy, for example, between your child's level of verbal comprehension and spoken language with their ability to learn how to read. Or you may notice limited language skills but an unusual knack for nonverbal tasks, such as solving puzzles and mechanical acuity. The possibilities and combinations are many, but the overriding question regarding any child is: Are there areas where they seem to be lagging behind? Complicating this question, of course, is the fact that all children develop at their own unique pace and along their own path.

My own mother got an inkling that something was going on with me around the time that I was four years old when she started noticing that I would meander or look out of the window when we played specific games related to learning the sounds of letters. Whereas I was an enthusiastic participant in physical activities, music, art, and verbal learning games, I would noticeably check out when she was trying to teach me the written alphabet, often enough that it seemed more than just a passing mood.

In my practice, parents most often seek me out years later, when their child is between eight and nine years old. The child may be reading markedly slowly or below grade level, struggling with spelling, finding writing or homework assignments particularly laborious, falling behind in their schoolwork, and/or possibly even having meltdowns while they attempt reading or writing assignments. This often occurs in contrast to other skill sets that would indicate that they should not need to struggle to the extent that they are.

You may notice that your child:

- reverses letters or numbers while reading or writing;
- finds sounding out words especially difficult relative to other children their age;
- has trouble spelling;
- can be unusually unfocused or is easily distracted;
- may be unable to get through tests in the allotted time they are given at school; or
- may have to read and reread texts multiple times because their comprehension is poor.

Common Indications of Dyslexia

Whether your child has a genetic predisposition or not, a bright child with dyslexia often lacks certain skills that one would typically expect them to have. Here is a list of common signs or clues to look out for:

Preschool Children (Ages Three to Five)
- struggles with pronunciation of words and speaking correctly
- difficulty learning to write their name
- lack of interest in learning how to read

School-Age Children (Beyond Age 5)
A child may exhibit the following **behavioral clues**:
- a dislike or a severe lack of enthusiasm towards school
- resistance, refusal, or lack of interest in learning to read
- avoidance of reading homework or games that require reading
- distractibility or struggle in engaging with schoolwork
- attention or learning issues in school
- a noticeable shift in a child's mood: exhibiting anxiety or depression that may or may not seem associated with schoolwork

Difficulty with the following **academic clues**:
- recalling sound-symbol associations
- writing letters and words properly
- sounding out basic words
- reading—taking an extreme amount of time to sound out words or process written language
- rhyming
- isolating sounds at the beginning or ending of words
- separating or combining words (like "base-ball")
- learning how to spell

- written letter or number reversals well past age seven
- reading comprehension
- learning to add and subtract or memorizing mathematical concepts or equations
- expressing ideas in written form

Difficulty with **temporal organization**:
- reviewing the events of their day in sequential order
- reversing left and right
- learning to tell time
- sequencing days of the week or months of the year
- recalling short number sequences (three or four numbers)
- organizing things such as their room or their time

While none of these issues alone definitively indicates that your child is dyslexic, they may tip you off to a problem. Regardless of whether or not their teacher has picked up on the issues, you will want to keep an eye on your child's progress and do further investigation (more on this in Chapter 2).

Helpful Definitions

Temporal Organization is the understanding and/or utilization of time concepts, which is another area that may be difficult for a dyslexic learner. This may be manifested, for example, in the inability to correctly sequence days of the week or months of the year or understand and/or utilize time concepts such as before/after or first, second, last, or beginning/middle/end, etc. Difficulties with temporal organization may also affect the ability to sequence numerals, sounds in words, sequence words in sentences, and/or organize sentences in a paragraph.

Attention Deficit Hyperactivity Disorder (ADHD) describes a set of behaviors that can include difficulty with sustained attention, hyperactive behavior (being in motion or not being able to sit for periods of time), and impulsivity (acting on things without thinking through consequences). Many people assume ADHD and dyslexia go hand in hand; I'll talk more about the correlation below.

Executive Functioning Skills are skills that include working memory, such as the ability to: hold more than one thought without becoming distracted, focus, manage time, organize, prioritize, and exercise impulse control.

Dyslexia, ADHD, Anxiety, and Depression

If your child *has* recently received a diagnosis of dyslexia, you may be aware that many studies show a significant overlap with ADHD, and in some cases with anxiety and depression or other mood disorders. Although this book talks exclusively about dyslexia, it is relevant to note that estimates show that 40 percent of children with dyslexia also show symptoms of ADHD.[3]

If your dyslexic child has also been diagnosed with ADHD, many of the exercises in this book will address its symptoms. These include strengthening executive functioning skills (such as organizational and time-management tools), as well as incrementally building up focused attention. Parents whose children have received a dual diagnosis of ADHD will therefore want to pay special attention to these skill sets, as they will have special relevance for their children. (Note that I do not directly address the issues of impulsivity or medications for ADHD in this book, which may be best addressed by a licensed psychiatrist.)

Anxiety and depression can also be frequent symptoms for dyslexic learners, presenting a classic chicken-or-egg question: That is, do children get depressed when they find schoolwork relentlessly frustrating and/or they aren't able to keep up with their peers in school? Or, alternatively, does their different wiring alone somehow cause a dyslexic learner to be prone to anxiety and/or depression?

Either way, my own clinical experience has shown that if a child has already been given a dual diagnosis with dyslexia (like ADHD, anxiety, and/or depression), there is a chance that over time, with academic progress, they may emerge less anxious and depressed, and their symptoms of distraction, for example, may also diminish as their academic abilities improve.

It can also be true that if a child has to expend significantly more energy concentrating on reading what a standard learner might breeze through, they will require more breaks to move around and expel energy to relieve frustration and stress. If a standard classroom cannot easily accommodate breaks for a dyslexic child, they may be inappropriately judged as "acting out" or disruptive. Distinguishing genuine attention deficits from the release of pent-up frustration can be particularly challenging in these situations.

In the case of any individual child, it may take a substantial amount of time to tease out answers since we all develop and learn in our own unique way. Regardless, ADHD, anxiety, and depression can all be significant barriers to a child's self-regulation, and I urge parents to keep a close eye on these vulnerabilities and to seek appropriate professional attention for any marked decline in your child's mood or functioning.

The Growing Dyslexia Community

When I was a teenager, I longed to know that there was hope for dyslexic kids like me and wondered if there were others who had gone through what I was enduring. I had heard about some dyslexic actors and politicians, but

I really yearned to know if there were other dyslexic people succeeding at the highest levels of all different professions.

Today there is a "Success Stories" page at the Yale Center for Dyslexia & Creativity website listing some of those individuals, offering encouragement and permission for dyslexic children to dream of whatever captivates them, reminding them that they are truly not alone (https://dyslexia.yale.edu/success-stories).

As neurodiversity has become increasingly mainstreamed, with more and more celebrities, entrepreneurs, and leaders speaking out publicly about their own challenges of growing up with dyslexia, the chance for dyslexic learners to emerge without devastating self-esteem effects seems to be within sight.

Likewise, as educators increase their awareness of the significant number of dyslexic learners in their classroom, hopefully they will become more attuned to the early signs, leading to earlier detection and intervention to minimize academic and social isolation for this vulnerable group.

While the stigma that dyslexia held in the past is slowly diminishing, there is still plenty of room for improvement. Universal education for administrators and teachers is likely the thing that could do the most to dispel any associated shame. I am hopeful that this generation will come to approach dyslexia as just another diverse attribute among individuals, as neutral as one child being more or less athletic, musical, or good at math.

Making the Most of Available Resources

In a perfect world, school systems would have ample and equal resources to meet the needs of *all* their students; educators would be attuned to and informed about the indicators that signal a learning difference; and the requirements of all types of learners would be equally prioritized. Sadly, of course, the reality is otherwise. Today, not even independent schools are universally welcoming nor understanding of neural differences—though many have made and continue to make big gains.

Generally speaking, these disparities can leave parents, and particularly those with less economic means, to manage and monitor their child's ability to learn on their own. Progress is happening, but it is slow—so for now, it is often up to parents to educate themselves and to seek answers if they notice their child is showing signs of struggle.

Whether or not you have the economic means to send your child to the best schools or provide special tutoring, if warranted, there are still plenty of options that exist today to enable you to support your dyslexic child in getting them the educational resources they may require. By aligning with your child's school's learning specialist or school psychologist, you will likely find programs in place to help children with financial need. Nearby teaching hospitals with centers for learning and/or developmental disabilities may also offer programs for candidates who qualify and can provide more resources to tap.

But the reality remains that if you need financial assistance, it will require your legwork, both in your community and online. Everyone Reading (https://everyonereading.org/) is an example of one route to take if you need help. It is among the national organizations that may be able to provide programs and special resources to empower parents. Governmental agencies may also have special funding for different learners in your area: https://sites.ed.gov/osers/category/grants/osep-grants/. There may be scholarships and financial aid set up for economically disadvantaged students that can pop up in unexpected places. Finding the right knowledgeable people in your school system or area may help streamline your connection to these resources.

One crucial thing to keep in mind, however: The emotional support and unconditional love that you as a parent can provide is one of the most essential aspects of setting a solid foundation for your dyslexic child. Your support and belief in them, as well as the perspectives you express, can have a huge impact to bolster their experience of learning. Ultimately, I believe a supportive family or a parent unconditionally championing their child can have the biggest impact.

Progress in Supportive Technology

The emergence of so many new technologies available to help children learn is a further optimistic sign and a reminder of the large dyslexic population to be served. Never before have there been more ways to get extra support for children in the classroom. These new tools have the potential to not only make extra help more accessible to all learners but they also minimize the disadvantages of income disparities. Significant resource differences can no doubt have an impact, but today they need not derail a parent's ability to help their dyslexic child scholastically.

The democratizing technological resources today are a significant improvement for any child with internet capability. For dyslexic learners in particular, this may also mean the possibility of avoiding or lessening the need for tutors in lieu of free or low-priced apps, websites, and devices.

Among the most recent tools with applications for dyslexic learners are:

- transcription devices for note-taking in class,
- narration devices and libraries of reading materials and audiobooks,
- apps for test preparation using custom-generated quizzes and flash cards,
- apps and programs that help with grammar and punctuation, and
- tutorials for math, science, foreign languages, etc.

A word here, though: You should note that with the fast pace that technologies are emerging, it is impossible to be as up-to-date as one might wish in this format. The Resources section in the back of this book (page 237) is meant to be used as a starting point for your own investigation into finding the best technology available to meet your child's specific needs.

Beyond the learning websites, apps, and research-driven tips, there are also online support groups, websites, and chat rooms—all there to offer help, give advice, provide recent local and governmental resources, and remind you and your child of the accessible community surrounding you. Above all else, I want to underscore the importance of reminding you and your child that you are by no means alone in coping with a learning difference. If you are not finding the resources you crave in your community, you might consider creating your own group, whether online or in person.

Supporting Your Child's Ability to Reach Their Full Potential

I always remind the parents I work with that, from the beginning of this journey, they need to understand that dyslexia is not a condition that will be neatly "fixed" or "cured." The mission for your child is to understand and embrace their significant and important strengths while they simultaneously work to build compensatory skills throughout their life. While our brain's circuitry may make it more arduous to acquire certain skills early on, hard work and dogged focus can greatly improve lags in processing times, reading comprehension, and writing. Yet as I experience daily, dyslexia continues to run in the background, obvious mostly to those of us who are ever-aware of how our own natural processes diverge from the world of more "standard" learners.

During a different era of education, my own experiences confronting ignorance within my independent school regarding my learning issues inspired me to work with children, hoping to equip them with the tools to get through high school, without the drama and shame related to their brain's wiring. As a kid growing up in the 1980s, I recall trying to convince myself that I didn't care if I earned my high school degree or not; I fully recognize now that not only would I have deeply disappointed myself if I hadn't, it would have dramatically altered the course of my life—and thwarted my potential.

I do believe that for the vast majority of us, the reality is that it is likely harder to succeed in today's world without a high school degree. It is for this reason that I work to help dyslexic children remove barriers to learning and try to minimize their struggle in order to help them reach their full potential. At the same time, the purpose of this book is to encourage your child to live their best life and develop and discover their own talents—wherever they may lie, and regardless of the level of formal education they may or may not desire. Therefore, my only agenda in these pages is to *remove impediments* for your child so that they can chase all they can imagine for their future, to go as far as they wish to go in life, in whatever direction they are courageous enough to dream.

To that end, I hope you will note that in the chapters about high school and beyond, the many suggestions listed to address special considerations for college admission (and later, graduate school) do not represent a bias towards higher levels of education. Rather, these detailed tips are included to provide actionable information for a path that many will choose.

Yet for a group that may start off their relationship to school fraught with extra challenges, it is easy to imagine a dyslexic learner opting to pursue a career that bypasses further academics in favor of work that may better align with their interests or aptitudes. But just as with *any* type of learner, it's important to note that an alternate career or educational path need not be a "lesser" choice in any sense.

The post–high school advice discussed in later chapters also applies to any training or job opportunities, technical school, college, or graduate school pursuits that your child may be inclined towards. They are also a continuation of the comprehensive skill set that I outline throughout this book. These adaptive life tools and work-arounds will help your child wherever they may decide to put their energies going forward.

The Gifts of Dyslexia

While research now shows that regardless of the country of residence, age range, or ethnicity, dyslexic learners represent a whopping one-fifth of the population generally, the impact of an initial diagnosis can still require an adjustment period for you and your child. It may seem a stretch to believe at the beginning of this journey, but I can assure you that, in time, you and your child will come to understand that dyslexia offers very real gifts. You will also come to recognize how much the world has benefited from different thinkers like us, even if your child's talents may not fully coalesce for many years.

Along with the challenges that can accompany the diagnosis are unique endowments that your child will come to discover as a result of their brain's different wiring. Far from being an affliction or a disease, dyslexia can be a portal into a world of original insights, perspectives, creativity, skills, and talents—no better nor worse than a standard learner's process, but one that requires more adaptation, extra time, attention, and targeted strategies to navigate within the sea of more traditional learners. All that extra effort can also come with the gift of cultivating a strong work ethic, grit, and resilience.

While one might not likely volunteer for these important character gains, dyslexia can actually help develop the tenacity and the ability to confront problems, straight on early in life, that adulthood so often requires.

Dyslexic children, as I cannot say often enough, are typically very bright and grow up developing unusual talents and clever compensatory skills. Occasionally, these can be less obvious abilities like an acute aptitude for reading people, a knack for collaborating with others, an unusual depth of compassion, or an ability to see the big picture in problem-solving, among countless others. More obvious abilities, like an acuity for complex planning, graphic design, architecture, and creative thinking, are among the countless possibilities.[4] Whatever special skills your child may end up cultivating, they will likely emerge in unique ways, long after they have managed to catch up academically—and can yield real advantages for a lifetime.

Eluding the trap of perfectionism may well be yet another gift of dyslexia. By the age of five or six, a dyslexic child may have already started to struggle to keep up in school and has had to confront the reality that they are not "perfect." In this modern era, the freedom to depart from that notion, particularly in school, can unwittingly unburden them. While difficult to accept, it may at least partially disarm the fear of not succeeding at something and may therefore encourage them to try new things.

For a dyslexic learner, sidestepping what can often be the impossible pursuit of a perfect GPA may allow more space for their experimentation and self-discovery early in life. If the frustrations of dyslexia aren't too extreme, early failures or disappointments in school can allow a child's own well of patience and resilience to emerge, helping them understand, as only experience can teach, that a defeat is truly not the end of the world. The hard-earned gift may be in learning that regardless of a weakness, there is value in persevering; that with real effort, one can overcome big obstacles.

Managing Your Inner "Super Parent"

All told, the experience of being dyslexic need not define your child—but it may just strengthen their character and supply them with the fortitude and confidence that they can accomplish anything they set out to do. But in the first brush with acceptance of this diagnosis, and then facing the immediate challenges that lie ahead, it is natural for a parent to feel concerned or overwhelmed.

While there are added burdens to be sure, with the crucial ingredients of your support and encouragement, your child will come to learn tenacity in applying themself, and with time, likely glimpse how much they are truly capable of. Knowing that neither of you are alone in confronting the challenges that lie ahead may help you both keep perspective during difficult moments. Your willingness to champion them with patience, love, and a constant, dedicated belief in their abilities, reframing their perspective to avoid shame, and reminding them of what makes them special, will make the biggest impact on their future success and happiness.

Along with all you endeavor to provide, striving to be a compassionate, attentive parent who takes on extra duties for a neurodiverse child is no small feat. Creating a safe, nurturing family environment, staying alert to emotional vulnerabilities, navigating new technologies while juggling the many responsibilities and realities of parenting today is its own kind of heroism and can take its toll on anyone—even the most overachieving among us! Add to it your own sensitivities and triggers, possibly from learning challenges of your own, and you may find *yourself* anxious or depressed.

Therefore, implicit in these pages of advice is the very real necessity of a parent's own self-care in the form of being attuned to your own struggles and vulnerabilities as you do your best to be there for your child. It no doubt takes practice to trust that your child can survive if you are not perfectly able to meet their needs at all times. But just as you hope to help your child avoid the trap of "perfection," the recognition of it as unattainable is a place to start for yourself as you seek to find balance in attending to your family and yourself. Learning your own real limitations and respecting them are certainly part of the journey of parenthood in general. By doing so, you will simultaneously be nurturing your child's emotional maturity, demonstrating for them what it looks like to be courageous enough to forgive oneself for one's own limitations and imperfections—a message that will likely have particular resonance for a dyslexic learner throughout their life, as it does for most humans.

CHAPTER 2

Diagnosing Dyslexia

As previously stated, many dyslexic children appear to be quite bright to their parents and teachers; they often grasp new concepts quickly, are highly creative, and demonstrate an impressive curiosity about the world around them. But dyslexia can show up at different times in a child's development in sharp contrast to their obvious intelligence and aptitudes.

Parents naturally hope their children will hit all the important milestones in life without any hiccups. But if you sense there may be a problem or you've been asked to seek testing at the request of your child's school, there is understandable concern. While you may be tempted to think it's a phase or your child will grow out of it, unfortunately, ignoring the situation or putting off an evaluation may only postpone the inevitable. Gathering information from testing is often the absolute best remedy—and the sooner the better.

The best case to be made for getting an evaluation is that if your instincts are telling you that your child is having an issue, you are likely correct. Denial, avoidance, or ignoring signs of a learning problem may compound the issue as time goes on. If you ignore the problem, it will eventually become the elephant in the room; the unspoken obstacle that your child is dealing with. Their teachers will likely know that your child is struggling and undoubtedly so will your child. A thorough evaluation can provide a much-needed answer.

Accepting a Dyslexia Diagnosis

If you're concerned about the repercussions of a formal diagnosis, it may help to know that children with dyslexia or other learning differences are better understood today and most schools have more resources available to them than ever before. By addressing a potential problem earlier rather than later, you facilitate the opportunity for your child to get the help they need and minimize undue suffering. Following this path can enable access to accommodations (like extra time on tests, removal of second language requirements, permission to use a calculator, taking tests in a quiet room, etc.) if required. Determining appropriate remediations from a thorough evaluation is the most humane approach to give your child the best chance to reach their full potential and keep pace with their peers.

At the same time, a good diagnosis and the best interventions are not a guarantee that a child will be a great reader any time soon; that may take years and lots of persistence. Gains may be made slowly as a child matures. Reading fluency takes time to develop and requires lots of exposure and practice.

Fear of Being Labeled

For parents who are reluctant to have their child made aware of a dyslexia label, it's important to mention that hiding a diagnosis from your child (or their school) may inadvertently and unwittingly add to their self-consciousness, shame, and embarrassment. The likelihood is that your child has already suspected, whether consciously or not, that they are struggling relative to their peers. Approaching the topic with them with clarity and honesty can lift the veil of confusion and the anxiety they may be quietly experiencing.

Knowing that there are supports in place to help them is usually a big relief and offers hope. Gaining an understanding that dyslexia is not related to intelligence and framed within the context that it is something that can be worked through can also minimize any potential shame or fear.

As I often remind my patients, there are lots and lots of really smart and successful people who have dyslexia and lots of widely available resources to help dyslexic learners. For inspiration on tough days, I recommend visiting the Success Stories page at the following website to get a glimpse of the many accomplished dyslexic learners and their contributions to society: https://dyslexia.yale.edu/success-stories.

Evaluations for Older Children

If a child's learning issues are not identified until they are older (middle school and beyond), then their self-esteem may have already suffered and they may seem angry, belligerent, and/or uninterested in learning. I see this all the time in my practice. Many children would prefer to be labeled "bad" as opposed to "dumb" and they often unconsciously act out their inner turmoil rather than ask for help or reveal how vulnerable they are feeling.

They may also be in denial, having developed strong compensatory skills that have allowed them to get by undetected. Some of these children have amazing abilities for verbal memorization, among other clever work-arounds. One of my patients explained that he managed to avoid reading assignments for years using his excellent verbal skills, manipulating conversations with his teachers to gain substantial amounts of information to complete his homework and deftly diverting his teachers' attention away from his deficits.

But if a child has made it to an older age undiagnosed, they have unfortunately most likely internalized a notion of being "stupid" and may act out with anger, become depressed, or withdraw from others, masking the fear that they cannot learn. In cases like these, once a child has a diagnosis and understands that they are not "stupid" and can be helped, the anger usually subsides. In these situations, I often find that a diagnosis provides palpable relief and validates suspicions that the parents had grappled with previously. Then the diagnostic report provides recommendations that are generally comforting, supplying a comprehensive path forward.

Partnering with Your Child's School

Regardless of their age, if you are considering having your child evaluated, it's essential to start the process by asking yourself what you hope to gain from the evaluation: Are you looking for information about your child's learning style so that you can understand it better, but you do not want to share this information with the school? Or are you trying to enable your child to get help in school? These questions are relevant to consider up front because if your child's tests indicate that they indeed have learning differences, there will not be much that can be done to help them in school if you don't share the diagnosis.

From my perspective, the goal is to have your child *thrive*, not just survive their education. That means minimizing potential struggles by creating the most supportive environment possible. This starts with getting an evaluation so that you can have the right interventions put into place that not only level the playing field for your child right away but also substantiate their need for supportive services and relevant accommodations later on. The team that is assembled will likely be involved with your child for some time, so you'll want to do your best to forge good relationships with them.

If you choose not to share evaluation results with the school, and therefore forgo services, you may find it much more challenging years later if, for example, your child is confronting a language requirement that they are unable to meet, or if they cannot complete their exams within the allotted time. Even further down the line, if they decide to consider taking college entrance exams, it may be more difficult to obtain accommodations without a well-documented history of learning issues.

Terminology to Know when Advocating for Your Child

It can be helpful to familiarize yourself with some of the essential rights you and your child have when seeking an evaluation or other services from your school district. The interventions and accommodations your child will be given may well last many years. Therefore, it's a good idea to be familiar with some of these basic terms:

Free Appropriate Public Education (FAPE) is the US law that states that every child is entitled to a free education with an appropriate individualized program to meet each child's specific needs as outlined in the IEP, in a public school.

Individualized Education Plan (IEP) is required after a child is tested and meets the standards for special educational needs. The plan takes into consideration a student's current level of performance in school, what yearly goals they should aspire to, and the services to be put in place to help them attain their benchmarks. If these targets cannot reasonably be expected to be met in a regular school setting, then alternative recommendations must be made.

Individuals with Disabilities Education Act (IDEA) is a federal law protecting every student's right to an education from age three to twenty-two (or until they graduate from high school, whichever happens first). It addresses specific needs and entitlements and related services to accommodate every child's unique needs to prepare them for their future success. Each state writes its own regulations, but in general, the law requires that parents be "equal members" of their child's IEP team and specifically aims to stop any schools from excluding or minimizing a parent's input into this process. Also, as part of IDEA, there must be a transition plan in place for a student who is aging out of school. To ensure equity for IDEA, there is a mediation process for resolution of disputes. Agreements made are in the form of a written contract signed by both parties (which is where a lawyer can be handy). Visit the US Department of Education's website for more information: https://sites.ed.gov/idea/.

Section 504 is a federal civil rights law prohibiting discrimination against persons with disabilities and guaranteeing that their specific needs will be met in public school in as close to a normal setting as possible. If you were to need to make a case that your child met the criteria for Section 504, you would want any and all school records and assessments related to your child to help establish their level of performance and needs for support in varied settings (group, friends, peers, etc.), social and emotional challenges, relationships, work and play, etc.—any and all input from professionals that paint a realistic picture of how your child navigates the arenas in their life.

Section 504 Plan is a plan generated by the Committee on Special Education after a child has been tested that specifically addresses the services, class placement, or accommodations they are legally entitled to in school

The Committee on Special Education (CSE) is also known as the Child Study Team (CST). This committee has different names depending on the state; I will refer to it as the CSE throughout this book. The CSE decides "eligibility" for special classroom placement, related services, and the child's eligibility category as well as coordinating and carrying out the special education plan for students. CSEs serve families in the district where a child's school is located and the committee is responsible for evaluating all school-age students (ages five to twenty-one) who are suspected of having a learning difference and identifying what the difference is if there is one. If a parent or teacher requests an evaluation, the schools generally have thirty to forty-five days to respond in writing to a parent's request.

The CSE is also charged with recommending placement and the type of special education programs and/or services within sixty calendar days (in most states) of the date of receipt of consent for evaluation. Referrals for an evaluation can be made in writing at any time during the (twelve-month) year by a parent, teacher, or administrator. If the teacher or administrator initiates the referral, the school district must promptly request parental consent to evaluate the student.

Informed Consent (part of IDEA) requires the school district to inform parents about specifics regarding any/all evaluations that are to be conducted, allowing parents to dispute the process. Parents are also required to receive official procedural safeguards annually (or when filing a complaint or a dispute). When dyslexic children turn eighteen, these rights transfer to them.

A **Prior Written Notice (PWN)** is required when there are any changes to a child's IEP or there are requests to evaluate a student. This is to ensure that parents are informed of what is happening with their child's educational plan.

Least Restrictive Environment (LRE) is the concept that a child should, whenever possible and appropriate, be educated in as close to a general education setting as possible. A parent must always be part of any decision regarding their child, which includes having access to their child's academic records. In the event of any disagreements, parents are always entitled to request mediation.

Inclusion is the guiding principle upon which LRE is based to minimize the differences in a child's educational setting and curriculum from the norm. To the greatest extent possible, a child should be kept in a regular classroom setting with neurotypical and neurodiverse peers.

For more comprehensive information about special education, your rights, and what's available in your area, please consult your state's Department of Education website or www.understood.org.

Evaluation Process: Public School or Private

In terms of testing, an evaluation set up by your public school district differs from a private evaluation in length and scope. School evaluations vary from state to state and from district to district; however, there are plenty of areas of overlap.

An Overview of Public School Evaluations and Your Rights

You have the right to a free evaluation through your public school's CSE. You can ask your child's teacher to make the referral, but even if the teacher disagrees, you have the right to request the referral, yourself, in the form of a letter (that is usually sent to the director of special services). An evaluation through the Board of Education is provided at no cost to parents.

Public school districts perform limited and varying evaluations that can include a hearing and vision screening, a developmental history, a full or abbreviated intelligence test (using only certain subtests), limited educational testing (to get a sense of reading, math, and writing grade levels), and possibly a speech/language evaluation and occupational therapy or physical therapy evaluation if they are required.

Once the evaluation is completed through your child's school, the CSE meets with a guardian or parent(s) to decide if their child is eligible for classification and qualifies for services. If they are, an IEP will be created to specify which special education services will be provided. Services may include a resource room, Specialized Education Teacher Support Services (SETSS), speech, counseling, and occupational and/or physical therapy. The IEP will also include any needed accommodations such as extended time and/or use of a calculator. (Of special note: one parent I interviewed for this book reported that one should *always leave an IEP meeting with a copy of the IEP in hand.* Her particular district made changes that were not agreed upon once the meeting ended and before she received the written IEP.)

Every year thereafter, the IEP will be reviewed in a meeting called an Annual Review with the parents present to determine any modifications or revisions. The teachers will also assess if the child has met their goals for the current year and set goals for the following year. Additionally, every three years there will be a reevaluation to update functioning and determine if there is still a need for services.

Supplemental Evaluations

Testing in public schools often does not automatically include evaluations for issues such as attention, memory, language skills, and social and emotional functioning. If you sense that your child is having trouble with any of these issues, you will need to specifically request additional evaluations from the CSE in your district. You may need to contact someone from the CSE to see how to formally request these evaluations and to find out if there is an appropriate staff member in the school district who can perform the evaluation being requested.

Making the Most of the Annual Review Process

Your child will have an Annual Review at the end of each school year. This is your opportunity to ask their special education teacher or the school psychologist to assess how your child is doing in the specific areas in which they struggle, such as reading fluency, comprehension, writing, and math skills, etc., as well as what progress they have made. This will help you and the school personnel working with your child determine what interventions worked and any adjustments needed for the upcoming year. There will also be reevaluations every three years that will be more in-depth and can determine if new accommodations are appropriate. For example, as academic rigor increases, your child may require extra time that they did not qualify for initially.

Summary of the Public School Evaluation Process

1. The child is identified by parent or teacher as possibly needing special education and related services.
2. Referral is made to the Committee on Special Education (CSE).
3. Parents or guardian give written permission for evaluations to be conducted.
4. The child is evaluated.
5. Eligibility is determined by CSE.
6. If eligible, an Individualized Education Plan (IEP) meeting is held with parents and an IEP is created.
7. The child receives services.
8. An Annual Review is held at the end of the academic year to determine progress made and create goals for the following year.

An Overview of a Private Evaluation

Private evaluations are a very thorough and time-consuming process that can be extremely expensive. Most private evaluators do not take insurance. If that's the case, make sure they will provide you with a proper receipt that includes testing and diagnostic codes if you choose to submit them to your health insurance company. You'll want to consult with your individual insurance company directly to see what is required with respect to your coverage.

After completion, you can expect to receive an in-depth, lengthy report that offers a detailed analysis of your child's strengths, weaknesses, and educational level, and recommendations for remediation, as well as any accommodations deemed necessary.

How to Choose a Psychologist for the Evaluation

The purpose of a private psychoeducational/neuropsychological evaluation is to determine if a child has learning differences, and if so, how their particular issues can best be addressed. It is therefore critical to ensure that the person performing the evaluation is a qualified and experienced professional who can work well with you, your child, and the school.

If you opt for an independent evaluation, you may want to get a referral from your pediatrician, who may know local experts, or you may prefer to contact a child psychologist in the area who conducts psychoeducational/neuropsychological evaluations.

National organizations may have lists of providers in your area. These organizations include but are not limited to: Smart Kids with LD, the International Dyslexia Association, and the Learning Disabilities Association of America. If your child attends an independent school, they will very likely provide a list of professionals that they refer to regularly.

For those who live in small towns or rural areas, your best bet may be a hospital clinic. Many hospitals have clinics within their pediatric department that offer comprehensive developmental and educational evaluations. The advantages of having your child evaluated in a hospital clinic can include access to a multidisciplinary team (e.g., social workers, psychologists, psychiatrists, neurodevelopmental pediatricians, speech and language therapists, occupational therapists, physical therapists, etc.). In addition, the clinicians can prescribe medication, if warranted, and follow your child, if indicated, reevaluating them every few years to track what progress has been made and what new recommendations are required. Most hospitals also accept insurance.

The disadvantage of using a hospital-based clinic is that the process can be long and drawn out. It might involve a long wait before you get started, followed by numerous appointments spread out over many months.

If you're in a city or suburb, you'll likely have access to select from a number of psychologists who conduct psychoeducational/neuropsychological evaluations privately. Having a choice is advantageous—but it does require that you to do your homework to ensure that the psychologist is a suitable fit for you and your child. The following questions can help guide you to select the right psychologist for your child's situation.

Questions to Ask Before Selecting a Psychologist:

1. **What degree/qualifications does the psychologist hold and how long have they been practicing?** For these in-depth evaluations, look for a licensed individual with a PhD or PsyD, in psychology. Be sure to ask how much experience they have with testing children for learning differences.
2. **Does the psychologist do all of their own testing, or do they use interns to do some of the testing and/or report writing?** If the latter, dig deeper to help determine your level of comfort:
   1. **What is the intern's experience with testing?**
   2. **Does the psychologist observe testing sessions?**
   3. **How much supervision does the intern receive?**
   4. **Who makes the diagnosis?**
   5. **Who writes the recommendations?**
3. Will the psychologist offer specific recommendations to help with remediation? You want to make sure that the psychologist is equipped to not only make a diagnosis but also to offer recommendations of what interventions are needed.
4. **How many test sessions are required and how long will each session last?** Depending on your child's needs, you may prefer multiple shorter sessions that allow your child to sit for less time or opt for fewer but longer sessions to minimize the amount of school missed.

5. **How long will it take to receive the final report?** The time frame for receiving test results depends upon the professional you select and can take anywhere from a few weeks to a few months. Ideally, you'll want your report within four weeks' time.
6. **Is there a follow-up appointment to go over the results and recommendations?** Since the most important part of an evaluation is finding out the diagnostic results and recommendations for your child, make sure there will be ample time to review the report with the psychologist to have all of your questions answered.
7. **Will your child hear the results?** If your child is age six or older, they should have a separate session with the psychologist to explain, in age-appropriate terms, areas of strengths and weaknesses and any suggestions. This meeting is important for your child to gain an understanding of their diagnosis and the interventions that will be put in place for them. It's likely that your child will be more apt to agree to the remediation plan if the explanation comes directly from the psychologist rather than from you.
8. **Will the psychologist speak to the school psychologist, tutors, or learning specialists if there are questions going forward or if questions arise with remediation?** At the end of this testing process, the psychologist will understand your child's strengths and weaknesses better than anyone else. Occasionally, questions arise once remediation starts and the psychologist should be available to answer these as part of their initial testing fee.
9. **Will the psychologist be willing to treat some information sensitively?** There are times when the report has information about your family that you may want to keep confidential and will have no bearing on your child's education. In that case,

you'll want to be sure the psychologist is willing to generate a second report that offers the most relevant information to the school while protecting your confidentiality.

Style Matters

Some psychologists are warm and friendly, offer flexibility during testing and allow a child to have a snack, walk around, or take a break if needed while others take a more formal approach. You'll want to get a sense of the psychologist's style when speaking to them on the phone to determine if they'll be a good fit for your child and if they are someone you feel comfortable with and can trust.

If your child is defiant, difficult, or very active, a formal person may be a good fit, whereas if they are shy and hesitant, you may need someone who is warm and more nurturing. You'll want to discuss these concerns up front as you interview a practitioner, to see how adaptive they are willing to be.

Whether to Bring Your Child's School into the Loop

Although you may be reluctant to involve your school in a private evaluation, for fear it could negatively skew perceptions about your child, there are some real benefits to consider. For example, the psychologist who tests your child will be able to glean information directly from teachers to get the best possible understanding of their learning style as well as their strengths and weaknesses in the classroom. Your child may behave very differently in school than they do at home, and their teacher can offer invaluable insights. Keeping the school in the loop regarding the evaluation and allowing the psychologist to speak to the teachers directly can enrich the understanding of what your child is experiencing in the classroom.

In addition, if they are starting elementary school and you give your permission, there are times when a psychologist may go to your child's classroom to surreptitiously observe their behavior. (This occurs *prior* to the evaluation so that when the child sees a stranger in the room observing the class, they are unaware that they are being watched.)

Possible Components of Your Child's Evaluation

Once you select a psychologist you're comfortable with, they will tailor the evaluation to your child's individual needs and presenting problems. Not all of the components listed below are part of every evaluation; public schools, in particular, do not include some of these sections unless they feel they are specifically warranted or if it is requested in writing or at a meeting by a parent or guardian.

Developmental History. It is important to rule out things that could potentially cause learning failure, such as a hearing deficit, visual deficit, medical illness, excessive school absences, etc. This evaluation will include a detailed review of your child's medical, educational, family, and social background to help rule out any other causes for a child's inability to learn to read, write, do math, sit still, etc.

Cognitive Assessment. Also known as intelligence testing or an IQ test, this measures verbal and visual perceptual skills as well as fluid reasoning, working memory, and processing speed.

Neuropsychological Assessment. These tests provide an examination of executive functioning, such as attention, memory, sequencing, planning, and organization. Most public school districts do not do neuropsychological tests.

Academic Achievement (also called Educational Testing). To determine academic areas of strength and weakness, these tests indicate the grade and/or age levels at which your child is functioning in reading, writing, and math. It will also assess your child's processing speed (how fast your child can complete these tasks as compared to their age-mates).

Receptive and Expressive Language. These tests highlight whether a more in-depth speech/language evaluation is warranted by assessing current expressive (speaking) and receptive (listening) language ability.

Social-Emotional Functioning. Often the psychologist will want to speak to the teachers to get an understanding of how a child is behaving in the classroom and their relationships with peers. There may also be additional tests or questionnaires given to the teacher, the parent, and, depending upon their age, the child themself, to help determine if there are issues that could include attention deficit, depression, anxiety, and/or oppositional defiance.

Summary and Conclusions. You should expect a lengthy summary bringing together all of the information gathered about your child, drawing upon the evidence of how and why a particular diagnosis has been made.

Recommendations and Accommodations. The recommendation section from a private evaluation should include specific suggestions as to how to help your child in each of their areas of weakness. It will also state what accommodations they will require in the classroom as well as when taking exams and standardized tests.

If you have a private evaluation and your child attends a public school, you will want to submit the report to the CSE. After they review the findings, there should be a meeting with the CSE to determine eligibility.

Sharing the Report with the School After a Private Evaluation

While independent schools all work differently, most will not generate an IEP. Once the report is complete, you should find out whom to send it to, and they will set up a meeting with the appropriate school personnel, possibly including the school psychologist and/or learning specialist, parents, a teacher, the principal, and the student (each school varies). This meeting will address eligibility as well as determine possible interventions and accommodations that your child will receive in school.

How to Explain an Evaluation to Your Child

I have found that many parents enter this process anxious about how their children will feel about being evaluated, but if presented calmly and positively, I can tell you that the overwhelming majority of my patients actually report enjoying the evaluation process.

Here is a rough idea of how you can explain the process to your child to prepare them for testing:

If your child is being evaluated in public school: "You know how there are times when you find that reading is difficult for you, or it takes you a long time to complete assignments or tests (or whatever your child's particular issue may be)? There are ways to help you with these tasks so that they will be less of a struggle. Over the next few weeks, you will meet with some people who specialize in figuring out how children learn best. Then they will communicate with your teachers about how they can help you in a way that will best support your learning style."

If your child is being evaluated in a private practice: "You know how there are times when you find that reading is difficult for you or it takes you a long time to complete assignments or tests (or whatever your child's particular issue may be)? We are going to see someone who specializes in figuring out how children learn best. You are going to do all kinds of games and activities with them that will help them understand how *you* learn. After you meet with this person, they'll be able to make suggestions for your teacher as to how to teach you in the best way possible."

CHAPTER 3

Moving Forward After a Diagnosis

Having your child evaluated can feel all-encompassing and overwhelming. Undergoing the evaluation, reviewing the results and recommendations, and meeting with school personnel is time-consuming and possibly anxiety-producing. Ultimately, however, a diagnosis can bring tremendous relief to both you and your child, providing answers to why learning has been such a struggle.

The thing that's important in all the hubbub of arranging for testing is to make sure to invite your child in and explain what is happening. This will help make the process less overwhelming and make it more likely for you to garner their cooperation. Just like you, if at all possible, they need to feel some measure of control in this process.

The Importance of Being Honest

In my many years working with families going through this process, I have watched parents worry and fret about how a diagnosis of dyslexia will affect their child. Some are even hesitant to share the diagnostic results with them.

What parents sometimes fail to realize is that children know that they are having difficulty in school and, likewise, when they go through the testing process with a stranger for the evaluation, they are aware that something is up. To fail to include them in the process instills doubt and uncertainty. Inclusion, however, sends the message that their struggles can and will be addressed. It is for this reason that I feel it is imperative that a diagnosis be shared with your child.

If your child received a private evaluation, typically the psychologist will go over the results and tell them their diagnosis directly (as discussed earlier). If they were evaluated through the school, they may be invited to attend the IEP meeting. But if not, it is your option to ask the school psychologist to talk to your child about the findings.

Either way, since their buy-in is paramount going forward, your child will need to be knowledgeable about their strengths and weaknesses to fully grasp why they have been encountering problems. If they are not included and continue to struggle or begin to receive extra help, they may leap to their own worst conclusions—likely assuming that they are not smart—rather than understanding the reality, which is that they have significant strengths and with help can work through their specific issues.

Receiving the information directly from a psychologist can make it more palatable for a child to face tasks they may have been avoiding, such as reading. Getting an accurate picture of what their learning difficulties are can also equip them with extra motivation and hopefully reduce their anxiety. Best of all, understanding that their issues will improve by following a clear path will likely be a big relief.

These are the things your child should come away with after their evaluation:

1. assurance that they are intelligent (not using IQ numbers) with a specific understanding of their strengths
2. an explanation of areas that need development or improvement
3. an explanation of dyslexia (or whatever their diagnosis is) and what it means specifically for them
4. the knowledge that they can learn well but they will likely have to work harder than their peers at times
5. assurance that with hard work they can still be high achievers

I know for my own family, receiving the information of my diagnosis answered so many questions. It also made sense out of what I was experiencing and helped prepare us all for what was to come.

Most importantly, I have often seen that the best way for a child to accept the extra work required of them is to get a keen grasp on how they will benefit from the extra effort. They may be more willing to sit with a parent or tutor or review math nightly if the evaluating psychologist explains that this is *their* recommendation (and not their parents' idea). In fact, some of the most helpful aspects of deferring to a "professional," whether a private or school psychologist, is that it can avoid a parent-child power struggle.

Parents may be surprised to learn that children customarily meet with the psychologist privately to hear their results. There are a few important justifications and upsides to this: The psychologist will be offering a child direct, honest feedback about strengths as well as, in a gentle way, weaknesses. While it may be hard to hear this information or to absorb it on one's own, chances are that as your child has struggled, you have sought to bolster them by telling them they were smart, and it's likely they did not fully believe you. This meeting is a chance for a complete and objective stranger to discuss what areas your child excels in as well as what they need to work on. The time with the psychologist can also offer an older child the privacy to share their own academic concerns, unfettered by parental oversight.

A Crucial Omission when Speaking to Your Child About Testing

One huge caveat must be mentioned: When meeting with a child, whether with or without parents, it is important that the psychologist and the parents avoid using numbers in their explanations, particularly for IQ tests. Intelligence tests are still a standard part of any evaluation whether done through the Board of Education or privately. Their results can change over time and have a margin of error when they are measured, which children will not fully understand. Parents need to hear IQ scores and grade equivalents in order to understand the overall results of a comprehensive evaluation, but children may process this information inappropriately.

How to Talk to Your Child About IQ Scores

In my opinion, children should never know their IQ scores. Your child can get plenty of information and insight without specific numbers. When they are school-age, gaining a sense of their results by being told descriptors is most useful. The psychologist might say to the child, for example, "Do you remember when we worked together at our previous visit? I learned that when compared to other children your age, you need more time to read something and understand it. However, when we *talked* and I asked you questions, you were able to express your knowledge quite well—in fact better than many people your age. What this tells us is that your ability to express your knowledge verbally is a strength. So, class participation is a great way for you to demonstrate to your teacher that you understand what is being taught."

Despite facing what could be an anxiety-provoking experience, hearing about one's strengths and weaknesses from a professional can actually be gratifying. It is uplifting and encouraging to receive insight into one's natural skill set and hear in-depth information about one's own learning processes. This is particularly true if your child has already internalized fear and embarrassment regarding why they aren't keeping up with their classmates. In that context, weaknesses can feel less devastating. Now they have a framework for understanding, which can hopefully reduce frustration and shame.

Later on, once they are eighteen years old and possibly heading to college, and having to advocate for themselves, your child will inevitably read their own reports and see their numbers. By then, they will more likely have the perspective and maturity to appropriately process their own IQ information.

Providing Context for Your Child

Your child must understand that a learning difference is just that, a difference—not a denunciation of their intellect. They need to know that weaknesses can be overcome and compensations can be made over time with hard work. Dyslexia may cause slower processing but has nothing to do with an individual's capabilities, creativity, or intelligence.

In fact, this is the moment for you to step in and enhance your child's understanding of their brain's inner workings. By educating them about the many other successful and accomplished dyslexics in society (via websites and films), they can begin to understand what dyslexia is all about. While it's true that they may need to work harder and longer than their peers in school, it's crucial that their diagnosis underscores their significant strengths and potential to gain a true appreciation for their capabilities and talents.

How you and your child choose to embrace this challenge can result in gaining confidence and self-esteem to face all of life's hurdles. Although it may be too early to fully understand and embrace, the importance of hard work and patience for both of you cannot be overstated. Your understanding of what their diagnosis means and how you frame both the positives and the challenges of dyslexia for your child can have a huge impact. The confidence and encouragement that you convey, as well as your expectation that your child can and will succeed, will help bolster and reassure them at their lowest moments. While it may take them more time and effort and cause extra frustration, they need to know that they are expected to learn and can learn well.

Framing a Diagnosis for Your Child: A Teachable Moment

"Everybody has strengths and weaknesses. We are lucky that we now understand what yours are. Moving forward we have all the information we need to use your strengths to help build up your weaknesses—and we'll all be there helping you. Like everything in life, the things that are hardest for us take the most time and attention to learn, but you'll get there. People with dyslexia have so many special talents—and have made so many great contributions in all different areas of society. You may need more help with some things and sometimes need more time to do your work than your classmates, but that doesn't make others smarter than you, it just means that they have different strengths."

It can also be reassuring to know that there are lots of other children like them who have successfully worked through these issues. As stated previously, the 20 percent of the population who are dyslexic include an abundance of accomplished individuals who have risen to the top of their fields in a huge variety of disciplines, so your child can be assured that not only are they very capable but they are far from alone.

You can also remind your child that they have a strong, loving support team at home (whether a single parent or a multimembered group), ready to help them get through the challenges that lie ahead. Along with their family, they may want to access support groups, whether local or online (with a parent's supervision) as well.

It's also important to check in with your child after a "feedback" meeting to help them process the information they have received and include them as part of the decision making regarding how to move forward. Rather than sugarcoating the information, offering emotional support and injecting the perspective that difficulties can be overcome together can be genuinely comforting. Typically, from my experience, a diagnosis offers a lot of relief—but regardless, allowing everyone to acknowledge their feelings is validating and gives way to adjusting to the new reality.

It's important to note that the last thing one wants testing to do is to make a child feel more alone and adrift from family support. This is a time to lean in, even if your child is a teenager and is forcefully pushing you away. It is also a moment to acknowledge and celebrate the strengths that have just been uncovered during the evaluation. Rather than dwelling on a feared weakness, it's an opportunity to practice real courage and acceptance. Most importantly, it can be an occasion to remind your child of how lucky they are that you can now understand what has been giving them trouble, so that they can get the help they need.

Moreover, I strongly believe that it's crucial to learn early that everybody needs a hand occasionally along life's journey, and that there is no shame in seeking help at those times. It's also an opportunity to reassert the importance of your family team and remind them that when we face adversity, we don't need to do it alone.

Classroom Settings

Depending on where you live, the types of interventions a school has for dyslexic children vary significantly. Your child may stay in the same classroom, but the school might place a SETSS (Special Education Teacher Support Services) teacher in the classroom to offer supplemental instruction and support for your child.

Alternatively, your child might enter into an Integrated Co-Teaching (ICT) classroom, which combines a general education and a special education teacher to provide instruction to a class with a mix of children with and without IEPs. Schools may also offer extra help in the form of a Resource Room for certain classes, but the type of support varies state to state and district to district. It's important to note that a dyslexic child might need more individualized attention than these settings offer.

Therefore, you will likely need to do research and investigate your school's resources by contacting Student Support Services (the exact name of this office varies across the country) and requesting to speak to the school psychologist, social worker, or learning specialist to learn more about the available services.

I also recommend researching the assortment of school options available in your area, including local charter schools, to see what type of reading support program they offer. There are also specialized independent schools scattered around the country, catering specifically to dyslexic children (but they can be very costly).

Comparing Teaching Methods for Reading

The thing to know first and foremost is that dyslexic children need to be taught to read using a phonetic approach like the Science of Reading. If your school does not use a phonetic approach, and you cannot find or afford a tutor, there are websites (like www.IXL.com) that can help you help your child.

There are two ubiquitous learning methods for reading used today; the general differences between them are as follows:

- **Science of Reading** is a vast, interdisciplinary body of scientifically based data from research compiled internationally over decades that found the optimal method for teaching children how to read. Their findings emphasize phonetically based learning methods that include phonological awareness, phonics and word recognition, fluency, vocabulary, and oral language comprehension as well as reading comprehension. The

Orton-Gillingham Approach is one such philosophy that was developed in the early twentieth century and was one of the first systematic approaches. Its structured, systematic, and multisensory approach to teaching reading, writing, and spelling uses a phonetically based system in a specified order.

- **Balanced Literacy** is a teaching approach to reading that started in the 1990s, blending phonics with the whole language approach, which emphasizes context and pictures to recognize unfamiliar words. Its popularity spread rapidly, with its focus on promoting a love of reading rather than adequately providing children the phonetic skills to sound out the words. This method has recently come under fire as it was discovered that dyslexic learners in particular, along with significant numbers of neurotypical learners, fell behind in reading as a result of underdeveloped phonetic skills. Currently, many schools are abandoning this method in favor of the Science of Reading curriculum.

Common Accommodations

Whether in a public or independent school, if your child has a diagnosis of dyslexia, they may qualify for special arrangements, or "accommodations," in school that are case specific and tailored to their diagnosis and individual needs (in public school these will be part of the IEP and 504 plans). These are meant to appropriately "level the playing field" so that dyslexic learners (who, for example, may process information more slowly, especially when it comes to reading) can perform to the best of their ability. Some of the more common accommodations are:

- **Time and a half.** A student may be granted 50 percent more time to complete tests, exams, and standardized tests as

compared with neurotypical learners in the class. This can also include the ACT/SAT, GMAT, LSAT, GRE, MCAT, bar exam, medical boards, etc.
- **Audiobooks.** A student may be given free access to audiobooks or other apps that read textbooks and other materials aloud. Make sure to have your child follow along while looking at the text and let them stop to take notes and annotate important material as needed.
- **Livescribe smartpen.** Permission to take notes using this computerized pen that converts written notes to text while simultaneously recording.
- **Permission to opt out of a language requirement** or take it on a pass/fail basis.
- **Use of a calculator** for exams and tests.
- **Use of a computer** for note-taking and/or test taking.
- **Use of spell check** for exams and tests.
- **Preferential seating** in the front of the classroom.
- **Permission to take exams in a quiet room.**
- **Permission to record lectures.**

While it can be an adjustment to have this shift settle in for both parents and children, there doesn't need to be any shame in accepting these accommodations, particularly if your child has struggled to finish tests within imposed time limits. Framing challenges within a context that reminds them of their intelligence and gifts rather than dwelling on the fact that they process things more slowly than standard learners can be helpful.

In addition, you may need to expose your child to more activities to help shore up their sense of self as well as to galvanize your family to bolster your dyslexic child's success. Within a proper framework, outlined in later chapters, these efforts will likely yield dividends in many unexpected ways for them in years to come.

How to Explain Accommodations to Your Child

A child should understand why they qualify for accommodations. Whether they are receiving permission to use special technologies or getting extra time or provisions in class or for taking tests, the most basic explanation is that accommodations level the playing field for dyslexic learners, offering them extra time or tools to provide them the chance to complete their work as their peers do.

How a Child Can Explain Their Accommodations to Classmates

When I have a patient who is embarrassed about getting extended time because other kids in their class say it's unfair, I offer advice on how they can explain it to their peers: "Think about a thing you really hate doing like going to the dentist, and then imagine doing it for ninety minutes rather than an hour. How would you feel?" "I want to get that thing over with as fast as possible just like you do. I read at a slower pace and need more time to think things through. Just like some kids are faster or slower runners. It just gives me a fair chance to complete the work and show what I know."

Ultimately, your child is apt to learn that they have strengths that they would never have imagined and that they have more resilience than the average child. But they will not likely come to this understanding on their own; you will need to be their champion and help them develop and uncover their special strengths.

Building a Support Team from the Start

Once a problem is revealed, meeting with psychologists, school administrators, and other learning professionals offers another crucial opportunity: that of building relationships to begin to garner support in the community. These connections with your child's teachers and administrators may prove to be extremely valuable down the line as you embark upon advocating for your child. Therefore, I strongly advise that you always put together a list of questions prior to your meetings and use your meetings with faculty to not only get answers but also to gather phone numbers and email addresses from individuals who seem to be knowledgeable and invested in your child, as well as taking notes on what transpires during these meetings to keep tabs on the process. Don't forget that, whether public or independent, your child's school is an essential partner in getting the accommodations, services, and attention that your child will need.

Within this new arena, you will also want to take note of the hierarchy or chain of command of the various players involved. Forming positive relationships and alliances with the decision makers in your child's case can only help. After all, you may well be working with these contacts for years to come.

You can also make the most of your in-person meetings with the faculty by inquiring about available resources in the school and in your community. There may be support groups for parents as well as for dyslexic children themselves to help you both connect to peers with similar struggles. Doing your own research may also help you locate local and state parent advocacy groups, whether online or in person (see Resources on pages 237–242).

Advocating for Your Child, aka Being a "Bulldog"

One thing I've seen repeatedly with parents is that it can take a great deal of time and energy to advocate for a child amidst the bureaucracy that exists within a school system. I wish it were not the case, but the reality of education today, with budgetary pressures, etc., is that there is a large range of special provisions for children that exist across the United States. This is where doing your research ahead of time, then being armed with information and having the will to be persistent, can sometimes be the only way you can get what your child is entitled to by law.

While it may not be an issue where you live, it is an unfortunate predicament for children with dyslexia: Parents need to be informed and equipped to confront resistance at times from their school system. This is where your understanding of your child's abilities and intelligence is so essential. It can be a parent's tenacity that carries them through to get the proper services. One such mother who had a lot of pushback from local administrators dubbed herself "a bulldog." She understood this was the only way her daughter was going to receive the appropriate help for her education that she was entitled to, so she took her role as an advocate seriously. This is another aspect of how your relationships with and access to experts in your area can be so valuable.

Finding a Properly Trained Tutor

If you or your child's school think that your child would benefit from a tutor, the school, PTA, and/or parent groups will most likely have a list of learning specialists/tutors with knowledge of how to teach dyslexic students that they can recommend.

If finances are an issue (and even if they aren't), there are free apps available that can help to build phonics skills at different levels. I recommend KhanAcademy.org (but there are many others that continue to come online) to start with early literacy and go all the way through to high school and also help with SAT/ACT prep later on. You may want to inquire with dyslexia groups on social media to find extra support and learning tools that are a good fit for your child. Keep in mind that some children fare much better working interactively (in person) with others. As an alternative, you may want to utilize the tools you find online *with* your child, at least initially, as they adapt to working on a computer device. (See Resources on pages 237–242.)

Taking Stock of Yourself in the Aftermath of a Diagnosis

While surely parents are most concerned about their child's well-being after the impact of a new diagnosis hits, there is a secondary component that should be addressed, as well. The emotional effect on a parent, after navigating the testing process, can be significant and may even be a trigger from their own childhood (since dyslexia can have a genetic component). Facing a learning difference can understandably bring up all kinds of worries and concerns ranging from anxieties about the unknown to, in many cases, evoking recollections of one or both parents' own educational past.

Furthermore, along this journey, the confirmation that your child is dyslexic may be a paradigm shift away from the standard emphasis on academic super achievement and grades. Depending on the expectations that you as a parent bring to the table, this may initially require a big pivot as your child gets the help they need to catch up to their class. Reframing how you measure success, therefore, emphasizing effort over grades and keeping in mind that your child's results may be inconsistent in the short term, is a place to begin.

My message to parents who have received a new diagnosis is to try to stay flexible and model adaptiveness for your child. Since a diagnosis may indicate a long road ahead for remediation, be prepared to do some self-care in addition to addressing the impact on your child. Use your own support systems or seek out new ones, if need be, to be sure to take care of yourself. Remember, the good news is that you all now know the work that needs to be done—and you are primed and ready to get your child the help they'll require.

CHAPTER 4

Enhancing Skills from Home

This comprehensive chapter explores some relatively simple but valuable, supportive methods that may make an appreciable difference in your child's progress as a dyslexic learner, regardless of their age. Whether or not the skills discussed have been highlighted as weaknesses in an evaluation, or if they have not yet gone through a diagnostic process, your child may still benefit from reviewing the exercises covered here. They include: articulating words accurately, blending sounds together, isolating and identifying beginning or ending sounds of words as well as the ability to tell time, executing sequencing skills, developing organizational skills, and understanding directional concepts like left, right, north, south, east, and west. Attempting these games and exercises can ensure that they have mastered the underlying prerequisite skills required to improve their ability to learn to read.

While a nondyslexic learner may acquire these skills through more casual exposure, a dyslexic child, no matter how old, will often need to be taught more directly. So, after your child has received a diagnosis, you can review these areas with them to ensure that they have mastered the skills described below. But even if they have not yet been diagnosed and you are sensing a problem, the exercises can be useful. It's a quick check—either they can do them or they can't—and if you find any areas where they're struggling, you can work with them to strengthen their skills through repetition.

If your dyslexic child has never been introduced to these exercises, you may be pleased to find that they have already picked up many of these concepts listed without any formal effort. You may be equally surprised that your school-age child may *not* be able to do them. While these exercises may seem like they are geared toward younger children, some dyslexic learners will still struggle with these skills, possibly into adulthood. So regardless of their age, it's a good idea to check in and make sure that they have competence in these areas.

If your child pushes back, explain to them that if they are struggling with any of these tasks, it is important to master them to improve reading and spelling.

Please bear with me as I walk you through how to best work with your child before you embark upon trying these important exercises. Many of these suggestions have specific relevance for dyslexic learners and will also apply to helping your child with homework over time, as well.

Approaching Exercises and Games with Your Child

In order to avoid undue pressure on anyone, it is important to consider your own skill set, interests, and level of patience before deciding if you are the right one to be engaging in these exercises with your child.

- You'll want to be able to be calm, particularly because it may well take your child extra time to process information when you start to work together. This can require quite a big shift in pace for busy parents charging through their day.
- Try not to panic if their progress doesn't align with your expectations, as each child develops at their own individual pace.

- These exercises can be especially challenging for dyslexic learners, and it may be helpful to remind yourself that these deficits have no bearing on your child's intelligence.
- If these games do not feel comfortable for you, there is no shame in calling upon others you trust who may have experience in this realm. I've certainly seen many children who do not work well with their parents and vice versa. Whoever is ultimately part of the designated team to work with them, the thing to keep in mind is that these are strictly *casual*, fun exercises.

It's important to note that your child will likely be sensitive to whether or not they are meeting yours or other adults' expectations. Therefore, the ability to remain relaxed and calm will help them avoid embarrassment and stress—it may even help them to be more patient with themselves.

Being Sensitive to Signs of Resistance and Shame

Starting off, I advise you to proceed with care and let your child know that it's okay if they don't know something or if they're struggling. The last thing you want these exercises to do is turn your child off to learning in any way or make them feel uncomfortable about exposing weaknesses or vulnerabilities to you. Particularly if you are in a family with other high achievers, children can be extremely sensitive and attuned to disappointing you, as stated previously. So, if you decide to introduce these games, here are some other tips that I like to keep in mind when I work with dyslexic learners:

- **Follow your child's lead with regard to pace:** You certainly want to encourage, but never to push, with regard to their speed in responding. With time you will likely get a sense of their cadence.
- **When in doubt, tread lightly and try again later:** Listen to your child and be attuned to signs of any type of resistant

behavior. Keep in mind that there are a variety of activities offered so if they seem to show reluctance with one type of exercise, you can move on to a different one. But if they are not engaging, my rule of thumb is try again another day.

- **Be alert to signs of stress or resistance:** If your child is showing signs of agitation such as crying, yelling, or withdrawing, they are letting you know they feel frustrated and you'll want to ease off. Similarly, outbursts, tantrums, or more subtle indicators like ignoring you or being easily distracted can indicate needing to choose another time to try to engage. They may be tired, hungry, or self-conscious—or possibly embarrassed because of a perceived failure.
- **If your child is not particularly receptive, avoid taking their reaction too personally.** In truth, one never knows why a child may sometimes prefer working with a different adult; the important thing is that they can be engaged to participate.
- **You may find that your child is capable in some areas and lagging in others.** That is not unusual. Some children are quite verbal and will pick up on these language games at a very young age, while others will need more time. If you find that they are grasping the exercises easily, you can move on.
- **If you can't get through their resistance for certain activities, take note of it.** You may want to wait a month or two to try again and see if they will engage. If they don't, you will want to talk with their teacher or the school psychologist because this could be a sign that this is a real struggle for them.

Methods to Engage Your Child

Your primary goal here is to help your child feel safe and excited to learn. Parents can incorporate the games and exercises below relatively painlessly, particularly when they discover that their child enjoys participating. Most are fairly simple and aimed at developing certain basic concepts.

Depending on how good you are at multitasking, many of them can be done while cooking, driving, etc. and can become a fun way to engage with your child.

You may want to begin the exercises when siblings are not around if it will put your child more at ease. They may prefer more focused time, devoid of any distractions from others. Regardless of when and where, you'll want to encourage their progress and effort and keep the mood light and fun (and less like a lesson).

- **Start out easy to give them an early win.** I like to err on the side of ensuring that things start off well so they experience success right away. I recommend you do the same so that they feel confident and good about themselves. Once they're enjoying an exercise and they have experienced success, you can slowly make the exercises a little more challenging.
- **Feel free to encourage and help as needed.** Use little hints and repeated nudges to sustain their engagement when playing the games and doing the exercises.
- **Your excitement will help energize their desire to learn.** Your positive energy and affirmations when they grasp a new concept will set the stage for a fun and playful experience for both of you.
- **Avoid using a reward system to engage your child.** I like to present these exercises as a fun way of interacting rather than offering any kind of tangible incentives to do them. I never want a child to feel they are being judged or that the exercises are a chore or a competition.
- **Incorporate examples that are of special interest.** If they love dolls, cartoon characters, superheroes, princesses, fire engines—whatever it is, use these to tailor the games to make them more engaging. Use your own creativity to make the games and exercises fun and interesting.

- **Once they show signs of progress in a particular area, you will want to check back at a later time to make sure it has been retained.** If they seem stuck, it can also help to bring back some of the previous exercises to reestablish prior progress and offer them success once again.

These skills and concepts work in tandem and along a progression rather than a direct, straight line forward. In other words, your child may develop some of these skills before others, so their progress in different areas will not be linear. Last but not least, remember that you are *not* expected to be a learning expert—and you won't need to be to do these!

Introducing the Critical Building Blocks of Language (Ages Five to Ten)

These following categories will briefly explain the underlying concepts related to the exercises and games for your child and will allow you to entertain and engage your five- to ten-year-old child while you lay the groundwork—or build upon the groundwork for the development of language and reading skills. When done within a fun and playful atmosphere you'll also be teaching your child the basic pleasures of using their brain and paying attention.

Language Immersion

Being as fully present as possible and exposing your child to new vocabulary when speaking helps develop language skills. Having a robust vocabulary is key to enabling a young reader to decipher written words as well as bolstering reading comprehension at any age.

> **Exercise: To expand their vocabulary, repeatedly incorporate new words into casual conversation. Make sure they know what the words mean, and use them often.**

Developing Phonemic Awareness

The following exercises are meant to build phonemic awareness—the ability to distinguish, hear, identify, and manipulate individual spoken sounds to pronounce words correctly. *Phonemic awareness is a prereading skill that is essential for children to learn to read and pronounce words correctly.* All of these language exercises are meant to develop your child's phonemic awareness—that is, their ability to distinguish distinct sounds that make up words.

How to Progress Through the Exercises

The best way to set your child up for success is to methodically demonstrate by example what you'll be asking them to do in these exercises. For example, "First I'll want you to tell me if two words rhyme. Do you understand what rhyming means? It's when two words sound alike but are also different, like 'house' and 'mouse.' You'll tell me if they rhyme by saying 'yes' or 'no.' In this case, we know 'house' and 'mouse' do rhyme—so you can say 'yes.'" For each new task you cover, you'll want to go through this process to be sure that they understand the task clearly before you start.

1. **Start by demonstrating what you are teaching,** for example, "House and mouse are words that rhyme."
2. **Ask them a yes/no question,** for example, "Do 'house' and 'mouse' rhyme?"
3. **Progress to open-ended questions:** "What rhymes with house?" Give them an example of what you mean before you ask them to provide an answer.
4. **Finally, let them ask you a question:** "Now, you ask me to find a word to rhyme with a word you choose."

Helpful Definitions

Phoneme. The smallest unit of sound in a language that distinguishes words from one another. For example, the "b" sound in the word "bat" or the "ch" sound in the word "chunk."

Decoding. Associating symbols to sounds or groups of symbols to sounds, such as digraphs (ch, ph, etc.), and blending those sounds together to read a word. For example: "ch-a-t" = "chat."

Sight Words. Words that cannot be decoded or sounded out. Children are customarily taught to recall these words instantly without sounding them out. Examples of sight words that cannot be phonetically decoded include: the, she, would, around—to name a few.

The Importance of Rhyming

You may assume that your child already knows how to rhyme, but children who are dyslexic often struggle with this task. Knowing how to rhyme contributes greatly to grasping the relationship between words that will ultimately make reading fluency easier. As an example, if a child is learning to read and struggling to decipher a word such as "could" but they have learned to read the sight word "would," strong rhyming skills will automatically help them with reading and then, later, with spelling.

Exercise: To see if your child has acquired the ability to rhyme, start by asking them if different words rhyme: For example:
- "Do 'sing' and 'ring' rhyme? 'Sing' and 'song'?"
- Have them find words that rhyme with "like" or "cool," etc. Progress to harder words as they improve.
- Once they can distinguish between rhyming and nonrhyming words, have them generate the question: "What rhymes with 'mug'?"

Articulation

Articulation is the ability to produce clear and distinct sounds. No matter how old your child is, make sure they can say difficult words correctly. You can help them with articulation throughout childhood by speaking slowly, exaggerating how you make each sound with your mouth, then by asking them to repeat the words you say. If your child is struggling, have them watch your mouth as you speak to help them see how to produce sounds correctly. Having them look in the mirror so they can see what their mouth is doing can also be helpful. The strategy is to develop your child's awareness of phonemes so that they continue to distinguish between the many sounds in words.

As their vocabulary grows, you can have them try to say more difficult words like "philosophical" and "cornucopia," slowly breaking up the words (chunking) into more manageable syllables.

Digraphs (two letters representing one sound) like "th," "sh," "ch," etc. are more challenging. Therefore, you will want to enunciate digraphs especially clearly and make sure your child can see your mouth so that they can more readily imitate the sounds. (Note that trouble with articulation may, but does not necessarily, imply dyslexia.)

Identifying Beginning Sounds

Learning to identify *beginning* and *ending* sounds that form words is a skill that can often be challenging for a dyslexic learner; so, you'll want to pay particularly close attention to helping your child differentiate between the variety of sounds that make up a word.

Starting with sounds that are very different, or easy to distinguish between, you'll want to focus on identifying the beginning sounds of words. Distinct from teaching a child to read and identify *letters*, distinguishing *sounds* is part of building phonemic awareness. A dyslexic learner may struggle with this and may not be able to grasp the concept.

Exercise: You can start by saying, "bat" starts with the sound for "b" (spoken slowly and exaggeratedly, saying the sound, not the letter). Zebra begins with the sound "z."

- Then ask them to identify the sound a word begins with.
- Once they can identify beginning sounds, graduate to comparing sounds and identify if they are the same or different. For example, "bat" and "kite,"—do they start with the same sound? "Stop" and "flop"? Remind them that "stop" and "flop" rhyme, but they do not start with the same sound.
- Start with initial sounds that are very dissimilar, such as "man" and "kite," then progress to initial sounds that are more similar to each other, such as "bat" and "put."

Identifying Ending Sounds

Only *after* a child has mastered the ability to identify beginning sounds, should you progress to ending sounds.

Exercise: Doing precisely what you did with beginning sounds, you'll now want your child to cue into hearing ending sounds. For example:
- Ask your child if words like "lid" and "pot" end with the same sound.
- "Do 'pot' and 'hot' end with the same sound?"
- "Do 'book' and 'mitt' end in the same sound?" Try assorted examples with and without using the same sounds.

Blending Sounds

As your child gains mastery of beginning and ending sounds, they can progress to blending sounds.

Exercise:
- Say the sound "b," then say "at," then say "'b' plus 'at' says 'bat'"; "'p' plus 'en' is 'pen,'" and so on, again making sure to say the sound not the letter.

- Once they master blending beginning sounds, have them blend ending sounds. "Coa-t" becomes "coat," "coo-k" becomes "cook."

Visual Cues for Blending

From my experience, dyslexic children do better learning to blend sounds if you use your hands to offer a visual cue. Bring up one hand and say the sound "s," then bring up the other hand for "ink," then bring the hands together while saying the word "sink." This visual cue effectively communicates how different sounds come together to form words. (Search YouTube using terms like "teaching blended sounds.")

Isolating Sounds

The ability to isolate sounds can be difficult for some children but is another essential task to develop.

Exercise: Have your child repeat a word without the beginning sound. Here's how I introduce the exercise:
- "I'm going to say a word, then I will say it again without the beginning sound." "Baseball" without the "b" sound is "aseball." Kite without the "k" sound is "ite." Now offer your child the chance to do this with a new word.
- Do the same with ending sounds: "Sun" without the "n" sound becomes "su." Make sure you are saying the sounds the letters make and not the name of the letter. "Start" without the ending sound becomes "star."
- Next, ask them to say a word without the ending sound.

This continues to build phonemic awareness and helps a child generalize their ability to sound out words.

Chunking Sounds to Form Two-Syllable Words

Another prereading skill that teaches a child how to blend sounds using their auditory skills involves chunking.

> **Exercise: Select words with two or more syllables: you say "num" "ber," then ask (and help) the child to blend it together, "number." You say "pen" "cil" becomes "pencil," etc.**
>
> **The idea is to break down the sounds they are hearing and speaking, to raise their awareness of how words are formed. Eventually, when learning to read two-syllable words, this can help break down words to decode them.**

When your child eventually progresses to reading, the phonemic awareness they develop from these various exercises in blending sounds together will make learning to read easier.

Encouraging Directional/Spatial Concepts

Besides struggling with language, dyslexic children can also struggle with spatial and temporal organization. Here are some games you can play with your child to strengthen these areas.

Learning to Distinguish Laterality

Not all dyslexics have trouble with left and right; everyone is unique and has varied strengths and weaknesses. Those who do not establish a dominant side may still write with a specific hand or favor a foot for various activities. Typically, though, children have an established dominant left or right side by their seventh birthday. It is worth noting that the absence of a dominant side by age seven is considered a neurological soft sign of dyslexia.

> **Game: Traditional games like "Simon Says" or Twister are great for practicing left and right and crossing the midline (meaning to**

go across their body). In the game Twister, the child spins a dial and might for example be asked to put their left hand on their right knee or right hand on their left ear.

Persistent Laterality Issues

If your child already knows how to write the letters of the alphabet and they are still reversing left and right, one way they can remind themselves of the difference is by identifying the "L" on their left hand with their index finger and thumb extended. Forming the "L" is the age-old method that works for some. But if a child continues to reverse left and right, there may not be a foolproof trick to resolve the issue, or it may take many years. In some cases, it may never be natural or automatic, as it is not for me. But repeating the games and exercises listed can really make a difference for most.

Directionality Basics

Once your child fully understands the concept of left and right, you can introduce them to the challenge of learning directions (north, south, east, and west). To assist a child struggling with directionality, you can introduce them to a mnemonic like "**N**ever **E**at **S**oggy **W**affles" to remember the order of directions (North, East, South, West). You can explain that once they know their orientation, they can proceed by turning their body to the right, using the mnemonic to determine the directions. For instance, if they start facing north ("**N**ever,"), they can recognize that east ("**E**at") comes next (to the right), then south ("**S**oggy), and finally, west ("**W**affles") as they continue to the right to close the circle. This approach helps them associate their orientation with the directional sequence in a memorable way.

>Game: The games Rush Hour Junior (for ages five and up) and Rush Hour (for ages eight to adult) are fun, educational ways to teach

directions such as left/right, up/down. (They are also available to play online, but I recommend the actual physical game.) The idea is to get an ice cream truck out of a traffic jam in a logical progression. Sit next to your child and encourage them to tell you what they're doing while they move the toy cars around traffic to become cognizant of each move they're making and practice verbalizing the moves to reinforce the concepts.

Number Recognition

This is a skill that is helpful for children with dyscalculia and can help any child practice number recognition.

Games: If your child confuses numbers, playing a physical game with numbered blocks or playing hopscotch and saying the numbers aloud as they jump into each box can help develop number recognition.

Time Concepts (Ages Five to Eight)

Telling time using an analogue (not digital) clock (ages five to eight) is still an important skill, and learning it has the additional benefit of helping teach the concepts of clockwise and counterclockwise, which can also reinforce directionality. Generally speaking, instilling the importance of time is relevant for children to learn as they enter school and begin to take on responsibilities. Likewise, the underlying concept of time is foundational and can be difficult for dyslexic and ADHD children.

Exercise: If your child has never had a clock, you'll want to get a digital clock for their room to familiarize them with numbers and time.
- Teach them to notice what numbers the clock reads when they wake up, and help them learn what time they need to go to bed.

- Once they have mastered a digital clock, introduce an analogue clock and teach them how to tell time (if you need help, refer to a YouTube video).

Developing Temporal Sequencing Skills

Creating an awareness of how things happen in *sequences* related to time is a key skill to acquire.

Exercise:
- Practicing simple sequences, like first you wake up, then you brush your teeth, then you eat breakfast, etc., can start your child off in recognizing the order in which things happen.
- Similarly, a child also needs to understand the timeline or sequence of a story. At bedtime, have them tell you what they did today in order of how things happened so that they start to be aware of the order in which their day unfolds and they learn to conceptualize that things happen in sequences.

Doing this regularly with your child can eventually help them generalize this skill. Ask them questions that require a sequential answer: "How did you create that art project?" Help them start to recognize methodical steps in performing and approaching tasks in a logical sequence.

Dyslexic children may also struggle with ordering numbers from lowest to highest or with tasks like recalling phone numbers or codes correctly. Try teaching your child important phone numbers that are relevant to them, such as your phone number or that of a close relative.

Exercise: You can begin by introducing them to smaller chunks of a phone number and slowly work up to the entire phone number.
- Have your child repeat it, look at the numbers, and practice dialing it. If need be, you might want to try putting a string of numbers into a song.

While cell phones may no longer require memorization of phone numbers, it is still a good idea for children to know this information by heart and to have the ability to remember number sequences.

Struggles with sequencing skills can present themselves when one is asked to recall the days of the week, months of the year, or the alphabet. While committing these commonly used sequences to memory, a song can be helpful (there are many options on YouTube set to popular tunes). It's not unusual that without the framework of the song, they may be lost. Ask a dyslexic child "What letter comes after J or before G?" and they may not be able to answer or it may take a very long time. Poor sequencing skills may show up later on in school as poor organizational skills.

Sequencing Exercises:
- If your child does rely on a song for certain sequencing tasks, like the days of the week, you'll want to ask them questions with some frequency.
- Ask, for example, "What day comes after Wednesday?" to have them work on fully integrating the order of the days.
- It's important to note that once they have mastered after, you can then move on to what day comes before: "What day comes before Thursday?"
- If your child is struggling, write the days of the week on index cards and lay them down in order from left to right. If they cannot recognize the words for the days of the week, draw pictures or use photos of unique things they do on each of the days.
- Later, move on to the months of the year—but make sure they can recite the months in the correct order before asking them which month comes after a certain month.
- Again, once they know what comes after, you can progress to what month comes before a month chosen at random.

Finally, progress to the sequencing of the alphabet. It may seem counterintuitive to work on the alphabet last, but sequencing what letter comes before or after a letter picked at random can be very difficult, particularly for dyslexic learners. Since the alphabet has twenty-six letters, as opposed to the seven days of the week or twelve months, sequencing the alphabet at random without relying on the song can be very tricky, and many dyslexics struggle with this throughout their life.

As children get older and are comfortable with ordering the alphabet, you can start to play the "Picnic Game" together. This game not only helps with sequencing but also short-term memory and concentration. Start with an item that begins with the letter "a" and then progress in alphabetical order. The goal is to get through the alphabet without forgetting what has been said before.

> **Sequencing Game:** To play the "Picnic Game," you and your child take turns saying what you would bring on a picnic or trip. Each one of you must recall what was said in the past and think of a new item to add, even if it's something silly. Person 1 might start by saying, "I am going on a picnic, and I am taking an apple." Then Person 2 continues, "I am going on a picnic, and I am taking an apple and a ball." Person 1 then has another turn: "I am going on a picnic, and I am taking an apple, a ball, and a cat," and so on.

Conceptual Language Development

These next concepts are essential building blocks for a child to master early on. There are endless ways to encourage playing with these ideas to help children gain mastery.

Categorizing (Ages Five and Up)

Dyslexic children tend to have difficulty with organizational skills. Starting your child out early in categorizing and sorting is a good way to begin the process of developing their ability to organize their world (which will be essential in years to come). If your child is five or older, they might already understand the concept of categorizing similar or related items and grouping objects together.

> **Exercise:** Find opportunities that are age appropriate for your child to categorize and then put into subcategories of items in their world. For example, animals (farm animals, sea creatures, bugs), food (fruit, vegetables, dairy products), and so on. Don't be afraid to be creative and increase the difficulty when your child is ready.

Identifying Emotions

If your child is dyslexic, emotional awareness and the ability to verbalize their feelings will have special importance for their emotional well-being going forward. I say this because from my experience, a school-age dyslexic child may encounter higher levels of frustration and possibly depression more consistently than a nondyslexic learner. Helping them learn to verbalize their feelings, therefore, is a skill that is going to serve everybody well.

Identifying, acknowledging, and understanding one's feelings is a lifelong process and starting early is one of the most beneficial things you can do as a parent for any child's emotional well-being. Providing your child with emotional descriptors can help them communicate to others what they're feeling and raise their awareness of their own emotional states. Some families like to use a feelings chart (available online) to offer visual cues to identify feelings when children are quite young.

In a best-case scenario, you can use conversations when they arise spontaneously and even use yourself as a model by identifying your own emotions in a variety of situations as a natural part of your conversations together. For example, you might say, "I had to give a presentation at work today and that made me feel anxious because I did not know if I would be able to answer everyone's questions." Or "Today the cafeteria was out of my favorite sandwich. I felt sad." Or "When I was reading instructions, I felt confused and then became frustrated because I couldn't understand how to fix the problem." You can also ask your child to imagine what another child or adult is feeling when they behave in a certain way. If your child snaps or is rude, you might want to ask them how they are feeling in that moment that made them react to you in that way.

These discussions also help introduce the concept of emotional awareness, not only of ourselves, but of others as well. They can lead to better emotional intelligence, which can add insight and perspective. Perhaps just as helpful, learning to understand and label our own behavior can also introduce the idea of empathy towards others. Ultimately, the more proficient your child becomes in articulating their emotions, the easier it will be for you to help support them to self-regulate and manage their own moods.

When to Seek Professional Help

Take note if your child is continually resistant to any of these games or exercises. Their reactions may help identify an area of weakness and can provide good information for remediations going forward.

If your child has not yet been diagnosed and is having trouble progressing with these games, discriminating sounds, articulating words or rhyming, and/or difficulties in general with expressive and/or receptive (speaking or understanding) language or speech, it is important to consult with your pediatrician, who may suggest that you seek a free speech/language evaluation through the Board of Education in your state. Even though your child may have already been diagnosed, these skills may or may not have been addressed during the testing and may not be part of the interventions suggested. They are very specific to language and many evaluations have a limited language component.

You should also note that if your parental instincts are telling you there is an issue, you have the right to request the speech and language evaluation even if the pediatrician does not think it is warranted.

If they haven't done so before, children who are struggling to develop any of these skills can also be referred to the local school district for evaluations, which may include a speech/language evaluation. Private evaluations can also be done (but this can be a costly option and may or may not be covered by your insurance—refer back to Chapter 3 for a refresher on testing and evaluations).

It bears repeating that seeking help early gives your child the best chance for remediation. If you suspect there is a problem or your child has just been diagnosed with dyslexia, and you are concerned that the experience of getting an evaluation may impact them emotionally, I will remind you that from my experience, the overwhelming majority of my patients truly find comfort in the evaluation process. Receiving a specific diagnosis and learning that there are interventions available to help can offer a huge relief.

THE PARENTS' TOOLBOX
Enhancing Skills from Home

This toolbox is meant to be an easy reference tool for summarizing the many skills discussed in Chapter 4 (and not meant to teach your child how to read). Be sensitive and follow your child's lead as to what they are ready for and avoid pushing them.

It is important to note that dyslexic children are going to have trouble with some or all of these exercises. It is for this reason that it is so important to practice with your child to acquire these skills so as to give them the biggest advantage possible. Remember to always start by demonstrating, then ask them questions with a yes/no answer, progress to open-ended questions, and finally let them ask you the questions.

Developing Phonemic Awareness

- Rhyming and Auditory Skills (distinguishing between different sounds): Practice rhyming games; start by asking rhyming questions, such as "Do 'sing' and 'ring' rhyme?" Later, ask them to gradually rhyme more difficult words: "What rhymes with 'mug'?" "What rhymes with 'could'?"

- Practice identifying *beginning* sounds: Demonstrate two words that start with the same sound, like "lollipop" and "lemon." Ask them if they start with the same sound. Finally, have them say two words that begin with the same sound.
- Then focus on identifying a variety of *ending* sounds. Teach them with examples: "ball" ends in "l," "coat" ends in "t," etc. Make sure to say the sound, not the letter. Ask if "ball" and "coat" end with the same sound, etc. Progress to asking them, "What sound does 'hat' end with? What sound does 'zebra' end with?"
- Once they can identify beginning and ending sounds, then progress to blending sounds. Say the sound "b" then say "at," then say "'b' plus 'at' says 'bat'"; "'p' plus 'en' is 'pen,'" again making sure to say the sound not the letter.
- After blending sounds, have them *isolate* beginning and ending sounds: "sun" without the "s" becomes "un"; "kite" without the "k" sound becomes "ite."
- Next, chunk sounds of words with two or more syllables: for example, "num"-"ber," then have them combine the two (or more) syllables. Visual cues can help a child see the relationship between the sounds.

Developing Directional/Spatial Concepts

- Reinforce laterality by practicing daily identification of left and right. Play progressively challenging games like Twister and "Simon Says."
- Reinforce directionality with games like Rush Hour Junior (for ages five and up) or Rush Hour (for ages eight to adult) to help teach directions such as left/right, up/down in a logical progression. Sit next to your child and encourage them to verbalize each move. Once they have mastered left/right, progress to north, east, south, and west (a mnemonic device may be helpful).
- Number recognition (good for dyscalculia): if your child confuses numbers, engage them with games using numbered blocks or hopscotch to familiarize them with the written numerals.

Developing Temporal Concepts

- Once your child can recognize numbers, teach them time concepts with an analog clock.
- Build sequencing skills (putting things in order) by having your child review their day, in order, before bedtime: What came first, next, and last? Ask for more detail as they improve.
    - Teach your child phone numbers. Break them down by chunking the first three digits, then have your child try repeating it, practice dialing it, seeing it, and writing it. If necessary, making a song may help.
    - Introduce the concepts of the days of the week and their sequence. Later, introduce the months of the year in order.
    - If they struggle, use songs from YouTube to help (search "twelve months of the year songs" online).
    - Once they know the days/months, choose a day of the week and ask, "What day comes *after* X?" Once mastered, ask, "What day comes *before* X?" Do the same with the months of the year. Always start with asking your child what comes after in a sequence before you ask what comes before.
    - Finally, progress to the alphabet and ask what letter comes before or after a certain letter picked at random.

Conceptual Language Skills

- Show your child the concept of categorizing and sorting similar items with examples to develop their organizational skills.
- Help them with emotional awareness by giving them the vocabulary to identify and verbalize their feelings.

PART 2

Adapting to Dyslexia's Challenges

CHAPTER 5

Building the Foundation for Your Family Team

Once you have established a remediation plan, you will want to begin to put the right support systems in place. You may want to consider making the most of your own family by establishing an atmosphere of collaboration. This premise audaciously assumes that rather than *burdening* family members with helping a dyslexic learner, that the special attention required is an *opportunity* for a more collaborative experience and a closer bond for the entire family. It's also an opportunity to educate family members about dyslexia, to convey compassion, galvanize support, and diminish shame.

A Note About "Family"

Families have become so much more diverse and complex today—and as such, when I speak about them, I mean to refer to whatever group is part of your daily or weekly support team. That can comprise any constellation of close individuals, whether related by blood or not—whomever you have in your child's orbit that you trust and depend upon as part of your family's close support circle.

While not everyone can have the benefit of two parents or multiple tutors and therapists, I have seen that a strong "family team," even if it's just one parent and a child, can be a solid core to work from.

The important thing to remember up front with these suggestions is that you are not chasing perfection—rather finding a balance and a style that works day to day for you and your family. The best plan is the one that is realistic and practical for you so that it has the best chance of really sticking.

That being said, I want to encourage you to try your best to be present for your child's needs when you can and not be too punitive towards yourself when you're past your limit. Perfection is not a realistic pursuit for any of us—but awareness and genuine effort over time will make a huge difference. On a good week, you may be able to manage a few of these suggestions below—it all depends on you and your family situation and the demands you juggle. Doing our best is all any of us can shoot for.

Having had the experience of growing up dyslexic myself and then later on, getting to work with so many families that have their own struggles, I have seen that there are practices and perspectives that can be consistently helpful. Dyslexic children may present themselves in so many ways like any other child, but shame can cause self-esteem challenges to quietly take root. So, these family practices, along with consistent messaging, will remind your child about the positives that come with dyslexia's challenges. They are meant to support and bolster your child's foundational sense of security, hopefully before corrosive experiences in school can chip away at their confidence.

Family Rules

A secure home life presents an opportunity to create a safe harbor to develop your child's sense of themselves and their abilities. Structuring that home space, with implicit family rules like those my parents set for us growing up, can create an emotionally stabilizing atmosphere of support. While my academic journey certainly was not always pretty, the security and values of our family foundation were the backbone that allowed me to weather so many storms (and continues to do so to this day).

Emotional Safety

A basic tenet of a happy team is that everybody's emotions are welcome. That requires acknowledging everyone's feelings and allowing them their perceptions of their own unique experiences, early on, even if they do not match up with yours, or are inconvenient at a given moment. We all want to be part of a family built on trust, unconditional love, and the freedom to feel safe to express emotions. The important thing to establish for your child is that, at the end of the day, your family is a team that encourages and supports each other.

Some parents become agitated when young children cry because they think that they are overreacting or being too dramatic. It is your child's right to feel that way. Even if you don't relate to what they are experiencing at that moment, acknowledge that you understand that they are upset. You can show compassion or empathy by accepting their feelings and then giving them some time to express themselves. Whether or not it seems like an overreaction can always be discussed later when they have calmed down, but hearing them out and validating their experience first is essential. This may also be a way a child subconsciously expresses that they need some extra attention, when they don't know how to ask for it.

Avoiding Sibling Rivalry

Bypassing rivalries reinforces the idea of the family as a unified force within the larger context of the outside world. A win for one is a win for everybody (except perhaps in an occasional board game or sport)!

Avoiding competition should start early. While there is a natural rivalry for what are perceived as limited resources in any family, children need to be reminded, likely repeatedly, that they are not favored over each other, that love is not a limited resource, and that they do not need to compete with their siblings for their parents' love.

One mother of a dyslexic learner spoke candidly about sibling rivalry in her family, reporting that she finds herself talking about each child's strengths quite often, in an attempt to balance out praise. She offers explicit examples, calling out the child who struggles academically for his emotional intelligence when the other child is proudly displaying a good test result.

In my family's case, having my younger sister surpass me in school was particularly difficult for me. After struggling as I did each day in school, my parents were mindful not to set me up to feel wounded again at home. Confronting and acknowledging the imbalance (that only got bigger during junior high school and beyond) actually provided a profound sense of relief. Instead of competing against each other, communicating openly allowed us to foster a more harmonious relationship.

While my parents did not magically extinguish our competitiveness completely, they did greatly diminish the friction in the house and reframed how we thought about each other. By early grade school, my sister had already become an important part of my home "team," championing my accomplishments and helping me study when she could.

Acknowledging Dyslexia's Day-to-Day Impact on Your Family

When dyslexia is part of the family dynamic, acknowledging learning differences sensitively within the group and taking care not to use hurtful language or convey shame in any way are key. Explaining and modeling for other family members what dyslexia means, how it will impact your dyslexic child as well as each family member individually, and how it can bring the family together to help are certainly important steps for aligning the group.

They all need to know that they'll likely be called upon to help out, and that you may have to spend extra time helping your dyslexic child with their schoolwork. You want to let them know to be sensitive to their sibling and that "we don't mean tease."

It is also unrealistic to imagine that siblings will be endlessly available and cooperative with each other. Their receptiveness may vacillate depending on their age, time pressures, or mood, but if you can effectively manage to encourage the general ethos of helping each other in your family, it can create a wonderful spirit of teamwork.

Furthermore, the more information that siblings have, and the more candor that they can express (possibly privately), the better one can expect your dyslexic child's needs to be supported by their brothers and sisters. If managed well, dyslexia can invite and expand the spirit of caring and generosity within your family—but you'll do best not to expect perfection!

With regard to parents' contributions to working with their dyslexic child, I was extremely fortunate that my mother was willing and able to teach me and that we worked so well together. I know now how unusual that is. Most children would prefer to work with anyone *but* their parents.

Yet it is important to note that there are many ways to support your child's ability to succeed other than by directly tutoring them. My father's contribution was to take me out for fun study breaks and spend hours and hours with my sister so that she did not feel alone while my mother worked with me. He also consistently celebrated my effort as opposed to my grades and worked extremely long days to pay for the tutoring that I also required.

No doubt, all this time and effort with me took a toll on my parents' time together as well as my mother's availability to my sister. The decision to invest so much effort into helping me was one that impacted the whole family. This is where the family values were clear: Helping one of us was meaningful for everyone; one member's accomplishment was that of the whole family, which required buy-in from each of us. But the realities in your family may be quite different, and it's worth trying to accurately and honestly assess everyone's abilities and limits to best meet the needs of your own family situation.

Managing Family Inequities

If the scales tip toward a dyslexic child receiving extra attention, as they often can, it's also helpful for parents to be aware and try to balance out time and attention for each child when possible. But it can be even better to invite the other members to help so that everybody gets to enjoy being part of a group effort. By acknowledging inequities and then explaining the disparity in your availability, you can allow each family member permission to express their feelings. Whether or not it is convenient or comfortable or easily remedied, validating everybody's experience is an essential part of a safe family space.

This does not mean that all parties need to hear each other's feelings. In fact, it may certainly be appropriate to shield your dyslexic child from having to listen to their sibling's complaints. But being sure to acknowledge the disparities at play in the family dynamic and making a conspicuous effort, on occasion, to remedy the imbalances can go a long way.

Acknowledging your other children's experiences can also prevent them from acting out against the dyslexic family member. The resentments can run deep—offering a teaching moment that exposes some of the difficult truths we all need to accept in life: that things cannot always feel or be "fair" and sometimes others' needs come before our own—and when they do, to not take it personally.

Furthermore, while it may not be optimal, it doesn't take long for these types of imbalances to become somewhat normalized in a family, as happened in my home. But either way, it's a good practice to attempt to remedy a chronic imbalance of attention (and the alliances that can develop as a result) by creating special bonding experiences so that nobody feels left out.

Without putting oneself under undue pressure, the parent tasked with helping one child in particular might try to arrange bonding time with the other child(ren) at some regular interval (even if it can't be frequent intervals). That might mean going out for a special activity or just spending extra time at home doing things, planned around what the other children enjoy. Putting intention and effort into cultivating close connections with all your children can go a long way towards balancing out unavoidable disparities and make everyone feel cared for and important.

Of course, every family approaches inequities differently. One parent of a dyslexic learner that I spoke with has been surprised that her children's needs have "flip-flopped" so dramatically at different stages of their young lives. She expected that the little one, who was dyslexic, would be consistently needier, but at times it has worked out to be the reverse—and continues to change. She talks honestly to both of them about inequities and explains that they need to be patient and wait sometimes while she is tending to the other—asking for them both to make a compromise during these moments. Afterward, if the imbalance was too extreme, she tries to spend special time with the other.

If your children fight or struggle with any of these issues, remember that you are not a failure. Conflict is a completely natural part of family life, as we've all experienced, and everyone is bound to hit rough patches.

Being aware of deeper conflicts and protecting an overall healthy and respectful environment are critically important—and as a parent, it is your job to protect that family dynamic. The hope and the goal are to make each member feel loved, safe, and heard.

Forging a Special Relationship with Your Child

Depending on your skill set and patience level, taking on the role of helping your child with their schoolwork may be one you want to consider. Being a parent is certainly pressure enough, so being a key player in their academic support team may feel overwhelming. But you will likely find that one of the unexpected benefits of putting in this effort is the opportunity to forge a close relationship for you both.

Still, it is important to be real about the extra effort and the potential for a wedge that these needs can cause over the long haul. Part of forging a supportive parental role can be preparing yourself with a realistic anticipation of what a dyslexia diagnosis could mean: more hands-on academic contact with your child; giving additional attention, time, focus, and structure to special aspects of their education; and potentially de-emphasizing grades. If this is far from your own educational experience, it will likely require an adjustment of your expectations as well. But if you can come to see yourself as a compassionate ally to your child, you may create an opportunity to help them form a more peaceful relationship with dyslexia rather than battling it.

By lending yourself to this task to whatever degree you are able, you may expand your own notion of yourself and your capacities as a parent while nurturing a supportive, loving relationship with your child at the same time.

Throughout my career, I have taken note of parents who seem to be able to steer clear of classic pitfalls of trying to work with one's child. From my observation, the most important thing is simply this: to make a sustained and conscious effort to manage your own stressors so as not to become excessively reactive or frustrated by your child. While this may be "simple" advice—clearly it is not easy! What it requires is keeping a handle on one's own feelings and anxieties before going in to help your dyslexic child—and trying to maintain that calm during extended periods.

It may be helpful to remember that one's own children may possess the ability to push your buttons like few others. Having a child with a learning difference can be extremely triggering—whether it's because your own experience in school was so similar to theirs or, conversely, because your learning styles are so divergent. Either way, it can be genuinely overwhelming and frustrating.

While none of us is perfect at this, going through the extra step of consciously taking stock of one's own mood and feelings, before requesting anything from your child, not only benefits your child, but can also help prevent you from projecting your mood or feelings onto your child. Approaching them with less anxiety or frustration spilling in from other parts of your day can free you up to bring more humor, patience, joy, kindness, and understanding into your interactions. This basic but challenging practice serves to help protect everyone from self-attack and sustain a calm atmosphere in which everyone can thrive.

Of course, as your child gets older, challenges like power struggles are likely to be harder to avoid, but having the clarity that you don't want the extra demands of dyslexia to eclipse your connection or turn you into a controlling or nagging voice can provide a rudder.

Fortunately, setting up a good time-management system early on (which I will describe in detail), and putting your child in charge of their own tasks as soon as they're ready, will empower them to drive their own success. You being well organized is a significant part of this effort, too, and can thwart resentments from the added time they may require from you.

It's also important to note that if you are a dyslexic learner yourself, homework and readings may be stressful or uncomfortable for *you*. Sharing the experience of your own struggles can be a supportive means to connect with your child and reinforce to them that they are not alone. If you are able to move past your own discomfort and anxieties, you can provide a bolstering and understanding voice from one who has been there.

But regardless of what type of learner you are, choosing to approach your child's dyslexia from the vantage point of presenting an *opportunity* for a deeper relationship can create space to sidestep controlling behavior and allow you to focus on being the parent that you want to be.

"Humor" Versus "Teasing"

Perhaps because of the big disparity in mine and my sister's academic situations, humor became an indispensable tool to break the tension from all the extra pressure I felt from the long hours I needed to work. When my anger and frustration occasionally bubbled up and became disruptive, my mother often suggested mood-changing family breaks. Sometimes this meant playing a game or having a snack together, which often evoked humor. These family moments allowed us all to laugh at ourselves and helped me to dispel the shame and embarrassment I was hiding. Even just changing the energy helped me shift gears and expel tension. The good-natured atmosphere of acceptance made all the difference and actually managed to bring joy into what had previously been a stressful moment.

Teasing, as distinct from humor, is another matter. While teasing is an entirely natural and fun way that kids interact with each other, it's helpful to create boundaries around it, particularly in your home. So, if one child unkindly teases the other related to being dyslexic, you as a parent can step in to make it clear that you won't tolerate "mean teasing." You can also point out strengths and weaknesses that we all have, to diffuse the sting of hurtful comparisons or words. You have the power to shut down the negativity within your family dynamic and you should. Your ability to role model how to identify when someone has crossed the line, and then to intervene, can teach your child to fend for themselves in other settings. Demonstrating this at home will also convey to your child that they do not need to reflexively absorb harsh words elsewhere.

From my own experience, as I got older and had encounters with mean teasing, I learned to cope by acknowledging my dyslexia and trying to infuse humor. It was fruitless to pretend that I wasn't having issues in school, but it took years before I had the fortitude to relax my ego and accept my struggles in front of my peers. That's when self-deprecating humor became my own personal social life raft.

Of course, each individual is different in this regard, but in talking to a variety of dyslexic learners, I often hear about their own rush to point out their dyslexia ahead of anyone noticing it first. Whereas I don't recommend drawing attention to oneself *in advance* to point out weaknesses, if a learning difference becomes conspicuous, humor can lessen the self-consciousness and soften the embarrassment.

For me, after many years of taking on shame, I learned to call out my challenges in a light way rather than become avoidant of participating in class or be self-conscious with my peers. In the final analysis, I now realize that hiding my deficits was so much more stressful than just acknowledging them with humor.

Everyone Brings Something Special to the Table

One central principle that my parents instilled is that everyone, regardless of learning style, needs to feel valued and important. Encouraging partnership in the family and highlighting each member's strengths dissipates jealousies and makes everybody feel appreciated. In keeping with this idea is the benefit of giving each family member small tasks and chores to make them feel valued and needed from a young age.

On a most basic level, inclusion in everyday family tasks serves to instill cohesion. When applied to making dinner, or on special occasions, for example, it means letting the child who can spell and has nice handwriting write out place cards, allowing the musical family member to take charge of picking music, the artistic one to arrange plates of food, etc. If your child is physically strong, they can help bring in the groceries and lift pots. If they enjoy cake decorating but the cake doesn't turn out perfect, don't worry. Perfection or a major talent is not as essential as the rewarding experience of participation, whether big or small.

While they may not always be welcomed by your children, the tasks are important, not only to give you support and build the habit of sharing responsibilities, but because they provide opportunities to promote family participation and membership. So be creative in doling out small jobs; ultimately, tasks can be fluid, changing each day or week, but the message that everyone is truly needed and appreciated is paramount.

The Power of Inclusion

While your own family will certainly be unique in its traditions and special bonds, times of prolonged struggle for your child can be an opportunity to mobilize extended family members and/or friends to join in. Capitalize on each other's skills and temperaments to let everyone take part. Freeing up a parent so that they can, for example, quiz a child for a test, or toss a ball around during a study break, contributes to the core idea of lending a hand to lessen the workload. All are wonderful opportunities to forge connections and let each member feel valued in contributing time and energy to a unifying cause.

Rather than being a burden, when the extra effort is shared, you are creating a loving extended family team, which is a win for everyone. Along the same lines, you might feel that asking others for help is a sign of weakness or imposes a burden, but from a different lens, it can be viewed as an inclusive opportunity, conveying recognition of someone's competence in a special area.

The general American trend towards individuality over many decades has to some degree eclipsed the importance of feeling part of a larger group or something bigger than oneself. But bringing the focus back to promoting the family as a unit does not need to diminish each individual's push to do their best. In the best case, it can simultaneously elevate each member to feel the satisfaction and enjoyment of working towards the greater good of the group. Within this system of mutual support, you certainly don't want to ignore the needs of one child to cater fully to the other.

Once the value of contributing to the welfare of the family is understood and everyone is on board, with a little creativity, there are ways to encourage involvement from other family members that don't have to garner resentment. For example, the plus side of asking a sibling to take a study break with your dyslexic child can later result in recognizing them for being really helpful and kind. Or asking an older child to pitch in with homework might even boost *their* self-esteem—having been entrusted with an important task.

This kind of inclusiveness contributes to the demonstration of the concept of your family as a team rather than every individual managing solo. Participation can be deeply satisfying and empowering when we all realize that we can make an important difference for each other. Just as profound, the unspoken message is that if *they* were ever to have a special need, the family will willingly be there for them as well.

Getting your children's buy-in without them feeling pressured will help them work well together. But teaching generosity of spirit does not come overnight, which is why the culture and values of the family are so meaningful. These opportunities for inclusion promote the important life lessons around the pleasures of giving of oneself to those you love and care about.

As a side benefit, collaboration also inevitably adds opportunities for fun and humor. But don't forget to acknowledge your helpers—this will make them feel appreciated and reinforce their important role in the family. A heartfelt "thank you" is always welcome.

Managing Expectations and Celebrating Gains

Many times I've noticed that dyslexic learners put an immense amount of pressure on themselves to succeed. My personal observation is that they may be craving the positive reinforcement of a good grade in order to be acknowledged for all their hard work and perhaps even prove to themselves that they can succeed.

Even if your child does not earn the grade they are hoping for, celebrating the small successes along the way and setting up a feel-good work-reward system that prizes resilience and tenacity is what I recommend. Rewards do not have to be big—just recognizing an accomplishment verbally sometimes is most meaningful. Expressing that you are proud of their effort or offering a big hug might suffice. Doing something fun for a few minutes after a big study effort or after getting back a grade on a paper or test that you and your child find acceptable (it might not be an A) and that reflects hard work may be enough. At other times, a small treat like a sticker, bath bomb, extra free time, or a favorite meal for dinner might provide special encouragement. The important thing to remember is that being a dyslexic learner is continually tough—and recognizing progress and hard work, despite whether or not that effort translates into high grades, is meaningful for your child.

When a dyslexic learner studies diligently and gets a C on a test or paper (or in my case, a C- in chemistry), that grade may be a hard-earned accomplishment that deserves real recognition. If a nondyslexic child comes home with the same grade, you might want to know what happened and what they missed. Kids will understandably ask why you have a different standard for each of them. Without being patronizing, you can genuinely reply that *hard work and effort is the standard; less so, the grades earned.*

Talking to Your Child About Grade Disparities Between Siblings

Your child might ask why you celebrate their C but want their sibling to strive for a higher grade. I like to say something along the lines of *"The goal is to always do our very best. Everyone has their own unique strengths and weaknesses. Putting forth our best effort with hard work and discipline is what we value."*

If the grade is a disappointment, the next challenge is honing the resilience to shake it off in order to get up the next day and try all over again. Here is where your responses can be so pivotal. I find that kids tend to look to you for how to respond and often internalize your perspective. So if you don't overreact and instead say something like "This grade doesn't reflect your efforts, and that's really disappointing," they get the message that it's not the end of the world. Acknowledging and validating your child's emotional experience is an essential piece of helping them move through what can be gut-wrenching experiences. Then helping them reframe the disappointment and allowing them to let it go by reminding them of the bigger picture can help move this process along and prepare them emotionally for their next challenge.

These moments also offer a learning opportunity for your child to figure out ways to be more efficient and targeted with their study methods going forward, to learn from their mistakes. Remember that a lot of vulnerability goes into trying hard, so it's key to celebrate the courage and effort that your child expends.

Hopefully, with time, they will consolidate their gains and learn mastery of skills that are their biggest challenges now. The trick is in finding the balance between being realistic about abilities and knowing that with enough effort and perseverance you can also conquer things that don't come naturally. This is really what one hopes their dyslexic child can get from their education: the confidence that when they apply themself—even if it takes extra time and diligence—they know they can accomplish their goals.

Navigating Differing Opinions

Amidst the best circumstances, the challenge of raising kids can be stressful, so having a child who requires extra help with schoolwork will no doubt add more complexity. From my experience, I've seen how normal it is for partners to have differing opinions, sometimes radically different, regarding how to take care of their children's learning requirements and enforce rules fairly within their family. Objectively, there can be legitimate room for disagreement. If you both have not had to deal with academic struggles as a youngster, these may be uncharted waters that are hard for the uninitiated to navigate. Or if either of you have dealt with similar issues, raising a child and seeing them struggle as you have can certainly trigger a lot of strong feelings, fears, and concerns.

I believe that regardless of the debate, the essential challenge is to listen well to each other and work at respecting and giving airtime to each other's feelings and preferences. Of course, even when all parties share the best intentions for a child, there can be a wide range of perspectives. Each may need to make compromises to come to a mutually agreeable approach that is beyond the other's comfort zone. Patience with each other during these moments is important while one or the other member of a couple gets comfortable with a new approach.

From my own observation, in trying to resolve a variety of concerns of the parents I see in my practice, the key to raising a child is finding the happy medium between allowing flexibility in stretching rules and maintaining boundaries. Applying which one at which time is the trick. While couples don't always agree on where to land on that continuum, I like an approach where kids are heard. That doesn't mean that they will get what they want every time, but in a family with good communication, everybody's voice is valued.

Furthermore, applying rules (that are agreed upon by both parents) consistently is a key way to create emotional safety—but sometimes there needs to be an exception or a special reward. A lot depends on having a good sense of your child, when they're legitimately struggling and when they're just whining because they're hungry or tired—or both! Generally when you have a child with dyslexia, I do believe you benefit from the flexibility of thinking outside of the box to problem solve and deciding when to rigidly enforce rules.

If you are raising your child with a partner, make sure to take time to nurture that relationship; it's foundational for the whole family and models balance for everyone—so don't shortchange yourselves. The same is true if you are raising children on your own. Your well-being is vital. Either way, being able to assess if you or you as a couple need help is essential to everyone, so be mindful to seek help if necessary.

When tensions get high, trying to introduce levity can be extremely valuable. It may not be automatic at first, but if you can both keep in mind the importance of injecting humor during difficult moments, it can help everybody ease tensions and inject perspective. In the long run, this will make a big difference along your journey together as a family.

If you are raising a dyslexic child with a partner whom you no longer live with, chances are the previous advice is not going to be easy. It may be that all you can do is try to diligently enforce rules to protect your child while they are under your roof. But everything you model for them will likely register, so if you can find a way towards consistency, humor, and perspective, and allow your child the freedom to process their feelings, you are setting a good foundation, whether they are physically with you most days or not.

Finding Extra Support for You or Your Child

It is not unusual for parents to feel stressed when unanticipated needs emerge, and it is understandable to become overwhelmed. Fortunately, the number of available resources has expanded significantly in recent years, as the demand has increased. The stigma around utilizing these resources has also diminished.

If, at any point, you feel you need the support of a counselor, psychologist, or a support group for you or your child, whether online or in person, your child's school psychologist may be a good resource for individual help, referrals, and guidance. You may also find support partnering with a tutor, special education or classroom teacher, or another proactive parent.

Where to Find Help

The following organizations may be a useful starting point for finding tutors, psychologists, psychiatrists, and local support groups:

The Learning Disabilities Association of America:
   https://ldaamerica.org
The International Dyslexia Association:
   https://dyslexiaida.org

National Center for Learning Disabilities:
   www.ncld.org
SmartKids with Learning Disabilities:
   www.smartkidswithld.org

As mentioned previously, if all else fails and you are not finding the help you need, you may want to establish your own parent group to connect with others to share resources and ideas. One mother I know with a dyslexic child started an affinity group for parents of children with learning differences because she wasn't finding the support she craved in the school. Over the years, she was able to persuade the school's administration to attend some of the meetings, which ultimately led to their better understanding of children who required accommodations in the school.

Groups of individuals, going through related struggles, can have a powerful and positive impact on each other and can be a fantastic resource. Seeing that your peers are finding similar challenges can help anyone feel less alone and more competent as well.

While it took decades for me to fully recognize the gifts of growing up with dyslexia, my goal is to help you and your child discover the advantages early so that your child can grow up with a better frame of reference and mindset than I did. With the understanding that everyone's needs and resources are different, I want to underscore that I truly believe that beyond surviving a diagnosis of dyslexia, your child and your whole family can actually get to a place where you can thrive and be more connected as a result of putting the previous ideas into practice.

THE PARENTS' TOOLBOX
Building the Foundation for Your Family Team

- Establish family rules and practices for emotional safety:
    Everybody's feelings are welcome and are worthy of validation.
    Educate family members about dyslexia to convey compassion, galvanize support, and diminish shame.
    Try to stay compassionate and supportive by hearing each other out and validating each other's feelings.
    Call out and shut down sibling rivalry in a gentle way to minimize competitiveness, which risks being particularly hard on a dyslexic child.
    Help children vocalize their feelings and stay aware of resentments building from inequities in attention from parents.
    Speak honestly about perceived imbalances regarding a parent's time.

- If your dyslexic child requires a majority of the available parental attention, try to bring in other members (grandparents, close friends, and so on) to help rebalance.

- If a sibling is frequently missing out on attention, make a special effort to do something nonacademic to spend time with them.
    Establish a "no tolerance policy" for "mean teasing" within your household (especially with regard to a young dyslexic child's learning differences). This models how your child can manage similar situations outside of the house (when you're not there to protect them).
    As children get older, use humor in the family to demonstrate that it's okay to laugh at yourself to dispel shame and embarrassment and to help children build ego strength.
    Acknowledge each family member's value and importance by giving small tasks and chores to help everyone feel recognized in their contribution.

> - Giving everyone a role in supporting a dyslexic child can create family cohesion and shift each member's emphasis from their own wants and needs to that of the group's.
> - Help manage your child's expectations by de-emphasizing grades and celebrating effort, hard work, and small successes for your dyslexic learner.
> - If the grade is a disappointment, help your child review what they missed and gain insight into how to improve their studying process.
> - Hone the ability to shake off a disappointing grade as a lesson in resilience.
> - Praise resilience and tenacity and set up small rewards for hard work when it feels right.
> - When parental differences erupt, give airtime to each other to voice feelings. Find room for compromise.
> - Try to reach a happy medium between allowing flexibility and maintaining boundaries in applying rules for your child.
> - Preserving time for yourself as an individual or for you both as a couple is foundational and models balance for everyone. Don't shortchange yourself on seeking help if you or you as a couple are struggling.
>
> If necessary, seek assistance from a qualified therapist, tutor, and/or support group, whether in person or online.

CHAPTER 6

Promoting the Best Study Skills and Habits

Instilling basic organizational habits provides foundational skills for both dyslexic learners as well as children diagnosed with ADHD. Children with these diagnoses often have trouble organizing their time and physical surroundings, as well as putting writing assignments into a logical order. All of these related skills should be promoted as early as possible to successfully nurture a child's ability to manage their schoolwork and therefore develop their independence and autonomy.

Instilling Time-Management Practices

Simple habits of making lists, estimating time frames, and planning for when to accomplish tasks is the best way to launch your child into taking responsibility for managing their academic life. In order to build towards this practice, creating a chart (either with words or with rows of pictures of daily tasks like a toothbrush, hairbrush, bathtub if they can't read) of their daily responsibilities, to be checked off once completed, instills the positive experience of accomplishment.

As your child matures, you can create more precise lists to continue expanding their organizational habits as well as to introduce the concept of prioritizing. The beauty of these practices is that as a child learns to organize their time, they are simultaneously sidestepping the necessity of you having to remind them to do chores (aka nagging)!

These simple time-management steps begin to allow your child to have agency over their day and will go a long way as their responsibilities mount in school. Learning to prioritize what is most important to them helps build a firm foundation for executive functioning as well. So, if you expect your child to clean their room and take a bath but they want to go play, help them come up with a plan and a timeline to accomplish all three.

If all goes well, these habits should continue straight through high school and require less and less oversight.

Here's how to introduce this practice as soon as your child starts to be assigned homework in elementary school and continue on through high school:

- When children arrive home from school, allow them time to relax, have a snack, and unwind a bit before starting to plan for how to budget their time. Keep in mind that dyslexic children expend a lot of extra mental energy to get through a day at school and therefore may need real downtime before starting homework.
- Start your child off with an expanding folio or file folders with sections separating subjects to help them organize their returned assignments. (This folio can stay home and does not have to go back and forth to school.) This will prevent papers from being lost in the abyss of their backpack or desk.
- As their academic demands increase, new assignments should be written down. In order to organize multiple assignments and daily responsibilities, use Google Keep or a hardcopy

Promoting the Best Study Skills and Habits

homework planner. Have them check off items as they're completed.
- Remind your child to put each assignment in Google Keep or their planner immediately, as it is assigned in class, so they do not forget.
- Help your child estimate the time required to complete their different tasks and homework.
- Encourage padding their estimates since underestimating time required for tasks is a common problem for children who have yet to master a skill. You will quickly learn if they tend to over- or underestimate the time required.
- Encourage your child to think about prioritizing the order in which items need to be accomplished. This is a nice way to introduce them to the idea of thinking strategically about approaching their work.
- Weekend time management is important too. It's not unusual for students to ignore their schoolwork until Sunday night. You can avoid the stress of doing things last minute by setting a weekend schedule on Fridays, allotting time for recreation and homework.
- In middle school continue with Google Keep (or a paper planner if they prefer) to keep track of short- and long-term homework assignments and projects, planned activities with friends, appointments, chores, and extracurricular activities.
- Gradually, over months and years (if necessary), work towards having your child generate the timeline themself. Hopefully by high school this habit will be so firmly established that they will need very little input organizing their time and managing their responsibilities. You will want to extricate yourself from the day-to-day oversight role as soon as they're ready.

Simple though they are, these steps are invaluable for a dyslexic child's success in school and to help them become self-reliant. Planning tasks and giving consideration to priorities and timelines lay the foundation for developing sequencing skills to exert control over when things need to happen. As one who has been there, learning these skills meant I could accomplish tasks successfully without my mother nagging me, which made me feel more in control of my life—a huge win during school!

Organizational Study Materials

Aside from developing the habit of time management, your child will most likely need organizational supervision and guidance with their notes as they near the end of elementary school. Assuming that your child's school is still using handwritten note-taking, here are the school supplies that I suggest:

1. Notebooks: separate notebooks with different colors for each class or one large binder with separate sections for each class.
2. An expanding folio file folder: mark each section with individual subject names, then use the sections to place returned tests, papers, and homework separated for each class.
3. Pen/pencil case: keep writing utensils, including different color highlighters, in a case so they are readily available.

Along with overseeing the time frame of their assignments and deadlines, you'll want to set your child up to be able to clearly separate their papers, notes, and notebooks for each subject in school. Promoting the habit of dating their notes (whether on their computer or on paper) keeps things sequentially organized. To further instill these practices, it's a good idea to occasionally review your child's system to make sure they are diligently organizing on a regular basis so that things don't fall into chaos.

Organizing Lockers and Desks

If your child is very disorganized, they may need your help or the aid of a learning specialist or school psychologist who would be willing to meet with them before or after school to assist them in organizing their school locker. It's best to try to do this discreetly without other students around. This is especially useful for children with attention deficit disorder with or without hyperactivity.

At home, they may also need your help straightening out their desk. If you can help them build good organizational habits early on, and they experience how efficient and time-saving an orderly setup can be, hopefully they will be motivated to continue.

Organizing Writing Projects

Teaching your dyslexic child how to organize a paper is generally not an easy task—you may prefer to leave it for their teachers or learning specialists at school. If they require special help, you may want to see if one of their teachers is able to work with them before or after school. If this job lands on you, there are numerous online resources to consult that provide more detailed information and ideas (search terms in YouTube such as "scaffolding" or "mapping a paper").

Establishing Effective Study Practices

One of the key differences in learning practices for dyslexic children is the necessity to overlearn material so it can be easily and quickly recalled. The idea is that rather than cramming material right before a test, a child needs to review a subject intermittently over a few days to get to an automaticity of recall (similar to how easily they can tell you two plus two equals four).

This practice is important throughout school and is relevant not just for sight words and math facts, but eventually for studying any other subject.

Helpful Definitions

Automaticity. Ingrained learning that requires almost no conscious thought to recall.

Overlearning. Reviewing or practicing information or a skill repeatedly until it can be retrieved quickly.

To illustrate the importance of overlearning, here's how things went for me as a child: If I was studying spelling words for a quiz, I would work on each word at home and go into school feeling confident that I knew how to spell them all correctly. Then I would take the quiz, become a little nervous, and the next thing I knew, I would only spell half or three-quarters of the words correctly. At home, when there was no time pressure, I could slowly process a word and think about how to spell it. In school, when the pace was more rapid-fire, there was no time for my brain to recall the information. The more anxious I became, the worse the outcome.

This is typical for how a dyslexic child can do well with a specific word one minute and struggle with the same word a few minutes later. It's easy to misinterpret the mistakes as an attentional issue—but these inconsistencies can happen repeatedly and intermittently, even after big gains are made. The reality is that this inconsistency is typical for a dyslexic person.

Overlearning everything until it is automatic is a great way to combat these processing issues,[1] with the only downside being that it requires planning ahead. Rather than studying or cramming for a night, mastery will happen over several days or weeks, calling upon your child to retrieve the same information over a more extended period of time.

Knowing and accepting that a dyslexic child might take longer to recall information than a typical learner can better set expectations for parents. Patiently working within a calm, relaxed, noncompetitive, and noncritical setting and repeating the information or quizzing them often can encourage your child to commit material to long-term memory. Take heart that although they will likely take a slower path to process information, they will indeed get there.

Different Learning Styles

To help minimize the time and frustration of studying repetitively, a child can benefit greatly from figuring out which modes of learning are most effective for them. Keep in mind that as their classes become more demanding, flexibility and using a variety of approaches may be most beneficial. As an example, if your child learns best by *listening* to information rather than reading or writing it, they may find that listening repeatedly to lectures or narrations of books helps them to learn the material most easily. But once they feel they know it, it would still benefit them to take a written quiz or try to (verbally) teach the material to someone else (or record it on their phone). This allows them to practice and reinforce the material using different modalities.

The following list of learning approaches can help you help your child identify which modes they are naturally aligned with. They will likely benefit from using a combination of these approaches depending on the subject matter. (See Resources on pages 237–242 for a list of all tools mentioned.)

Visual learning. When taking notes or rewriting information, your child may benefit from inserting pictures or symbols, and/or using charts and graphs as helpful prompts. Underlining, highlighting, and using different fonts, and/or large type sizes, and/or colors will also help to organize information into categories.

Auditory learning. Audiobooks are one of the most helpful technological advancements for dyslexic learners, particularly if their own reading is slow and lacks fluency, which leads to poor comprehension. Your school's learning specialist should have a list of resources and accounts that allow your child free access to this wonderful tool. Being able to listen to text read aloud can help them get through a larger volume of reading in less time. *But be sure they read along while listening* to develop their reading fluency and automaticity in order to help bolster their reading skills (see Resources, pages 237–242). Children can also benefit from devices such as Livescribe smartpens, which transform both handwritten notes and audio into a digital format for convenient playback. These smartpens have an embedded camera to capture written content and a microphone to record spoken words.

Storytelling. Providing context and background for what a child is about to learn can be effective for all types of learners. Many students benefit from *scaffolding* new information into a story to offer context. (Scaffolding is a method used to help a student learn new information or develop a new skill by presenting background information.) Dyslexia experts Drs. Eide and Eide's research suggests that dyslexic learners may benefit even more than neurotypical learners using this style. Since material is not always presented in this way in school, you may occasionally have to be the one to help present it in this format. So, for example, if your child is about to learn a new topic in history or English literature, offering them a background story and a synopsis of what they are about to be presented in school can draw them into the topic and make it more comprehensible.

Experiential learning. Most children enjoy hands-on, tangible, interactive experiences to absorb new ideas and concepts. Using more than one sense at a time can stimulate different areas of the brain, which benefits most learners, including dyslexics, as well as enhance our ability to learn.[2] For example, when teaching the concept of addition or multiplication, tangible items such as marbles or M&M's can help make math fun and conceptually understandable. If you are working on fractions, you can divide a pizza, a cookie, a pie, etc., or involve your child in baking and use measuring cups and spoons to demonstrate.

This can also be applied for children when first learning to read and blend sounds together by employing a visual cue to *see* how two phonemes or words come together to form a word. This is done by using your open left palm (if your child is in front of you) to represent the first part of a word or sound, like "b" (the sound of the letter, not the letter itself). Then bring up your right hand and say the second sound "at." Then bring your two hands together and say "bat," visually demonstrating how the sounds are blended. This works with compound words as well; say "base" and "ball" as you repeat your previous actions and bring your hands together representing the two parts forming one word. (Search "Haggerty phonemic awareness" on YouTube to find helpful videos.)

Study Methods

Here are some effective methods to help a child study:

Teaching others. Some dyslexic learners, including those with dysgraphia (who have trouble with written language), can benefit from repeatedly reviewing information verbally. This can be done by explaining material to another person (or even a stuffed animal), or by recording oneself. It's a great way to assess if one really knows a subject thoroughly.

Working with a study buddy. Finding another student in the class to discuss and hash things out with can be extremely helpful. Reviewing notes in preparation for a test or a presentation together can be an effective and enjoyable way to learn material. Aside from the social benefits, it can also help students clear up any gaps in their note-taking or understanding of the material.

Creating quizzes and study games. If your child is preparing for an exam, one effective study method is to have them create a quiz for themselves. Whether manually or digitally, using websites like Quizlet, students can create different types of study guides and games from their textbooks to give them practice and make studying more fun.

Writing and rewriting notes. Rewriting notes in longhand, rather than typing them, can aid in acquiring information, concepts, etc. (This mode is not suited for students with dysgraphia.) Rewriting and continuing to condense class and reading notes can clarify and reinforce the information—the more times the better. It should be noted that typing and retyping has not been shown to be as effective.[3] Although typing may be neater and more legible, it unfortunately does not connect to the same pathways in the brain as handwriting does.

While I have not come upon research studies on this method, I personally discovered and recommend that writing information repetitively, making the last time right before going to sleep, can help reinforce the material.

Creating mnemonics. Some dyslexic children can see or hear something a few times or even once and be able to recall it. Typically, however, dyslexic children will have a difficult time committing something to memory and will require a lot of repetition and rehearsal in order for it to be memorized and automatically recalled.

Mnemonics are effective learning tricks to make memorization easier and less tedious. Much like when you taught your child the days of the week by singing a song when they were younger, you can utilize rhyming or association tricks, or a framework such as setting information to a song, or creating an acronym prompt to facilitate recall of new information. Other examples of mnemonic techniques, which can help make recall easier for any type of learner, include:

- chunking (the way we divide phone numbers into small groupings with the area code, three numbers, and then four numbers instead of just trying to remember a group of ten numbers)

- clustering (grouping similar items in a list)
- imagery (visualizing an image to help with recall)
- elaboration (telling a story about events in history to place the events in chronological order)

Using flash cards. Creating flash cards is beneficial for learning a wide variety of subjects and good for rote memorization, acquiring new vocabulary words, multiplication tables, historical facts, and more. Make them small and handy so they're portable and can be referred to easily in the car, during downtimes, and before bedtime, too. Flash cards can be reviewed even months later to ensure the information is still committed to memory. Plus, the process of writing out the cards is itself a good step in acquiring the material.

One student reported that she makes flash cards and then poses a question to herself based on the material. Then she records herself answering the question, and listens back to what she said while checking her notes to make sure that she did not omit any information.

Staying Aware of New Technologies

With so many new technologies available, dyslexic students are devising new and better ways to study centered around their specific strengths and needs. Schools have different rules around which technologies they allow in the classroom, so you will want to clear the use of devices before purchasing them for your child. For example, the ability to record lectures can help students to review their notes and make sure they were accurately transcribed, but some schools will not permit their use. Some math apps (including Photo Math, MathWay) solve math problems to allow students to check over their work in detail, to be sure they fully understand the steps, though some schools prohibit their use. Staying ahead of all the new technologies at your child's disposal as well as the ever-changing rules in school systems will help you both come up with creative ways to address their particular needs in the classroom and at home. (For more information, see Resources, pages 237–242.)

Tips to Encourage Your Child to Read

Whether for pleasure or for school, having your child read books to you or to themselves, or even listening to audiobooks, is a plus (but be sure to have them follow along in the book form). Tempt them with anything at all that sparks their curiosity and interests so they'll be motivated to read during their free time or at night before bed. Finding even just one special book, early on, that really captivates your child can lead to a lifetime love of reading. Comic books, graphic novels, book series, or even a specialized magazine targeted to their interests can be part of hooking a child into reading. If your child loves a book that has been made into a movie and they want to see the movie, you may be able to entice them to read if you apply a "book-first" rule. This was an idea one clever mother came up with to incentivize her dyslexic daughter to read. That child is now a high school teacher.

Working Towards Balance and Moderation

If your child has the correct educational support in place, as well as appropriate accommodations for their needs, they are primed to thrive in school. At the same time, prioritizing some basics is also a great idea. The way I like to explain it to parents is that if a dyslexic child is already taxed just trying to keep up with their peers, their brain may be more prone to short circuit from things that might not bother a nondyslexic child. For example, if your child comes home after a difficult day at school, likely unaware that they are maxed out, and they don't get the amount of sleep they require or they eat excessive amounts of sugar, they are working from a deficit. This is not great for a typical learner, either, but they may have a bit more bandwidth to fall back on. So, you'll want to be mindful to try to establish these important habits:

Technology. While it is certainly convenient as a parent to set your child in front of a screen to entertain themself, setting limits early on in their life will prepare them well for managing a balance in their relationship with technology, right from the start.

We all know that cell phones, tablets, social media, etc. have replaced a lot of the activities that kids historically spent their time doing. The teenage brain is particularly sensitive to novel experiences. Apps and technology feed into the brain's reward system in the form of dopamine that can lead to a struggle with regulation and maintaining moderation.[4] While kids are working on their computers doing homework, messages pop up advising them of emails, texts, new social media posts on Instagram and YouTube, and on and on. These devices are creating a type of distractibility in all of us, but children are particularly susceptible.

Every professional will recommend limiting a child's time on screens and social media to help teach moderation, minimize anxiety, and increase happiness. We all have to exercise discipline in taking time away from our devices and any parent can tell you this is rarely easy to enforce, particularly with teenagers.

While it is not realistic to block your children from devices forever, you can invoke constraints or blackout periods during heavy work times, as well as family mealtimes and family outings. Experts recommend coming up with a media plan related to a child's age, personality, and developmental age that includes encouraging time to exercise and facilitating getting adequate sleep.[5]

Certainly, the older a child gets the more difficult trying to exert control becomes, but helping them set boundaries for themselves early on is a great start. Your example can also inspire their self-control later, despite all their protestations.

By middle school, dyslexic children surely know that it takes them longer to do their work than their peers, so helping them set up parameters will greatly aid their own self-discipline. I recommend instilling a rule to turn off all notifications while they are sitting down to get work done. Let them know that this will help their efficiency so that they can get back to their social lives or at least "check in" sooner once they finish their work or during break time. Encouraging your child to put their phone in a different room while getting work done can further minimize distractions.

If you're not yet convinced of the real importance of limiting social media exposure for your child, the Academy of Pediatrics cites its connection to sleep deprivation, distractibility, addictive behaviors, obesity, behavioral issues, as well as leading to risky online behaviors like sexting, etc. Furthermore, multitasking online while doing homework can negatively affect schoolwork.[6]

If you find your child continually resistant to separating from social media, you may want to dig deeper and inquire into what they get out of being on their device. Sitting back and listening and allowing them to give thought to examining whether or not they are indeed getting what they're craving can be a useful bit of self-exploration. It may be a time to remind them that moderation in all things, regardless of what they see their friends doing, is actually vital. If they are not able to limit themselves and the parameters you set do not help them exercise self-control, you may want to seek professional help.

Nutrition. It's hard to say enough about the importance of what we put into our bodies and how that can affect cognitive functioning. While I am not a nutritionist, my observation for myself and my family is one shared by the American Dyslexia Association, which suggests that a balanced diet rather than too much sugar or processed foods is important for overall health and optimal mood. But I encourage you to do your own deep dive into what works best for your child.

When I was growing up, some of my long hours of work were rewarded by baking, which meant consuming sugar. Today, I push my children to find ways to relieve stress that are not food focused. If they do want to cook, I have them find healthy recipes or bake bread rather than sugary desserts. Likewise, instead of a sweet reward for a couple of hours of work, try to provide a healthy snack or, better yet, throw a ball around or go for a quick run or walk with them. If they've had an especially tough day, rather than using a dessert as a treat, I might offer to watch a sitcom together, play cards, do a puzzle, take a yoga or dance class online, or watch a few funny quick videos.

Sleep. One thing most everyone can agree upon these days is the importance of sleep for the brain and overall health. For a child's brain it is no doubt crucial. While no one gets enough sleep, particularly in high school, do the best you can. Some parents fear that allowing their teenager to "sleep in" on weekends, when nothing else is going on, will encourage laziness. I strongly disagree. If they don't have sports or other activities, let them rest; an adolescent's developing brain needs it.[7]

Also important is instilling the habit of no screens before bedtime to help your children fall asleep. If that is unrealistic, have them wear blue-light-blocking glasses or use screen filters on their devices in the evening, which have been shown to minimize sleep disturbances.[8]

Exercise. Getting involved in a sport or physical activity can be life-changing and build a habit that benefits overall health. Countless studies extoll exercise for brain health as well.[9] A strong body helps develop a sense of strength that goes beyond the physical, with the added bonus of releasing tension. If you feel physically strong and fit, you may well feel emotionally stronger, too. Plus, the endorphins from a good workout can deliver a sense of well-being and happiness for the whole day!

Humor. You know by now that I believe humor to be essential for thriving in most of life's challenging situations. Research supports that laughter improves mood, relieves stress, boosts immunity, and can even enhance our ability to learn.[10,11] Childhood is certainly not easy, and growing up with dyslexia can amplify difficulties—so remember to encourage your child to laugh and find humor around them. It will help everyone keep perspective and lighten up long nights of studying. Finding humor together as a family in simple things infuses a bit of joy and demonstrates a resilience of spirit every day!

Don't Underestimate Your Influence

I also recommend modeling these behaviors yourself; it will be infinitely harder to get your child to put down their phone or ignore a notification, be disciplined about eating well or getting exercise if you are continually distracted by technology and eat poorly. Demonstrate your values by letting them witness you putting your phone in the other room during dinner, avoiding devices when you're interacting with family members or while you're at a restaurant together. Exemplify restraint and conscious disconnection to prioritize your time together for everybody's mental health.

Likewise, modeling the ability to laugh at yourself demonstrates ego strength, while helping the family enjoy some fun together. Sharing your hobbies and interests can also allow them to see other ways to fill their time. Making sure that they see you do your own self-care, making healthy choices, like exercising, crafting, and reading, can make an impact, too.

Increasing Attention Span with Breaks

Breaks and downtime can be very effectively used for children with dyslexia (and ADHD). Determining the interval length that your child can maintain focus before they'll need a change of activity is generally a function of age and practice. For example, young or highly active children may sit for less than twenty minutes and then need five minutes to recuperate by running around or doing some jumping jacks, etc., whereas older children might work for sixty to ninety minutes or more and then need to shift gears for fifteen or twenty minutes.

Whichever works for your child is fine, but to find the best flow, you'll want to establish a reasonable (not excessively packed) schedule by trial and error. The thing to keep in mind is that the brain learns best in smaller increments.[12] Excessively long spans of work for a young dyslexic child can push them past their limit, leading them to become overwhelmed, so I suggest helping to build in breaks as needed. The balance of work to breaks will likely change and progress as their ability to concentrate increases over time.

If they have a large volume of things to study, it's best to separate the lessons into smaller parts and learn a little each day. For example, if they need to learn twenty spelling or vocabulary words, try mastering a few at a time and then tackle another small group. Going back and studying them again as a review after a few days will reinforce gains.

Benefits of "Low-Tech" Breaks

While there are many high-tech tools and games to entertain or help a child relax, children benefit from a balanced diet of screen time relative to low-tech activities. It is for this reason that I prefer that study breaks don't add additional screen time. In a perfect world this is manageable, although, with teenagers, it's likely they will want to connect with their friends, which may mean online contact. Since socializing is so essential for avoiding isolation, fostering connections, and building relationships, you'll likely need to negotiate for some balance as your child gets older.

Ivy Ross and Susan Magsamen, authors of *Your Brain on Art*, cite new data showing the benefit of low-tech pursuits like doodling, coloring, journaling, pottery, knitting, listening to music, dancing, singing, writing poetry, being out in nature, or even taking a shower. Break times after concentrated work are great opportunities for a shift in sensory experiences that these activities offer.

Science is now able to show supporting evidence that creating art (in a wide variety of forms) can shift our attention to distinct senses so that simple activities can calm the nervous system; reduce cortisol; generate dopamine, serotonin, and other mood-enhancing endorphins; and encourage increased neuroplasticity as well as enhance our ability to learn.[13] Research has also shown that children who regularly participate in arts are better adjusted socially and less prone to depression.[14]

Creating some form of art (regardless of one's intrinsic talent) is also a soothing way to recover from a tough day. With so many schools defunding art programs, parental support for these activities can be particularly important to nurture self-expression as well as overall health.[15]

Socializing and physical activities are also great ways for your child to let loose and connect. Encouraging them (if necessary) to spend time communicating with friends as well as developing their athletic skills are essential for their emotional and physical development.

Although the research is still in its early stages, teaching children relaxation techniques such as mindfulness, yoga, or meditation has also been found to be effective to help lower stress and anxiety.[16]

THE PARENTS' TOOLBOX
Promoting the Best Study Skills and Habits

- Encourage organizational skills for dyslexic learners:
    Instill time-management habits: make lists and budget time necessary for homework, big projects, chores, and weekend activities as well as break times. Help your child track their time estimates to improve planning.
    Use basic organizational tools like day planners (paper or Google Keep), file folders, and notebooks with color coding as a visual reference for planning and organizing.
    Help your child organize their desk and closet and, if necessary, (with discretion) their locker at school.
    Writing assignments can be particularly challenging and may require extra organizational help. Step in when needed without doing the work for them.
- Establish study practices that are most effective for your child.

>   Rehearse and repeat material, making sure to study in advance to allow for more review days, until material becomes automatic.
>
>   Encourage your child to use a variety of learning modes, if possible, to try to expand their ability to acquire knowledge using multiple modalities.
>
>   Use trial and error to find what works best for various topics or tasks, including auditory, storytelling, visual, and experiential modes as well as utilizing tools like writing and rewriting notes, teaching others, listening to material repeatedly, creating quizzes and study games, working with a study buddy, and creating mnemonics and flash cards.
>
>   Explore new technologies to augment and streamline your child's ability to function well in the classroom as well as to help them with study and homework practices. When using audiobooks, have your child read along with the text if possible.
>
>   Keep your child reading for pleasure with materials that relate to their interests. Series may help entice them to read multiple books and you may want to incentivize them to read with creative perks.

- Model balance, moderation, and the importance of self-care. Help support your child to make healthy choices with technology, diet, exercise, sleep, and hobbies.
  >   Set firm limits on social media and device time to combat distractibility.
  >
  >   Set up guardrails to support their own self-discipline by turning off notifications during homework hours.
  >
  >   Protect family time by establishing electronics blackout periods during meals and other bonding occasions.
  >
  >   Remember to keep a sense of humor and laugh together as

often as possible to help everyone lighten up and keep perspective.

Use breaks like physical exercise, art projects, and connecting with friends to give the brain a rest. This will help to build attention span over time.

Try for low-tech breaks to avoid too much screen time, especially before sleep.

CHAPTER 7

Practices to Bolster Self-Esteem

Countering the self-esteem hits that a child may experience daily must be included in any conversation about the potential lasting effects of dyslexia. As discussed previously, the first line of defense is to be that voice in your child's ear reminding them of the strengths and advantages of being a dyslexic learner. You'll need to encourage them to recognize their own talents and abilities regularly, despite the grades that they may earn—as well as educate them thoroughly on what dyslexia really is, and how many successful and talented dyslexic learners have made enormous contributions to society throughout history.

Internalizing these two confounding realities would be confusing for anyone, but it is the message you need to try to communicate to your dyslexic child: that you are smart and capable, even if there are times when you feel that the world is telling you otherwise.

This chapter explores practices to help encourage a child to thwart their own self-attack and inclination to take on shame that can start to develop at an early age. These strategies aim to both instill positive habits and perspectives that combat negative self-talk as well as build up different skill sets that buoy self-esteem and confidence.

The Importance of Nurturing Independence

A child's natural path to autonomy can be abruptly interrupted by requiring extra help getting through their academics. Over time the extra attention and supervision that a dyslexic child can need may interfere with their inborn drive to gradually move away from parental oversight. Just as with the organizational suggestions in previous chapters, there are some small conscious steps you can begin to take to encourage your child down the path towards building skills for self-sufficiency early on.

While they may have been sloppy at the beginning, letting them bake or clean with you, or do anything for that matter, helped foster a child who felt proud of their abilities. Similarly, when you allowed them to make small decisions about what they wanted to wear or eat, taught them to brush their teeth and hair, tie their shoelaces, etc., you empowered them to feel grown-up and capable.

Therefore, as they get older (and depending upon the level of safety where you live), finding opportunities to let them go out with a friend for ice cream or for a walk or a bike ride home after school can be steps towards expanding their independence. Allowing children some level of choice provides them with a measure of control and therefore promotes autonomy.[1] If children can continue to build self-sufficiency by demonstrating that they can handle themselves, and parents fight their desire to overprotect and gradually gain trust in their child's judgment, it will be much easier to promote self-reliance academically as well.

While I have observed a great variability between children in this regard, I believe that particularly with a dyslexic learner, even though it can be uncomfortable initially, it is your job to motivate and inspire their separation in many small ways, both socially and academically; the two go hand in hand. Of course, there are no hard-and-fast rules, but by keeping aware of their level of independence over time, you may be able to sense when to nudge their autonomy along.

While the desire for a parent to feel needed may be strong, what you ultimately want is to help your child feel capable of learning to do things for themselves.[2] So, just like we approached the exercises in Chapter 4, the idea is to start out by doing something *for* your child, then doing it *with* your child, then *watch* them as they try it on their own, and then letting them do it independently. This preserves a child's sense of independence while protecting a parent from "over parenting" and possibly even going past their own limits.[3] Remember, this is a process, and there is rarely a straight line towards progress.

Establishing Autonomy as a Teenager

My own academic dependency on my mother was quite extreme throughout my education, as she was the one who stayed up with me every night from middle school through high school. At times it was painful if I was angry at her yet still needed her to read to me in order to complete the next day's homework or to prepare for a test. She and my father saw the conflicting pulls I was wrestling with: the desire to be independent in the way my friends were (hanging out after school, staying on the phone for hours at night, or shutting themselves in their room to do homework alone for hours) versus spending the extra time I needed working with my mom and/or tutors.

My parents made a conscious decision to acknowledge my inner turmoil, and when the opportunities arose, they allowed me to experience a sense of autonomy and independence. But inevitably, as a teenager, I still became irritable and annoyed having to be so dependent and disciplined. Typically, articulating this tug of conflicting feelings was not easy as a kid and there were blowouts. It's obvious now that my emotions were part of the normal undercurrent teens experience individuating from their parents. Yet I can also better understand today that my situation was even more fraught because of my dyslexia.

If your child isn't craving much separation, I suggest encouraging them to test the waters to develop confidence in handling themselves on their own. It may be up to you to seek out situations that allow them to have experiences separate from you to incrementally build upon. If your child continues to acquire skills that allow and encourage self-sufficiency and parents are able to wrestle their own desire to overprotect, children can continue to build confidence in their own judgment. Even small mistakes can fuel great lessons for everyone: when a child figures their way out of an unplanned situation and a parent can see that they have the ability to think responsibly on their own, it's a good learning experience for everyone and builds self-esteem for the child.

To be clear, I am absolutely not suggesting leaving a child without support, but rather coaching them to manage new situations as you would normally want to, recognizing that a dyslexic teen may not have gained as much experience as their age-mates.

Teaching Your Child to Advocate for Themself

Acquiring the ability for self-advocacy at a young age further nurtures independence-building and is particularly crucial for a dyslexic child. While you may initially be the one who makes sure that their needs in the classroom are attended to, as they get older (I suggest somewhere between seventh and eighth grade), they need to take over your role and learn to advocate for themself in school, and beyond. These communication skills will not only serve them well throughout their academic life, but they also present another opportunity to develop a sense of autonomy and competence.

In the beginning of the school year, your child should arrange to meet with their teachers in classes that they anticipate will be a struggle for them. They will need to thoroughly explain their learning differences and why specific accommodations have been given to them: that they, for example, process information slowly, and they may not want to read aloud in class. Or perhaps they need to take class notes on a computer (instead of transcribing them). Along with whatever accommodation they require should come their promise to pay close attention and raise their hand whenever they feel they can answer a question. If they cannot avoid getting called upon for reading aloud, they should request receiving reading materials in advance.

As the semester continues, they'll need to learn to ask for help if they get confused. If they are unduly struggling or did not do well on an assignment, exam, or paper, they should be encouraged to approach their teacher, armed with specific questions, so that they can be better prepared going forward. If they have trouble paying attention, they can even request a seat change in the classroom to help them get dialed in. Being able to communicate in these ways not only empowers them to learn to advocate for themself, it also shows their teachers that your child is engaged and interested in their education and willing to work hard.

When Your Child Needs to Email a Teacher

Dyslexic learners may have more occasion to directly contact teachers as they navigate getting their needs met effectively in the classroom. An instructor's preference for students to contact them via email presents an opportunity to introduce your child to using a more formal mode for these communications (distinct from how they might email friends). Specifically, they need to learn to start with an appropriate salutation, then add a thoughtful opener like "I hope you are having a good day/evening," or "I hope this email finds you well," and then continue with the reason for the message. Finally, they should close out the note by thanking the teacher for their help and signing their name.

Listening Well and Delivering "Mantras"

Moving beyond consciously building independence, dyslexic learners may still experience a kind of isolation or feeling of separation from their fellow classmates. Everyone can feel self-conscious and see themselves as an outsider during times in their lives, particularly in the teenage years, so let's not let our dyslexic children think that they are alone in feeling different in the world. But taking time to really hear what they are going through and express themselves creates a valuable space for your child to process their own experience.

A perfect example of this was when one mother took note of hearing her dyslexic child call herself "lazy" when she was doing her homework at night. Curious about what inspired that negative self-talk, she asked her child what she meant. She then took the opportunity to explain to her daughter that her learning difference did not make her "lazy." She pointed out that she was not at all lazy, but rather her brain needed to learn things in different ways—no better or worse than her classmates—and sometimes that required needing more time. While it was not the first time that she had explained this to her daughter, by tuning into what her child was saying, she found a good moment to reiterate and reframe what her daughter was being told at school by a teacher who was clearly uneducated about dyslexia.

Listening well is a crucial skill for a parent and is part of building the safe home environment one hopes to provide for their child. Being attuned in this way leverages a valuable opportunity to assist your child in navigating potential challenges within school or elsewhere.

Beyond these interventions, after particularly rough days, we can all use reminders of the special things we bring to the world and that our uniqueness is often what makes us beautiful and special. Dyslexic learners are likely to need this kind of reminding and reframing, perhaps more than neurotypical learners, because they so often experience heightened stress, disappointment, and anxiety. So, when your child has occasional lapses of feeling down or frustrated, be sure to remind them of their special attributes and that they are far from alone. This is not easy stuff, after all.

Furthermore, since struggles related to dyslexia are unlikely to resolve quickly, a child can often need reminding that things will get easier. You don't want to judge them or make them feel self-conscious for admitting that they're struggling, and you may quite likely be the safest person for them to express their frustration to. This does not mean that you want to encourage your child to capitulate to their feelings of defeat, but rather it's an opportunity to be compassionate, validate their feelings, and let them know that they are not alone.

This war that wages inside must be shared by a caring parent, or parents, who see the struggle and believe in a child's intelligence and capacity for learning. Then by articulating to your child not only the things that they excel at naturally, but also those things that they are slowly accruing, like tenacity, spirit, eagerness, courage, and possibly even endurance, you are raising their consciousness to the bigger picture. Acknowledging the skills they are acquiring helps a child to recognize and validate their own efforts and provides them the language to actually understand and become aware of what their hard work has yielded. These are all strengths that will serve them extremely well and often come with big payoffs down the road as adults.

It is vital for your child to hear some encouraging truths about the difficulties they are confronting to remain optimistic during the tough moments. I call these scripts "mantras":

> "Because you do not excel at something in this moment does not mean that you will never succeed at it in the future. We all have our own strengths and weaknesses, and over time you will continue to make real progress. Just look at all the improvements you have made up until this point, mastering skills that were difficult earlier on [for example riding a bike, doing a cartwheel, etc.]."

> "Anyone can make mistakes or fail at something but not everyone has the fortitude to get back up and try again—and again. That kind of grit and determination is among the most important

things anyone can learn. Whether you realize it or not, you're building the kind of character and resilience that will serve you well throughout life's many challenges."

Assuring your child that things will not always be as they are today and that adulthood will likely bring some relief is also an important injection of reality that they may not be aware of.

"School can be rough, but it is temporary. It's not easy being judged and graded on things that you're struggling with each day. Later in life, whether in college or at a job, tasks will be more adaptable to your strengths and the things you enjoy. Remember that, for a dyslexic brain, it's all about the long game. Success will continue to build over time."

"While it may be hard to believe in this moment, when you eventually choose a career you love, where your talents lie, you will not have the same pressure to do things daily that do not come naturally, like you do now."

"I have found that kids who do not necessarily get the best grades can be excellent at 'life' with a gratifying career, wonderful friends, and a family of their own. What matters is that you are learning to work hard and apply yourself. Not being a great student does not necessarily mean that you won't be extremely happy in life. Skills will get easier for you and you will continue to make great strides—try to be patient with yourself. Your intelligence and diligence will pay off in the long run."

Dyslexic learners, who are forced to compare themselves regularly with more standard learners, require these kinds of reminders. These messages are not "pat answers" nor meant to merely pacify a struggling child. They are actually realistic and based on my personal observations of many dyslexic learners I have worked with and come across. They are important reminders for children to trust that their dyslexic brain develops differently.

I have shared these mantras with countless families who tell me they refer back to them repeatedly when their child is going through a particularly rough patch. While the exact message your child needs to hear may be somewhat different, I recommend keeping it at the ready!

Encouraging and Acknowledging Hard Work— Less So, Grades

Among the different experiences that a dyslexic child may encounter during school is the predicament of likely having longer hours and more supervision than a typical learner. Although we can hope that this doesn't happen to your child, they may also be quietly worn down by less praise and attention at school, possibly internalizing the experience of being "less than" on a daily basis. Without the ability to express or even recognize or understand their feelings, they may be left to retreat within themself and internalize self-defeating messages.

If your child is receiving less positive reinforcement in school, particularly in the form of grades, my general rule of thumb for dyslexic children is to celebrate *improvements* (rather than grades, per se). Depending on the specific challenges they face, grade comparisons to the rest of their class may not be particularly relevant. More pertinent is how well they apply themself and their burgeoning work ethic.

Seeing grade improvements will no doubt be an encouraging sign, but the most important thing to stress is that they are putting effort into their work and steadily progressing in the mastery of their studies. Mistakes present opportunities to pivot and understand areas of weakness so they don't continue to falter in the same ways. Frustrating though it can be, there may be classes in which grades may not at all reflect your child's effort and this can be continually disappointing.

At those moments, I like to remind my young patients about the big picture by referring to an all-important "mantra" again. But aside from the fortifying and motivating pep talks, you may also want to set up more explicit incentives to help your child through especially tough semesters, to keep their spirits up and their motivation intact.

My family had rituals of rewarding my hard work with ice cream sundaes—maybe not the best practice to promote today—but rewards do encourage and motivate us all to work hard.

However, in the hopes of helping a child orient themselves more towards their own intrinsic motivation, without debasing their effort with a material inducement, one approach I like is to shake up the reward system by inviting your child to choose a realistic reward for themself after they have reached a specified goal. Or, rather than a material inducement, they may choose a social reward—call a friend, play a video game (with a friend), have a parent take time out to kick a ball around, etc.

Above and beyond the rewards, though, your words of encouragement will be motivating to your child—and whether they admit it or not, they will naturally internalize your voice to sustain them through what can be emotionally and physically exhausting efforts. So, make sure your messages are authentic and uplifting, underscoring your child's aspirations to reach their higher self—and be sure they see how much you value their work ethic. Your positivity matters beyond measure and your acknowledgment of their efforts can be an important counterbalance to a rough day, week or semester at school.

Reframing "Failure" as an Opportunity to Learn Resilience

A prime opportunity for reframing your child's experience into a larger context relates to so-called failure. While it certainly isn't what anybody wants to aspire to, disappointing outcomes along the path to learning mastery can be formative in the best ways. Surely, we all want to set out children up for success, but sometimes that can actually mean allowing them the freedom to fail, particularly when the consequences are not devastating or emotionally harmful.

Just as babies regularly experience their own version of failure when they attempt to roll over, sit up, crawl, and so on, young children may flounder when they try to ride a bike, pronounce words, tie their shoelaces, etc. We encourage their resilience and perseverance, having confidence that their tenacity will eventually bring them success.

Yet when children get to school, parents can understandably feel that they need to protect them from negative or painful experiences, being loathe to risk their child feeling discouraged or defeated. But if your child hits a roadblock, remember that some level of challenge can help build fortitude. Allowing them the time to figure things out on their own will develop frustration tolerance and teach them to be patient with themselves. Offer a bit of guidance and lots of encouragement, yes—but don't be afraid to let them stumble—so that they can then discover that they have the tools to try again and ultimately succeed.

It is in this way that "helicopter" and "snowplow" parents can inadvertently circumvent important building blocks for their child's self-esteem and resilience by being too quick to remove obstacles for them. (A parent might even fear that it will reflect poorly on *them* if they don't rush in to help.) Yet if a child has no experience with disappointment or frustration, they may be more devastated when they are forced to confront challenges beyond your parental control.

Perhaps unexpectedly, the challenges dyslexic children face early on may ultimately make them better prepared for "real life" as compared with their traditional-learner counterparts. Being forced to abandon any notion of academic "perfection," because it will so often be out of their reach, helps develop the gift of resilience. Having to confront academic disappointments can push them to pivot and try new and better strategies and ease them into taking on measured risks further down the road—making them less fearful of failure.

Allowing Time to Heal After a "Failure"

But let's not forget that we all need time to recover after a gut punch like a big disappointment, particularly if we've put in a lot of time and effort. A child may need to scream, cry, and/or take time to vent their anger. It's important to allow them the space to move through their strong feelings and lick their wounds. Then be sure to help guide them back on the other end by reframing the experience as a life lesson for how they can improve going forward. You'll see that your child can demonstrate an eagerness to get back up when they are given the freedom to grieve and heal.

Building Frustration Tolerance

Similarly, the expectation of feeling "at ease" in the classroom may not be part of the school experience for a dyslexic child. This relative lack of comfort, ironically, may be what nurtures their ability to adapt to a multitude of rigorous situations. While this predicament is certainly not one that most of us would opt for, it may be an unlikely gift of dyslexia. That is, in the best-case scenario, being wired differently than standard learners may push dyslexics to stretch their capacity for tolerating and adapting to discomfort. If the extra stress or anxiety they experience becomes easier to handle over time with eventual successes, this may indeed better arm them with the confidence to meet new and bigger challenges later on.

All that being said, the reality remains that having a dyslexic brain can be frustrating! It can be arduous forming the cognitive pathways to get to the same place as one's neurotypical peers. It can also be exhausting having to put in so much time doing homework at night. One parent explained the predicament to her dyslexic child by setting their expectations this way: "It is okay if you find homework hard and frustrating. You do spend more time on it than other kids. Just like you get time and a half for tests, you should anticipate taking time and a half to do homework as well."

As an adolescent, I recall that as my frustration increased, I would often become angry. I now know that my emotional outbursts were not at all unexpected or atypical. Most dyslexic children I've spoken with have gone through some years of elevated frustration and explosive behavior that manifested in similar ways—lots of tantrums, anger, and crying, especially during late nights of studying during the mounting pressures of high school or possibly middle school.

It's hard to know the precise level of sustained frustration that your child may be experiencing—potentially compounded by feeling alone. Validating their feelings may help de-escalate their distress in the short term; or sometimes an energy shifting break or a hug might help. Occasionally, it may be the right moment to deliver the "mantra"!

As mentioned previously, contributing to the frustration of the additional hours of work is the extra remediation required for dyslexic learners. At some point they will likely and understandably begin to crave space. It may be a call to install more frequent breaks or budget alone time for them.

One mother found a way to provide her child a measure of independence by offering him his own locus of control. When her son started to melt down doing homework, she would tell him, "You don't *have* to do your work, but *you* will have to deal with the consequences. Either take a break and then finish your assignment or you will have to explain to your teacher in a note why you did not do the work." Betting that her child would be resistant to having to write to his teacher, she was confident that this would be an effective motivator to encourage him to self-regulate long enough to get through his work. But giving *him* the choice made all the difference.

As with anything, discussing the tensions in a supportive or empathic way can clear the air and help your child recognize that their feelings are understandable and natural. It may even diminish a possible urge to fight you or a tutor or teacher.

Helping Your Child Preserve Self-Esteem

Since your dyslexic child may be more apt to have occasional meltdowns than a standard learner, they will likely need your empathy and validation by helping them express their frustration. But at the same time, you want to be sure to be empathic rather than *enabling*. That is, regardless of the compassion you feel for your child, setting limits on their behavior has real value for them. Boundaries help preserve a child's self-esteem, whether or not they welcome the limitations during a heated moment. It's important to be clear that tolerating bad behavior will not make anyone feel good in the long run.

Setting consequences for acting out doesn't need to be made out of anger or demonstrated aggressively, but if done calmly and consistently, it will likely help your child rein themself in. These boundaries demonstrate care and offer reassurance when they're feeling overwhelmed and out of control.

Parents can feel like they want to give their dyslexic child some slack for bad behavior out of compassion, and perhaps, on occasion, that may be okay, but not correcting a child's repeated bad behavior can communicate to the child that the parent believes the child can't do better; it may even convey, incorrectly, that the parent doesn't care.

Regardless, whether a child acknowledges it or not, treating a parent badly registers within them, and if it becomes habitual and without consequences, it can have the profound effect of preventing the child from feeling good about themselves over the long run.

Here are three steps for intervening, setting boundaries, and helping your child self-regulate when they are losing control:

1. First check in with yourself to be sure you're coming from a place of strength and calm to ensure that you are not overreacting or bringing in baggage from your own day.
2. Stop aggressive behavior in its tracks (e.g., raising one's voice, slamming things, kicking) by saying gently but firmly

"That's not how we behave (or treat each other) in this family." Depending on their age, if you sense that your child is losing control of their behavior, separate them and give them space for a time-out. If they're older, suggest they spend some quiet time alone, take a shower, or do something physical to help them calm down.

3. Be sure to reconvene later to discuss their behavior and explore what is driving it. Helping them articulate the feelings that lead to the unacceptable behavior is important. Then you can discuss alternative ways to cope in the future. Let your child know that they will need to find a better way to process their feelings and not act them out.

Remember: this is not meant to be a punitive process—it is giving your child the tools they need to govern their emotions and allow them to consider better options for how to behave, laying the path for growth that will serve them throughout their life.

Lessons in Consequences

Rather than "punishments," setting boundaries serves to demonstrate that you care enough to do the tough part of parenting. Despite your child's protestations, following through with consequences communicates that you're willing to fight for what's in their best interest, even if it means some difficult moments in the short term. It also demonstrates that you are willing to do what it takes to help them recognize how their actions affect others (for example, hurting someone's feelings), thus enriching their ability to empathize with others.

Certainly, there are no hard-and-fast rules for what system is right for your child, and consequences may need to be applied in a nuanced way depending on a child's age and circumstances. For example, if your child forgets to bring their violin to school in third grade, as opposed to if they are in eighth grade, your response might be justifiably different. In the first case, you might deliver their violin to school to allow them to participate in music class. Afterward, you should probably institute the practice of creating a checklist for your front door so this doesn't happen again. In the latter case, with a list hopefully already in place, you might consider using the situation in eighth grade as a life lesson to help them see that they need to be more diligent in being responsible for themself. Abstaining from running to the rescue might actually be harder on a parent, allowing the consequences that promote self-reliance to play out. It's a decision that you as a parent are uniquely poised to make.

Likewise, it makes sense for a parent to check their child's homework in elementary school to be sure they have understood and completed their assignment appropriately and on time. This encourages good habits, time management, and responsibility. But when your tween reaches middle school, let them start to be more independent and responsible for themselves, regardless of whether they'll have repercussions in school when they don't do their work or make a half-hearted attempt to complete it thoroughly. If you are fighting about taking initiative, this is the time to let go and allow them to stumble without the fallout of devastating consequences.

By all means, get involved if they want your guidance with time management or homework. I am not advocating abstaining from helping, but some children will need more independence and want you to step away. The thing you want to avoid is becoming the enemy. So, retreat if they crave independence and let everybody see what happens.

In the best case, if your child survives a disappointing grade and learns that it doesn't mean a failed course, the idea of failure can become less scary. While that may at first sound like a negative, there is freedom in knowing that a school "failure" is survivable. Allowing a teen this kind of autonomy may propel them to examine the effectiveness of their study habits and figure out improved ways to approach their work next time.

Daily Gratitude Practices and Helping Others

When times get tough and there are moments to apply consequences, it's probably also the right time to start instilling regular gratitude practices for your child, if you haven't started them already.

Some of the best ways to avoid envy, anger, jealousy, and depression is to remind ourselves of how fortunate we are on a regular basis. Acknowledging our many blessings is an essential part of a healthy life perspective. Even during the toughest of times your child can probably find something, and hopefully many things, to be thankful for.

I feel so strongly about this practice that whenever it's feasible my family and I do a gratitude exercise during dinner. We go around the table and everyone tells the best part of their day or week, listing what we are thankful for and how we helped someone else that day or week. We also discuss the most difficult parts, which gives us all a moment to share the challenging things we may be facing. This can allow for an occasional reframing of a challenging situation: for example, not taking something someone said too personally or trying to be empathic to what a classmate might be going through that's causing their behavior.

Highlighting positive experiences during these gratitude exercises is a wonderful way to balance the natural tendency to dwell on the negatives we all encounter. This exercise has helped my family to keep perspective during good and bad times; my kids have learned to take mental note of special experiences during their day, to earmark them for our dinner conversations.

I like to preserve a time and place that is safe to share these thoughts and feelings; they often offer an opportunity for humor as well. Reminding ourselves regularly of all that we have to be grateful for can also be a good way to verbalize to each other how much we are all valued and appreciated. I highly recommend trying this in your family.

Be prepared, though: Ironically, this practice can become most challenging with teenagers when they are likely to need it most. So, during particularly rough days, when my kids have been vocally resistant to engaging in the exercise, I like to suggest fundamental things for them to be grateful for, like how lucky we are to have fresh running water, a home, and our health. I believe pushing through their resistance reminds them to keep perspective and hopefully helps to avoid a pity party.

Additionally, incorporating helping others as a daily intention is a wonderful way for children to build self-esteem. Since kids can be naturally self-directed, it may be a revelation to shift their focus towards considering others, even when they're going through something difficult themselves. Implanting this idea can invite them to reach outwards, raising their awareness to others' suffering, taking them out of their own struggles. Moreover, promoting the value of being of service to others early on nurtures compassion and encourages kindness, which can lead to building self-esteem at a core level.

Making Time for Extracurricular Activities

While it is not likely to be convenient or economical for parents to take on added commitments and responsibilities, dyslexic learners can particularly benefit from being exposed to extracurricular activities that don't rely on standard academic pursuits. Outside of the structure of school and without the stress of homework or grades, new activities present opportunities to discover unknown talents—not to mention added social outlets. Whenever it is practical and safe, I like to encourage diversifying skill sets to expand a child's notion of themselves in this way.

At the same time, listening to your child's input about what they are interested in and feel comfortable doing is important. For example, if your child has poor perceptual skills, you may want to start plugging them into activities that don't require strong eye-hand coordination in a relatively nonpressured environment, to build their confidence. Options like, but not limited to, swimming, fishing, karate, chess, gymnastics, dance, playing an instrument, art classes, and singing may be more conducive to their strengths. If your child is willing to try things they are not necessarily immediately gifted in, it's wonderful to offer them the opportunity to expand their skill set. Either way, you'll want to be mindful to not put them into a stressful situation in a well-meaning effort to build their self-confidence.

Owning Strengths and Weaknesses with Humor

Finally, along your child's academic path, they may go through periods when they are expending a lot of energy to mask or work through their academic weaknesses. Learning to own their shortcomings, rather than hiding them, can actually provide a huge relief. When we can all learn to relax our egos, find humor in situations, and possibly even laugh at ourselves, we are usually better for it.

I believe in starting that practice from an early age with a delicate hand. Keeping everybody feeling emotionally safe is a priority and you never want to disregard or not consider a child's feelings. Making sure to laugh *with* them as opposed to *at* them is especially important in those early years. (Certainly, it never feels great to be laughed *at* excessively at any age, in any case.)

Lightening things up in a family safe zone where parents can gently counter a child's sensitivity to embarrassment with affection in the form of a hug or smile or deliver some silliness or extra attention can be a way to try to begin to desensitize a child to some good-natured teasing about themself. This can model a path to building ego strength to hopefully bypass internalizing shame.

By learning to lighten up in the safety of one's home, it can eventually ease a child into doing the same in other social settings. To be clear, I am not suggesting that anyone can or should become impervious to *ridicule*, but that developing a sense of humor and being comfortable exposing our shortcomings (knowing that everyone has them) genuinely helps smooth out the edges of life for us all. But sensitivity levels can vary greatly for children, so for some of us this can happen in early grades, for others it may take years to be able to get enough emotional distance to be able to laugh at one's foibles. Either way, be attuned to your child's tolerance level so as not to make home an emotionally unsafe space.

In my own family, no one, including my parents, was off-limits, and while I was certainly more sensitive around my peers than I was at home, I eventually learned to laugh at my weaknesses at school, too. My parents made sure the joking was not excessive nor ever done with malice; it was okay to gently and lightheartedly see the humor in how many tutors I went through or that I was baking a stockpile of bread and cakes in weeks when studying was stressful.

Regardless of the mounting pressures in school, humor helped to keep the perspective that things did not always need to be serious or intense. By developing the ego strength to step back and gain some perspective, children can begin to grasp that things are often not as tragic or earth-shattering as they might initially feel. It helps, too, when one can learn to ratchet back their natural competitiveness and desire to be good at everything in all situations in order to lessen some of the self-imposed shame and embarrassment.

The habit of laughing in my family helped to disarm all of us, both emotionally and physically, because laughter can be such a visceral release. I still regard it as an actual necessary part of my day—particularly on hard days. Personally, having learned to find levity at my own shortcomings by high school was a tremendous gift. Being able to deflect embarrassing situations with laughter helped diminish the shame I had reflexively been absorbing for years.

Though risky, your child might discover, as I did, that other students begin to cheer them on after they see that they are strong enough to be honest in recognizing their weaknesses. So don't forget to try to look for ways to lighten up!

Confronting Bullying

Since having dyslexia can potentially open children to the possibility of being picked on by others, and with bullying being rampant across the country, I think it's necessary to discuss ways to consider handling a situation if it arises. In this context, I am defining *bullying* as: "abusing, aggressively dominating, or intimidating another with a real or perceived power imbalance."

It is worth noting that a child who is being bullied and a child who is having trouble learning in school can actually present in similar ways. For example, if you notice your child is starting to hate school, has become uncharacteristically apathetic in their classes, has become depressed or anxious, or is starting to isolate themself, they may be encountering a difficult situation in school that they are too ashamed to open up about at home.[4] These symptoms could realistically be manifestations of bullying *or* dyslexia, or both.

Similar to other areas of parenting, this is where listening well to subtle changes that your child may or may *not* be verbalizing can be key. While there is no simple, one-size-fits-all solution for confronting bullying, Jonathan McKee (*The Bullying Breakthrough*) underscores the value of parents prioritizing taking time out of their busy lives to be present with their kids and encourages them to demonstrate a real interest, concern, and compassion for their children on a day-to-day basis so that they're more attuned to potential changes in their behavior. Having frequent conversations in which a child can share about their day and reveal their interests may also open the door for them to expose more of their feelings and experiences when there is an issue.

If they are being bullied at school, rather than trying to fix the problem immediately, McKee's research points to first validating your child's experience and letting them know that they are not alone. He recommends demonstrating empathy for what it feels like for your child to possibly not feel safe at school—without minimizing or ignoring the problem—all of which convey that you are taking their feelings seriously. Only then should you discuss ways to manage the situation by involving school personnel and/or other relevant staff.

This conversation also can be instrumental in teaching different means to resolve conflicts in a thoughtful way. The key is that your actions should conform, whenever possible, to your child's wishes (unless they are at risk of being in any imminent physical danger), to allow them a measure of control.

Parents should also know up front that the reality of approaching school personnel is that they are often too overwhelmed to adequately handle these situations expediently. McKee recommends that, if you need to contact them, make sure to ask when you can expect results/action in advance so that you can keep them accountable by following up accordingly. This is a real occasion to find your "inner bulldog," if necessary, to advocate fully for your child—and to be persistent.

Regardless of the type of bullying, a hostile environment can have a great impact on any child's experience of learning. For a dyslexic child, it may be that much more important to protect their experience of school, especially if they already feel particularly vulnerable.

At the same time, they need to understand that bullying can happen to anyone and what the behavior says, more than anything, is that the bully, themselves, secretly sees themselves as "less than" and looks for others to dominate to make them feel better about themself. It's a tough lesson for a child to grasp, but it's one that everyone will likely have some exposure to during their life. Raising their consciousness to the fact that they don't need to cower to anyone makes this a real, although unpleasant, learning opportunity and underscores the importance of not giving away their sense of themselves to anyone for any reason.

Strong family support will significantly bolster your child emotionally. And real advocacy within the school may certainly be appropriate (and urgent) if there is any sort of physical threat involved. Your child may benefit from learning martial arts to help them build their own physical self-confidence and overcome the disempowering feeling of being victimized.

THE PARENTS' TOOLBOX
Practices to Bolster Self-Esteem

This chapter discusses strategies to instill positive habits and skill sets that combat negative self-talk. The first line of defense is to be a voice in your child's ear about the strengths and advantages of being a dyslexic learner. Remind them and have them recognize their own talents and strengths regularly.

- Your dyslexic child may become less self-reliant than a standard learner because of the extra attention and help they may require for academics.
  - If you see them overly dependent on you or lagging behind in the ability to feel confidence in their own judgment, seek opportunities for them to build skills for self-sufficiency.
  - If this process starts at a low level early on, it will be much easier to foster self-reliance later.
  - Motivate and inspire their separation in many small ways, both socially and academically.
- Between seventh and eight grade, teach your child to begin to advocate for themselves with teachers.
  - In difficult classes, have them explain their learning differences and why they have received specific accommodations for their dyslexia.
  - If they did not do well on an assignment, exam, or paper, have them approach their teacher, armed with specific questions so they can learn for the future.
  - If they need to email a teacher, aid them in using a proper format, more formal than they would use writing to a friend.
- A dyslexic child's struggles are not likely to resolve quickly, so they often need a "mantra" from you to remind them to remain optimistic that things will get easier in the future and that they are steadily building the skills they need. Highlight *the skills they naturally excel*

at as well as those they are quietly accruing: grit, courage, endurance, and the ability to work hard. They need to know that once high school is over, they will not confront the same daily struggles, whether in college or in their chosen career.

- Make room to really listen if your child opens up about the frustrations they're experiencing.
  - Check in with yourself to be sure to come from a place of strength and calm without baggage from your own day.
  - Validate their feelings and show empathy but don't let them forget that dyslexic learners are not the only ones who feel "different" in school or in life.
  - Reframe and normalize stress or challenges as something everyone goes through.
  - Remind your child that because they require extra time in school for tests, they should expect to have to put in extra time on homework as well.
  - Build capacity for tolerating frustration and discomfort to increase confidence.
  - Install frequent breaks at times of high frustration and long stretches of work.
- Celebrate improvements, with less emphasis on grades.
  - Some grades may not reflect your child's effort and can be continually disappointing.
  - Allow time to heal after a disappointment or failure.
  - Reframe small "failures" as an opportunity to learn resilience (particularly when the consequences are not devastating or emotionally harmful).
  - Offer a bit of guidance and lots of encouragement, but don't be afraid to let them stumble; they need to discover that they have the tools to try again and ultimately succeed.
  - Rewarding big achievements, when merited, can help your child feel appreciated and encouraged.
- Help your child preserve self-esteem by being compassionate while setting boundaries.

> Accepting mistreatment or bad behavior doesn't make anyone feel good in the long run.
>
> Validate their feelings but encourage your child to express themselves *verbally* to avoid having them act them out.
>
> Follow through with consequences to help them self-regulate if they cross explicit behavioral limits.
>
> Calmly stop behavior and give consequences to keep everyone's self-esteem intact. Rather than being punitive, this is to help your child gain the tools to resolve these situations in the future.
>
> If necessary, allow your child space for a time-out.
>
> Reconvene later to discuss the feelings motivating their behavior and alternative, more constructive options for the future.

- Acknowledging our many blessings contributes to a healthy life perspective. Use daily or weekly family meals to discuss what everyone is grateful for and encourage helping others each week.
- Extracurricular activities are especially beneficial for dyslexic learners to balance out academic challenges and discover new talents to build up their competence and expand socially.
- Help your child learn to use humor and own their strengths and weaknesses.
  > Owning shortcomings rather than hiding them can be a huge relief.
  >
  > Work to lighten things up in a family safe zone to gently counter a child's sensitivity to embarrassment, modeling a path to building ego strength and hopefully bypassing internalizing shame.
- If your child confronts bullying, they may not verbalize it to you. Signs of being bullied can resemble indicators of a learning difference: starting to hate school, change of behavior or mood (including anxiety or depression), isolating, as well as taking on shame. Showing genuine interest in your child can keep you attuned to these possibly subtle changes in behavior and encourage them to open up.

If they do share a bullying incident with you, take it seriously. Validate their feelings first, and show empathy without minimizing their experience.

Then discuss ways to manage the situation *with* them to increase their ability for conflict resolution.

If you decide to contact a teacher or administrator at school, inquire as to when you should follow up to keep them accountable. Then be persistent.

Reassure your child that bullying can happen to anyone and is generally a symptom of the bully feeling "less than" others, to underscore the importance of not giving away their sense of self to the bully.

PART 3

Navigating Challenges in School

CHAPTER 8

Skill Building in Elementary School

The beginning of school is an exciting time for everyone; it is also an important opportunity to be on the alert for signs of dyslexia. If a child is not yet diagnosed, new learning situations, like starting a new school or grade, can offer clues that were previously masked by a child's efforts to compensate for deficits.

Children can be very creative in hiding learning issues, but if they remain undiagnosed long enough, they may present with anxiety, depression, distractibility, or emotional outbursts that can be red flags, possibly (but not necessarily) indicating that they are struggling and starting to fall behind academically. If your child has not yet been diagnosed, review the "soft signs" of dyslexia (pages 9–10) and consider having them evaluated for a learning difference.

Minimizing Classroom Frustration for Your Child

Once a dyslexia diagnosis has been made, the best thing to do for a child is to try to limit the level of discouragement and frustration they encounter in learning settings to the highest degree possible. This is accomplished by arranging for school interventions and accommodations as well as by preparing your child for what they can expect going forward in school. The goal is to maximize the positive experience of participation and engagement and prepare your child for the extra effort they will need to expend to thrive in school (also see How to Explain Accommodations to Your Child, page 51).

The Importance of Advocating Early for Your Child

After a diagnosis of dyslexia, at the start of each school year in elementary school, I recommend meeting with your child's teachers to advocate for their special needs. For example, requesting that your child's teachers avoid classically embarrassing situations, like being called upon to read out loud in class. Explain your child's situation in depth, and ask that they only read if they raise their hand. If possible, you may also request that they receive reading materials in advance to practice with, at home, so they'll be better prepared in class.

Ways to Help (Established) Readers Read Out Loud

Once your dyslexic child begins to be a more fluent reader, they may still have trouble reading text out loud in front of others. Using a larger type size for, say, doing a presentation with notes can make a significant difference for many. (If available, books with larger print are also helpful.) Additionally, certain fonts, such as Courier, Arial, Calibri, Verdana, Gothic, and Comic Sans, among others, are often

Skill Building in Elementary School

easier for dyslexic learners to read (www.weareteachers.com/best-fonts-for-dyslexia/).

To illustrate how fraught these classroom dynamics can be for a dyslexic child, I offer my own, particularly vivid, early recollections: despite receiving my own diagnosis earlier than most (in first grade), there were no interventions or accommodations put in place by my school. This left me perpetually struggling to keep up with my peers and uncomfortable asking for help. It somehow didn't seem to matter that I was around watchful educators who were supposedly aware of my situation.

As the pace of the rest of the class's reading rapidly ramped up, I became self-conscious that everyone knew that I was falling behind. It wasn't long before I started to copy from the person sitting next to me. Likewise, I learned that causing distractions would help me divert attention away from anybody noticing that I was progressing slowly. Here's where creativity came in: The old round tables where we sat were held up by wobbly legs. I realized that I could discreetly unscrew the leg under my table while it appeared that I was reading. When the nut eventually fell to the floor, the table would fall over. This caused a dramatic disturbance, and the teacher would have to call in maintenance to put the table back together. I did this two or three times over the course of a few weeks until the maintenance men made it so tight that the leg would no longer budge. Fortunately, no one ever got hurt—and no one ever figured out that I was the culprit, or if they did know, they never called me out.

Of course, these antics could not disguise my reading issues indefinitely. I was reversing letters and words, struggling with blending sounds, and none of my teachers were teaching me the rules of phonics. In class, when we read aloud, I strained to sound out each syllable, and before I could even try to blend the letters, a classmate would invariably call out the word. I will never forget the feeling of my face heating up and my heart beating so fast that I could barely speak. I felt humiliated.

The Benefit of Phonetics

While a phonetically based reading curriculum does not guarantee ease or avoidance of embarrassing situations like those I endured, a phonetic approach, like Science of Reading (one that breaks down each word and then blends sounds together), is the most effective way to teach a dyslexic child how to read. (See pages 48–49 for an explanation of this learning approach.)

A parent can choose to call their local public, parochial, or independent schools to inquire about the type of reading programs available before making a decision as to where their child will attend. If a Science of Reading approach is not accessible, and there are no other options, you can supplement your child's reading education using content from YouTube, or finding a tutor trained in the Orton-Gillingham Approach, or something comparable that has a variety of ways to help children build phonetic skills.

Helpful Resources

Search for a Facebook page or other support group for parents of dyslexic children to get current recommendations of what other parents have found helpful. One current site posted by a teacher on YouTube, called Susan Jones Teaching, offers easy-to-follow instructions. Use YouTube search terms: "teaching phonics" or "learning phonics."

If you feel your child's school is not doing enough, it may be time to get creative and seek out other children who are at your child's reading level to share the cost of a tutor. Finding a well-trained person who has a solid background in a phonetically based approach is key. You might also inquire into whether there are parent or student groups dedicated to learning differences in your school or community. Finding other parents who have been grappling with these issues can help introduce you to excellent resources as well as connect you to an informal support group.

Keep Your Child Reading

- After your child has learned the basics of reading, it is helpful to have them continue to consistently read books for pleasure. Look for opportunities nightly, on weekends, and over the summer—even if it is only twenty minutes a day—to engage them in topics that they love. The more they read, the more recognizable the words will become and the faster they'll be able to process the words. Repetition is the key to building fluency. Simple words will lead to the more complex with practice, time, and patience.
- Have your child read at their appropriate level (this does not necessarily mean it is the grade they are in) or slightly below when they are reading independently. That way the words are familiar, making comprehension easier. At the beginning, it's a good idea to avoid difficult material that will cause excessive struggle and possible avoidance of reading down the road.
- If they are interested and insist on attempting books that are above their reading level and you see them starting to struggle excessively, you can read out loud together or have your child listen to the audiobook while they read along.
- When possible, use actual books and not iPads or tablets for reading. When using a tablet to read, there can be a tendency to superficially skim the pages. If your child has a large reading assignment, it is easier to plan ahead if you can physically see the volume of pages, to give an accurate sense of how much more they need to read. Also, if your child likes to read before bedtime, an actual book allows them to avoid exposure to blue light, which can inhibit sleep.

Multisensory Learning

When studying math or science, young dyslexic learners may also benefit from incorporating stimuli from various senses. Interacting with physical, tangible items to see, touch, and manipulate can be extremely helpful (for example, helping to understand multiplication tables using groups of items like popcorn or marbles).

Experimenting with your child to find the most effective tools for them can be advantageous, too, especially as the demands on their time and attention ramp up. In my case, my mother found an inroad for me to learn math concepts by commandeering our (erasable) Formica dining room table (it was the 1980s) to demonstrate geometric shapes and fractions. She also made the best use of pizza and fruit pies, which certainly captured my attention better than reading a geometry textbook. My parents were not familiar with the term "multisensory" back then, yet through trial and error, it turns out that we were intuitively employing this method. Mixing conceptual ideas with tangible aids helped me understand basic concepts like, for example, that I wanted one-third of a pie as opposed to one-fourth of it when there was a pizza in front of me!

Improving Sequencing Skills in Elementary School

Early on in school, dyslexic children's sequencing issues may show up as difficulty in organizing, alphabetizing, recalling the months of the year and days of the week, or possibly when retelling a story in sequential order.

This can spill over into challenges such as organizing their room and closet, doing homework, managing time, etc. Because of this prevalent issue for dyslexic as well as ADHD learners, it's extremely helpful to instill the habit of keeping an orderly room. Not only will this encourage organizational and sequencing skills, but it will also lessen the amount of mess that a child can generate. While everyone will have their own standard,

I don't recommend aspiring to perfection; rather, minimizing chaos is a good rule of thumb.

When advocating for tidiness, it is far preferable to have your child organize their own space (to give them the feeling of agency) than for you to do it for them. But if they need a helping hand (and they most likely will), don't forget to get their consent and then engage them in the process of sorting out their drawers, closet, desk, etc. I recommend trying to make it fun, using organizers found online or even (covered) shoe boxes labeled outside with a category name. Most of all, if possible, avoid making this process stressful or punitive. Just like the rest of us, children like to feel in control of their stuff.

The Importance of Learning to Tell Time

Related to sequencing issues, dyslexic children may have difficulty with temporal sequencing skills such as learning to tell time on analogue (non-digital) clocks. It's a good idea to teach dyslexic learners how to read an analogue clock with tangible hands that the child can manipulate (inexpensive toy clocks are available for purchase at toy stores or educational websites online). Along with learning a new skill, these clocks can also indirectly help with directionality by teaching clockwise and counterclockwise. Start by showing them simple concepts on the hour, such as 2:00; then progress to half-hour then quarter-hour increments. As they catch on, progress to harder concepts, such as 1:12, etc. To further reinforce sequencing skills, have your child relay the order of the events of their day to you, have them teach you something that requires sequential steps, or play the "Picnic Game" (see page 71).

Helping Your Child with Homework

Over the years, experts have gone back and forth about whether or not parents should step in and help their children at home if they are struggling.

For a dyslexic child who may be straining in the classroom, I recommend trying to help if you are equipped to and your child requests it. I do not endorse giving them answers or doing their work for them, but if they need clarification with a math concept or practice with reading, step in if you can and if it doesn't create a fight.

Teachers can vary greatly in the way they present new units in their class. They may not provide scaffolding or give adequate background information, which may make it challenging for your child to engage in a subject. Parents can offer context for a topic by using a story to scaffold and introduce background information.[1] While I do not suggest having a parent take on this task indefinitely, it can be a helpful inroad for a child who is struggling.

Building Your Child's Attention Span

Part of the challenge for young dyslexic learners is that they are attempting to do something extremely frustrating. fMRI imaging studies have shown that the way dyslexic brains decode language is more complex than a standard learner's and therefore can be laborious and even exhausting. Forming connections and acquiring knowledge takes extra effort that can require more breaks and cause emotional outbursts from fatigue and frustration.[2] Therefore, it is important to build up one's tolerance gradually, using intermittent breaks. As their ability to read improves, their attention span will also likely increase.

Certainly, if your child also has attentional issues (ADHD), you will want to help them develop the ability to sit and concentrate for increased periods of time. (See also Increasing Attention Span with Breaks, page 114.) Many parents ask me about medication for ADHD. While I advocate for all things natural and prefer to steer away from medication whenever possible, I have seen that it can provide significant benefits for some children. If you feel medication might be right for your child, I suggest consulting with a psychiatrist.

Introducing Extracurricular Activities

Along with offering alternative interests to motivate your child, extracurricular activities can be a great relief for the developing brain and excellent for cognitive development. Try sports, art, music, or any clubs that might appeal to your child's curiosity and interests. While it may be overwhelming for a parent, I encourage the effort, as these activities will be so vital for a child's self-esteem. Discovering new skills after struggling all day with academics may offer a big boost. Activities that access varied senses (like cooking, ceramics, running, etc.) can also reduce stress and cortisol. If the activities are social, so much the better.

THE PARENTS' TOOLBOX
Skill Building in Elementary School

If your child is struggling in school and has not yet been diagnosed as having dyslexia, be aware of indications and seek an evaluation as early as possible.

Once diagnosed, work to diminish your child's level of frustration in the classroom.

- Make sure interventions and accommodations are in place if your child has received them.
- Start a dialogue to advocate for your child with their teacher by explaining your child's situation in depth.
    If possible, ask to receive materials in advance to practice at home.
    Request that the teacher only call upon your child to read out loud if they raise their hand.
- Ensure they are being taught with a Science of Reading/phonetic approach; multisensory learning may also benefit dyslexic learners.
- Prepare your dyslexic child for the extra time and effort that will be

required to become more proficient in their reading fluency as well as to complete their homework.
- If you are able to help your child with their schoolwork (without fighting) by removing roadblocks and reducing their frustration, do it.
- Having a learning difference can be exhausting; allow time for breaks to increase attention span and build endurance.
- After they have learned to read, dyslexic children may benefit from using large print or different fonts for reading out loud.
- Promote reading for pleasure using any topics that grab your child's interest.
    - Read nightly—and whenever possible, actual (nondigital) books are best.
    - Use reading materials at or below their reading level to maximize the likelihood of a positive experience.
    - If they are interested in material that is more challenging, read the book with your child out loud (or use an audiobook) and have them follow along in the book.
- Time management and the ability to tell time (using an analog clock) are essential in elementary school.
- Instill the benefit of an organized room (perfection is not necessary) to begin to promote basic organizational skills.
    - Help them organize their drawers, closets, toys, books, etc. so they feel a sense of agency with their things.
    - Have your child tell you about activities in sequential order.
- Encourage extracurricular activities to support mental health, brain development, and self-esteem. Try sports, art, music, or any clubs that might appeal to your child's curiosity and interests.
- If necessary, find academic support locally or online.

CHAPTER 9

Adapting to Middle School

As everyone who has ever been a seventh grader knows, social interaction in middle school can quickly become every bit as central to your tween's day as academics. Middle school typically means a ramping up of academic responsibilities along with a new social landscape and a natural push toward needing more independence. Starting a new school, particularly during puberty, is a classic time of anxiety and extra stress. You may find your child acting out more, being grumpier, more needy or clingy, overwhelmed, or checked out and harder to reach. It will also likely become more difficult to get your child to open up to you about the challenges they're confronting in school.

What I have found with children, and especially adolescents, is that you may ask them how they're doing after a tough day, but they will choose to open up when *they're* ready, and on their own terms—like when you're making dinner or in the car together. Whenever it is, the important thing is to be there to listen—even if it's right as you're going to sleep. It's still important to ask the questions, but don't expect full disclosure on *your* time. Following your child's cues and allowing a conversation to flow naturally conveys the essential message that their health and happiness are a priority to you.

In the mix for a dyslexic child can be heightened academic frustration and self-consciousness, resulting in internalized shame and causing extra self-esteem challenges.

Transitioning Your Parental Role

Aside from all the hormonal swings and moodiness of young adulthood, your tween is likely to become less amenable to the style of parenting that they tolerated before. If you are still heavily involved in the management of their homework and schedules, middle school presents a good time to start to build up their confidence and competence by gradually encouraging autonomy.

Just as with the other important skills you teach them, retreating from helping to manage their responsibilities, to observing and stepping in with suggestions when needed, sets them on a path to accommodate their innate drive towards independence. That is to say that rather than continuing to actively partake in the supervision of their time management, organizing, or quizzing them, you'll want to take a step back and ask, instead, if they need your help. Rather than nagging, the idea is to start letting them run the show and release yourself from being the homework police.

To be clear, this is never about leaving your child high and dry. Just like any other skill they've been working to master during their early years it's about giving them the tools to effectively get things done, step-by-step, and weaning them from constant oversight. Part of the process is assuring your child that you know they are capable of taking on more responsibility for getting their work done well and independently, thereby encouraging them to gain confidence in themselves.

Talking Your Child Through Their Decision Process

If your child wants to go to a party Friday night but has a team practice Saturday and then a game on Sunday, here's an example of how the conversation can go. You can start by asking:

- "What's your plan for getting your work done?"
- "If you go to the party, will you regret it Saturday because you will be tired?"
- "How will you feel doing work on a Sunday night and not getting to relax before the school week starts again?"
- "How will you feel if you miss the party?"

Ultimately, your questions can help them do a cost-benefit analysis, prodding them to think through whether or not the repercussions are worth it. Engaging in an adult conversation without attacking or judging their choices may be groundbreaking for you both and allow your child to hear themself negotiate their priorities and consider consequences. Just as valuable, the exercise conveys a level of respect and trust to help nurture their emotional maturity.

Limit yourself to a few questions: "What takes priority?" "How long do you think it will take?" "When do you want to stop for a break?" Allow them to answer the questions to start approaching how they should be thinking of organizing themself and managing their own time. Assuming that the tools for independence are established, you are there to offer guidance—but not to *do*. Yet if they can't get things done on their own, you'll certainly want them to be able to seek your help.

Don't assume this will be easy! Letting go of controlling behaviors to allow your young teenager to rise to a challenge can be more stressful at first than helping. Yet this is the time that all the preparations, practicing time management, and organizational skills, as well as homing in on how they learn best, will start to really pay off. As you retreat and allow them to make their own mistakes, they have the opportunity to get an important education in learning the consequences for their actions. Going into school without their homework or not preparing for a test can let them see how they need to up their game going forward. When it is no longer you prodding them, they get a chance to experience that they can influence their own success, hopefully building a motivational loop to propel and sustain them going forward.

If they insist on going at it completely on their own, middle school is the perfect time. If they begin to miss assignments or are not able to complete them on time, they may have to meet with their teacher to figure out how to do better. Your contribution to this new phase might be to check in every other day as they segue to more independence. But if your child seems ready, it's a good time to shift the onus of their school responsibilities onto them going forward and let them rise to the occasion.

Finding Your Child's Drive and Motivation

Because the strategies outlined in this book are primarily based on the assumption that your child is naturally interested in learning and has just been unable to keep up because of their dyslexia, I have not discussed the possibility that they may *not*, in fact, be motivated academically. Whether your child is a dyslexic learner or not, children, of course, naturally exhibit a range of academic effort. Some arrive at school enthused and put internal pressure on themselves to achieve. Others are more reluctant and have little interest in doing things that are academically challenging or frustrating. Still others may require ongoing supervision until they cultivate greater initiative and discipline.

If a child is asking for help with their work, their level of interest may be more apparent. But more often than not, if they're struggling, parents may infer that they're just not as interested in learning. That assumption may be far from correct; their lack of interest may be masking frustration, avoidance, or a mild depression as a result of not being able to learn as easily as their peers. If they have not had an evaluation up to this point, now is the time.

If they are reluctant to engage and resistant to working hard, depending on their age, it may be an opportunity to have a frank conversation with your child, without being punitive or angry, to discuss what aspirations they may have for themself and what they can anticipate if they don't put their best effort forward in their studies. Inviting your child to make adult decisions about their own education can allow them to consider the effort required to step up and reach their goals. Approaching them as their ally can realign you—and give you an opportunity to offer your help.

That being said, sometimes children need to grow into an interest in academics and some may never find real motivation there. If your child is not willing to put effort into their schoolwork, I recommend continuing to expose them to new extracurricular activities and arenas to help them tap into their passions and curiosity, whatever those may be. If something truly sparks their interest, a real desire to learn may emerge.

Championing Your Child

As middle school ramps up, it may become more difficult for your child to maintain a positive mindset regarding their attributes and strengths without you as their champion. Before they can embody confidence independently, they will likely need you to help remind and reinforce for them that they are not alone in their struggles, nor are they defined by dyslexia. This is also a good opportunity to highlight the fact that, in life, everyone has hardships that others may not necessarily be aware of or recognize, and that they are in no way "less than" anyone else. They also may need to be reminded that the challenges they're confronting right now will get better over time.

Encouraging Your Child to Develop Their Own Motivation

Along with the shift away from overseeing every aspect of their homework and assignments, this is also the time to have your child begin to develop and own their motivation to succeed, steering them away from working hard for extrinsic reasons (like parental praise). By focusing instead on your child's intrinsic motivation (succeeding because learning makes them feel good about themself), you encourage their autonomy and make space for their own inner drive and curiosity to emerge. This requires reinforcing the idea that *they* are the experts on *themselves*. If it matters to your child, they will be more invested in succeeding.

According to neuropsychologist William Stixrud and test prep specialist Ned Johnson's research, if parents remain in their managerial role, they may be calming their own anxieties about their child's likelihood to succeed but inadvertently increasing their child's risk for anxiety and depression further down the road.[1]

On the other hand, for a dyslexic child, it can be difficult to sustain their motivation when they are working so hard and not getting the grades that match their effort. This is one of the real challenges that dyslexia can present—and you need to remind your child that they are doing all of this work for the sake of learning and their future and not for the grade. It may not be an easy sell. I like to explain to children that some skills (study skills, writing skills, etc.) are important conceptually and necessary to master, regardless of whether their effort yields a good grade or not. For example, they may not need to know about the Ottoman Empire when they're older, but they will rely on the critical thinking skills they developed when trying to write a paper about the topic.

The heightened awareness so many children have now, even early on in their education, particularly in competitive schools, is that the fast track to success or "winning" in life necessitates good grades to earn entry into prestigious universities. That singular focus can crank up stress levels, yet may not ultimately lead to the happiness outcome that kids or their parents imagine and may be at the cost of tuning out a child's own passions and curiosities. More preferable is motivating a child towards the experience of complete absorption in what they're doing, when their brain is in a state of high attention and low stress. (The one exception to this is video games, which can be highly addictive and therefore should be limited.) This sweet spot of total immersion from extreme interest is the ultimate goal for children to develop during their early years.[2]

Whatever their interests, children need the freedom to explore and experiment. It might be something you do not value, such as fashion or makeup, movies, video gaming, etc., but if that is their genuine passion, it can be used to build upon—an inroad to encourage your child to read, explore, do research, and enjoy that feeling of total immersion.

Particularly for dyslexic learners, I encourage you to expose your child to places and things that relate to their passions and interests like visiting factories, museums, a workplace, lectures, movies, or other experiences to excite their curiosity. Beyond just researching on social media, the internet, libraries, and bookstores, the more engrossed they become, the more they learn to honor the pleasure of pursuing their own interests.

If your child is excited by car racing, for example, it can be an entree into car mechanics, design, engineering, physics, strategic thinking, technical driving skills, statistics, and so on. Their fascination can propel them to explore, become engaged, and then build skills in the most organic sense, without any regard to a notion of "work." Endless focus from complete immersion can be a natural outgrowth from their curiosity, which can then help foster and develop a strong work ethic.

Nurturing this special spark also opens opportunities for the whole family to connect with them, not to mention expanding their social outlets to meet groups or individuals who share the same passion.

Interests will no doubt evolve and change, but the practice of recognizing and honoring what fascinates your child is a special, joyful experience to be highlighted. For different learners, these much-needed opportunities can enhance their educational experience, expand their own idea of themselves, and bolster their self-esteem.

Moreover, underscoring the process of recognizing and then pursuing interests also unconsciously nudges a child to tune into and value their own natural instincts. What fascinates them is not only fun but germane to unlocking who they are—and can engage them in the pleasure of learning, connecting to others with shared interests, and potentially helping them avoid isolation, depression, and anxiety.

Accepting Difficult Emotions

Meanwhile, since anxiety in dyslexic children can be higher than those of neurotypical learners, I believe there is reason to consider proactively buffering them from the most competitive aspects of education, particularly while their brain matures through high school. That is why, depending on the child, intentionally segueing to an intrinsic focus, preferably sooner rather than later, can be such a grounding approach. This is not to sidestep competition indefinitely for a dyslexic child but rather to further reinforce the value of what they are accomplishing from their own, more relevant, reference point.

Getting out ahead of what can be a big jump in responsibilities as well as academic and social pressures in middle school is also a great time to keep an eye on a young teenager's mood for signs of depression and anxiety. It makes sense for any parent to be aware, but since dyslexics may be more prone, you'll want to stay that much more vigilant.

At the same time, the well-known psychologist Dr. Lisa Damour makes it clear that some level of anxiety is expected and even productive for children.[3] This is also true for sadness—not to be confused with clinical depression. Managing the full range of normal human emotions is part of life, and parents need to give their child permission to experience all of their feelings (even if they don't always understand them immediately) so that a child can learn to move through them and recognize that they can and will recover. But when anxiety and depression interfere with a child's daily functioning for a prolonged period, it is time to seek professional help.

Symptoms of Anxiety

The following are symptoms of clinical anxiety: experiencing excessive fear and worry; feeling nervous, irritable, on edge; having a sense of impending danger, panic, or doom; an increased heart rate; breathing rapidly (hyperventilation); sweating and/or trembling; feeling weak or tired; difficulty concentrating; having trouble sleeping; restlessness; or experiencing gastrointestinal (GI) problems.[4]

Symptoms of Depression

Depression can present as, but is not limited to, feelings of emptiness, sadness, and hopelessness; feeling worthless; extremely low self-esteem; extreme fatigue or lack of energy; fixation on past failures; difficulty sleeping and or eating; or getting no sense of joy or withdrawing from activities that used to bring happiness. It is important to note that the above-mentioned symptoms can be part of the normal spectrum of human emotions at extreme moments. However, once these feelings interfere with daily functioning for a period of time or become chronic, it is time to seek professional help.[5]

Reframing Failure to Develop Self-Efficacy

Middle school offers an opportunity for your child to approach resolving their own problems before the stakes get higher in high school. This entails you as a parent remaining present to "consult," encourage, show empathy, and remind your child how much you love them—but allow them more and more responsibility for themselves, to give them space to learn from their own mistakes. This approach aims to create a safe, nonpunitive, and supportive environment without the fear of humiliation or shame if a child ultimately needs your help if things go wrong. It also helps to avoid the external pressure to be perfect so that a child won't feel they need to hide their scholastic challenges.

Though undoubtedly anxiety producing for parents (who want to minimize their child's pain and try to help them avoid making mistakes or developing bad habits), experts suggest that as their child reaches a certain level of maturity, parents should consider a shift in perspective. The idea is that if a child feels more confident and respected, they will feel comfortable seeking your help when they need it.[6]

When they do seek you out for help, you might be thinking, "How do you not know this?"—but keep it to yourself! Some of their inquiries may at first be more of an emotional test to seek assurance that you will still be there for them, without retribution, when they take big steps towards individuation and independence. Your job is to assure them that you will.

Furthermore, a tween or teenager (or, in truth, a student of any age) may or may not fully grasp that a single failure does not determine their capabilities. If they do encounter failure, they may be too scared to notice the grit and resilience they're accruing.

Based on the assumption that your child gave their best effort, I believe in disarming a "failure" right away with a nonpunitive response; instead, calmly and sympathetically explain that there are rarely dire consequences from a middle school grade disappointment. Guide your child to put genuine effort into learning the material they missed and analyze what they could have done better. Particularly in middle school, gaining the confidence that they can come back stronger after small defeats will be invaluable.

Sharing Resilience Stories

If your child has received a disappointing grade despite having put in a lot of effort, hear them out and encourage them to talk about what they're feeling. And don't be afraid to share your own life experiences of failure or disappointment and how they made you feel, to help them feel less alone. Knowing you have survived your own vulnerable experiences and were able to bounce back can make you more relatable and encourage them that they, too, can come back from a failure. Allow them time to recover, but remind them that life is about getting back up after setbacks to find another route to success.

While no one sets out hoping for their child's defeat, experiencing little failures/disappointments can have the counterintuitive benefit of a young adult confronting their worst fear in school. I learned early in life that once you've failed, the anxiety that surrounds it dissipates. Later, it can inspire you to step out of your comfort zone to try something new, knowing you're resilient enough to bounce back if the outcome is not all that you hoped for. The loss may hurt, but it will not be devastating. Eventually you can grow from it and learn to pivot in order to transform the experience into a win.

I often ask dyslexic children I work with, after a disappointing grade on a test, "What's going to happen tomorrow?" letting them acknowledge that their emotional reaction to a grade has little to do with the reality of what is at stake for a given singular failure.

So, if a child gets a poor grade, ask them what went wrong; make sure they are aware of what areas they did not understand and encourage them to review that material until they understand it—or to seek help from a teacher. Conversely, if they get a good grade, ask them how they studied and praise their effort. Make sure they know that both good and bad grades are ephemeral and do not influence the next test. The key is to step back and strategically analyze where they can improve and then make a specific plan for how to better prepare next time if they did not meet with success initially.

These moments are opportunities to demonstrate the importance of persevering amidst life's disappointments; "teachable moments" that serve to highlight that they can learn from what they may have missed today as opposed to dwelling in a negative mindset for long. Focusing on the value of building resilience and grit by choosing to pivot rather than wallow in self-defeating messages can become a lifelong practice.

Finding their own best mode for learning, continually being willing to adapt to better methods, and staying organized and ready to work hard are all pursuits that will reap great benefits in the long game of life. Being dyslexic may not change, but it doesn't need to stop a child from overcoming and gaining mastery. Ultimately, this process amounts to a class in Resilience 101!

A Caveat Regarding Failure

An important exception regarding failure is when you see your child making a big mistake that will actually hurt them with potentially lasting consequences. One way to help without instructing or lecturing is to ask guided questions. Despite a young adult's inclination to ignore the possible fallout of their actions, it's your job to prod them anyway. Just like a business consultant might do, prompt your tween to really think through their decision making and the likely results that can ensue.[7]

Choosing Your Battles

The start of middle school will no doubt present plenty of opportunities for your child to begin to push back against the amount of control you've had for years. Since it is their job to start the painful process of individuation, they are likely to provoke conflict unconsciously designed to make it easier for them to eventually go out on their own.

In my own case, since my mother needed to put so much effort into my academics, she made a conscious decision to begin to give me extra freedoms in other arenas around middle school. My parents understood my need to fit in socially, and starting in seventh grade, they wisely loosened the reins, allowing me to express myself through my appearance. This included the freedom to dress the way I wanted to, greenlighting the iridescent stars that I glued onto my temples as well as the washable purple and pink streaks I would put in my hair (that I could rinse out in time for school). My clothing was pretty wild but they affectionately laughed about it rather than choosing to yell about it. Their reactions felt liberating and also reassuring. Rather than telling me that I looked ridiculous, they told me that I looked cute! This built me up enough that on the occasions when they thought that I was overdoing it, I would take their opinion seriously.

Of course, the maturity level of the child must be considered, but at that time in my life, if my parents had not put up with my clothing, creative get-ups, or offbeat movie selections, it would have led to the typical parent-teenager conflicts. As it was, my school life was so frustrating, and my self-esteem was so low from how hard I needed to work for school, that I craved those outlets to let loose and assert my independence.

During those teenage years, my relationship with my mother also became more complex. It was hard to fight with her, then dramatically lock myself in my bedroom for hours, only to skulk back into her room later when I needed her to read to me. Fortunately, I learned that I could sit and be read to while wearing zebra-patterned pants and a purple streak in my hair, satisfied that I was an independent rebel in a different way!

The most important part of these experiences taught me that respect, compromise, and communication are extremely important—and this is true with all children, dyslexic or not. Self-esteem, self-confidence, and feelings of independence are hard to come by during adolescence, and children need all of the help they can get. Parents have to decide what is acceptable and what boundaries need to be created.

This is where I recommend the advice that the psychiatrist offered my mother when I was a little girl: Decide what is negotiable and what is not, and work from there. Every child needs to feel like they are being heard, respected, and that their feelings are being considered through open communication and compassionate understanding. Confronting a rigid rule structure on top of being so programmed academically would have been stifling. Furthermore, allowing me these small freedoms conveyed my parents' trust in my ability to make decisions, which helped build my self-confidence.

My family and I walked a fine line together, but the nonshaming and nonjudgmental environment in our house helped support my need for independence while simultaneously holding me in close contact with them out of necessity. These are principles that I suggest working towards to compassionately bolster your young teen.

Building Confidence by Avoiding Negative Generalizations

When a young adult starts to understand that by studying, or working hard and applying themselves to a task, they are learning the steps to gain mastery and are achieving what Carol Dweck calls a "growth mindset." This is the notion that the most important academic goal for a child is to expand their beliefs about their own abilities.[8]

Just as your child learned to walk and talk when they were too young to say to you "I am bad at walking" or "I am bad at balancing," learning new skills can be broken into steps to build upon to achieve mastery. Helping a dyslexic learner maintain this same mindset as their education progresses is particularly desirable. So, when you want to encourage your child to keep building their skill set, remind them of everything it took to learn to pronounce words, take their first steps, write their name, r de a bike, etc.; they have been succeeding in skill building for years.

Ultimately, the hope is that with your input, they will not fall prey to negative generalizations about their own abilities to learn. For example, avoiding the conclusion that they are "bad at math" in general if they struggle with a particular unit of math. Encouragement and the message that they are capable of learning can inspire perseverance and motivate your child to seek help from a teacher or friend or go online to find another approach. The important message is that while some students may have strengths in one subject or another, hard work and a positive attitude can win the day and ultimately lead to success.[9]

Succeeding Academically in Middle School

Being overwhelmed is a natural part of school for most kids, but a dyslexic child may feel it even more profoundly. As stated, there may be more frustration and a need to work harder and longer than their peers with less success. They may also require more time studying for tests, and they may possibly fail on occasion. Being cognizant of these transition periods can be stabilizing for your child and help them recognize that new demands require adjustment and patience. Helping them process the emotional component, with an extra dose of reassurance and empathy, can soothe anxieties. The bottom line is that these reactions are typical for all learners.

Here are some straightforward, effective tools to help your child greet their new academic challenges.

Middle School Organizational Basics

Time-management techniques like using planners, Google Keep, and lists continue to be key in keeping your child on track to adapt to the increased workload and responsibilities that come with middle school. Continuing to make your child aware of the importance of prioritizing their time will be more and more relevant as they progress in school. Keeping lockers and desks organized can also help quell anxieties that can arise from chaos and prevent your child from getting too overwhelmed.

As more sophisticated papers begin to be assigned, the need for systematic and logical organization becomes essential. Thankfully, personal computers and the internet have transformed the efficiency of some of the arduous process of organizing and writing research papers. After determining a thesis statement, preparing an outline for a paper is the next critical step. The essential task is to put complex information into a logical sequence.

I like to recommend "mapping," which is a method of brainstorming that helps one organize topics and corresponding ideas for writing a paper. Usually the thesis statement (or main idea) is put into a bubble in the center of a blank sheet of paper and related topics are entered into surrounding bubbles. Once your child can see what information they want to include, they can choose how to present and elaborate each idea in a logical sequence. It's a great tool to help children visualize and organize a variety of related thoughts to help bridge them together. There are various websites that can further help your child organize a paper (use search terms such as "tools to organize a paper").

Adaptations for Dysgraphia

If your child has dysgraphia and struggles to get their thoughts onto paper in a cohesive way, have them dictate their ideas into their phone or computer. Later they can manipulate the transcription by cutting and pasting and editing the document. Grammarly can also be a helpful editing software or app, similar to spell check but used for grammar. (Google Docs also checks grammar.)

Depending on your child's school, they may be allowed to take a photo of notes on a blackboard, or record a class (using their phone), or use a Livescribe smartpen that helps transcribe what a child hears as well as type what they handwrite. An added benefit of recorded note-taking is the ability to slow down the pace when a child plays back the recordings to catch anything they may have missed in class. Aside from the productivity that these technologies provide, they can also allow a child with dysgraphia to be more present in the classroom.

Another adaptation for writing issues relates to copying notes. While most children will make gains from writing and rewriting notes, as discussed previously, a child with dysgraphia is likely an exception. Since writing is laborious for these learners, I recommend they reread or listen to material and verbalize what they are trying to learn. This could mean repeatedly rehearsing the material out loud or recording themselves on their phone so they can replay it to hear what they may have missed.

Keeping Your Child Alert to Effective Learning Methods

The end of middle school is an important time for a child to focus on their best style for learning, as previously discussed, in order to minimize frustration and study time. Since classes are often taught using a range of methods (like readings, lectures, demonstrations, etc.), you can help your child to take notice of the varying techniques that work best for them (see also page 103). Refer to the Resources on pages 237–242 for supportive tools and technologies. Although your child may have no control over how information is presented to them, it can be helpful for them to start to become aware and be able to identify the methods that are most in line with their learning style. Potentially they will continue to build upon them for the rest of their lives.

Foreign Language Considerations

One area of struggle for dyslexic children can be trying to learn a foreign language. Just like with learning to read and speak English, difficulty with phonemic awareness, including issues with articulation, auditory discrimination, and sound symbol association, etc. can be particularly difficult for dyslexic learners and more so if the language is not phonetically based. It is likely that tuning their ears to a new language will be challenging—particularly if the class moves at a fast pace or the teacher uses language immersion to introduce the material.

Fortunately, there are many languages (with the exception of French), that are phonetically regular. So, if your child decides to (or must) learn a new language, Spanish, German, Italian, Latin, Mandarin, Japanese, Korean, Hebrew, Arabic, or any language with characters may be preferable. These languages are known to be simpler to decode because each letter in a word makes a (single) sound (unlike English and French). This is not to say that these options are in any way "simple," but they do have the phonetic advantage over English. As an alternative that puts more emphasis on visual learning, many schools offer American Sign Language as an option.

The decision of whether or not to seek a foreign language waiver depends largely on your child's drive and motivation level. If it doesn't evoke too much anxiety, middle school may be the appropriate time to discuss these decisions with them and their guidance counselor (or any other support personnel on their school "team"). If your child *is* quite driven and they want to try a foreign language, they may want to consider a pass/fail option if it's available. Reconsidering the foreign language decision again early in high school is advisable, as it may impact their college choices going forward.

Goal for Late Middle School

As your child is preparing for their transition to high school, you will want to make sure that they hit the important benchmark of getting their homework completed on their own without you nagging them. If this is unrealistic for your child, letting them experience the repercussions of not handing something in will hopefully incentivize them to step up and become more diligent before the consequences become more serious in high school.

Stress Relief for Middle School

Amidst all the angst and challenges in middle school, I became an avid fan of horror movies. Sitting and screaming on the edge of my seat was a great way to release the pent-up anxiety and stress from the school week. Everybody needs a way to decompress, and it's helpful to figure out what works best for your teen and to build time for it into their schedule.

I also had the benefit of working with a wonderful tutor for math and science in middle school who good-naturedly endured bargaining with me for my study breaks. If I worked for forty-five minutes, he would let me call a friend for five. If I did fifteen math problems, I could do a headstand for one minute. I realize now that the autonomy I felt in doing these activities was a key benefit for getting through many brutally long nights. I encourage you to create the right mix of custom incentives to energize and infuse some fun for your child while offering them a much-needed measure of control.

While the amount of homework may not yet be as overwhelming as it will be in high school, even short assignments can be time-consuming for a dyslexic child. Dividing information into small chunks and learning little bits at a time, with breaks in between (like doing physical activities or changing the energy up with art projects; light, fun activities with the family, etc.) rather than "cramming," is best for their brain's wiring. Depending upon what they are studying, taking a few days to learn and then review the information is far preferable (see also page 101).

Making Opportunities to Bond on Your Child's Terms

If you haven't done it already, middle school is a great opportunity to make a real effort to connect with your child about their interests and activities. Particularly if you're finding yourself too deeply mired in your child's schoolwork or time management, step back and make a conscious effort to try to get to know what excites them outside of school. Whether it's bonding over their music, videos, books, hobbies, or sports they love—anything that can help strengthen your parent-child bond on your child's terms can build a bridge and add an essential dimension to your connection and balance out your relationship. The more they know you take time and care about their lives, the more inclined they will likely be to open up about their struggles as well.

Keeping Perspective and Remaining Hopeful

Amidst the growing workload in middle school, the message that your child needs to hear constantly is this: struggling greatly in middle school does not mean they are doomed to a future of more of the same. While they will always be dyslexic and may likely not hit their stride before college with hard work they will consolidate gains each year and notice growth and improvement.

If they are unable to achieve to the level that they would hope for because of their dyslexia, you may not want to dwell on the school portion of their life. A more realistic scenario for a smart child who is struggling academically in middle school may be to encourage them to achieve their best without putting extra pressure on themself for grades. Beyond school, homing in on what they show an affinity and passion for helps to broaden their horizons to begin to find what captivates them.

As a reminder, continuing to champion your child through the harrowing changes of middle school and making good use of the "mantras" (see page 123) can infuse optimism for your young teen.

Learning to Laugh at Oneself

As the stress ramps up during these middle school years, the reminder that early failures do not need to be regarded as tragedies becomes more pertinent. Life's disappointments can be softened substantially with the merciful injection of perspective and occasional levity. While it can certainly be easy to get drawn into the drama of your tween's social life and want to rush in and relieve their emotional discomfort, you may both be better served in the long run by finding opportunities to infuse humor and a new vantage point. Gently pushing your child to look beyond their own reality bubble and remember that they surely do not hold a monopoly on insecurity or embarrassment during these years, even if it may feel that way, can be a relief for everyone. What may seem like a humiliation to a self-conscious middle schooler may present an opening for you to offer a shift in perspective.

While it is certainly true that plenty of adults have not mastered the ability to laugh at themselves, introducing a humor release valve during some of life's tough moments can help to develop much-needed ego strength, simultaneously encouraging your child to develop a thicker skin over time.

THE PARENTS' TOOLBOX
Adapting to Middle School

- Begin to segue from helping your child with organizing their time and schoolwork to encouraging their independence by observing and checking in when needed.
- This may be a good time to discuss what aspirations your child may have for themself and what they can anticipate if they don't put their best effort forward in their studies.
- Before your child can embody confidence, they will likely need you to be their champion.
- Help your child find their own inner drive and curiosity to learn the pleasure of learning and engage and motivate them to work hard.
- Anxiety and sadness are normal emotions, but it's important to familiarize yourself with the *clinical* signs of anxiety and depression so you know when/if to seek help.

- Step away and allow your child to make their own mistakes in middle school before there are lasting consequences.
    - A onetime "failure" or disappointing grade can be overcome and allow a child to come back stronger and build resilience—the exception is if there will be lasting consequences, in which case you'll want to step in.
    - Share your own stories so your child understands they are not alone.
- Avoiding micromanaging and choosing your battles help to build independence and convey your trust to your child, which can enhance self-esteem.
- Encourage a "growth" mindset. Push back on a child generalizing that they "can't" overcome a struggle.
- Academic Tips for Middle School:
    - Continue to encourage their own time management and incorporate tools like Google Keep and prioritizing of their time.
    - Encourage organization of their lockers and desks, as well as their research papers.
    - Continue to establish the most effective study methods for your child so they're ready for high school. Refer to the Resources section at the back of the book for supportive tools and technologies.
    - The decision to get a foreign-language waiver will depend on your child's motivation and abilities. Consider a phonetically regular language or American Sign Language.
    - An important goal for late middle school is to have your child be able to take responsibility for independently completing their homework without you needing to nag them.
- Stress Relief for Middle School:
    - Avoid "cramming" for tests and divide work into smaller chunks while incorporating breaks.

- Find and make opportunities to bond with your child on *their* terms by learning about their interests outside of their schoolwork.
- If they are struggling greatly academically, keep perspective that things will get better as they get older. Support your child in whatever ways you can and revisit the "mantras" when necessary.
- Remember, the tough times are important opportunities to find humor and laugh with your child.

CHAPTER 10

Thriving in High School

High school presents new challenges for everyone, but for dyslexic learners it can be especially tough. The added pressure of requirements like biology, physics, or a foreign language as well as the organizational challenges of writing long term papers, with possible college applications looming in the background, can all significantly magnify academic stressors. Whether or not your child is attempting to tackle a rigorous curriculum, scholastic pressure, mixed with the possibly dispiriting impact of working hard at school without a lot of positive reinforcement in the form of improved grades, can leave anyone understandably stressed.

A teen expressing a feeling of "hating school," as I did during much of my high school experience, may really be trying to express that they are struggling and frustrated and can't find a way to succeed. So, even as you increasingly give them the freedom to flex their independence, it's important to keep the lines of communication open so you can try to offer support. I recommend continuing to connect around their interests, allowing them to talk to you when *they* are ready, and doing your best to really listen without being judgmental.

Inspiring Your Child Towards Independence

While you may have been considerably involved in their school life thus far, it's an important time to consider and encourage the social and academic growth they'll require in time for college or the "real world." Although it may be hard to let go, you'll want to be thoughtful in assessing what you feel is right for your teen when they start flexing their independence at a faster rate than ever before—rather than reacting from your own fears.

As they naturally progress towards increased autonomy, being well organized can be key. Having the time-management skills and diligence to break down the tasks in front of them and then schedule their time accordingly is a great way to build that competence to meet deadlines and accomplish what they set out to do. With these steps under their belt, they have the tools to conquer new challenges. Their ability to organize will empower them towards independence.

If they are not able to see it yet for themself, make sure that you are *not* subtle in conveying that they will need to organize their time well and incorporate all of their extra responsibilities. Far from trying to stress them out, the message is to remind them that they have the skills they require to get everything done and they can reach out for support if needed.

Advocating for Themself in High School

Similarly, as they approach the new arena of high school, it's a great opportunity to encourage your teen to advocate for themself academically. Here are some suggestions of appropriate ways for *your teen* to communicate their needs at school and for how to conduct themself in the classroom:

- Clearly convey to their teachers which accommodations they receive and why.
- If they start to struggle with a certain topic, set up a meeting with their teacher to ask specific questions that they have prepared in advance.

- Sit in the front row, look the teacher in the eye, and nod occasionally so they know they are "actively" listening and are dedicated and serious about their studies.
- Anytime they feel comfortable raising their hand and showing that they are engaged, they should be encouraged to participate.
- Check to be sure all work turned in is neat and thoroughly checked over for spelling or other grammatical errors.
- Hand in all assignments early, if possible, to request feedback so that they can edit their work before the due date. Many teachers will be willing to look over a paper and offer feedback if work is turned in early.
- If work needs to be resubmitted, be sure it is on time.
- If they are unsatisfied with their grade, whether for an exam or paper, have them ask the teacher if there is a way to improve that grade with extra work.

Workload Tips

Coping with a bigger workload and being overwhelmed are typical parts of high school for most teens. A dyslexic learner may feel the impact more profoundly while they adjust to new demands and work through the emotional component of the shift to high school. Remind them that everybody in their class is working to step up their game at these transition times, too—so they are not at all alone in their experience. Review the "mantra" (pages 122–125) to let them know that they will get there by applying themselves; and that you and the family team will be there to help.

- **Boosting time-management skills.** While your teen may already be quite competent at managing their academics, chores, and other commitments, they may need help managing the stress and anxiety of the extra demands that high school brings. As the complexity ramps up, they may temporarily require some extra support with time management. Don't worry—your teen is not regressing but rather taking one step back in order to move ten steps forward.

- **Promoting strategic prioritizing.** There may be nights when it is impossible for your child to get everything done. These are opportunities to start them thinking strategically about prioritizing their many responsibilities and assignments. While it is important to get all assignments done, there may be times when your teen has an abundance of deadlines on the same day. If this occurs, they may need your help to figure out what to sacrifice (although planning ahead may prevent this). If they have a major test to study for and a paper to finish as well as smaller homework assignments, they'll need to figure out which tasks have a greater impact on their grade. The paper and test may be weighted more heavily while a homework assignment may have a relatively insignificant impact on their overall grade.

- **Utilizing all their tools to manage their workload.** To help handle the volume of reading your adolescent is required to do, continue to utilize audiobooks and textbooks. Many parents resist letting their teen listen to books because they think their child needs practice reading. Unfortunately, with the time pressures and the volume of reading required in high school, it is typically not a realistic opportunity for them to get their reading up to speed. They may need books read to them in order to keep up and fully understand the content.

- **Consider language waivers early.** A very driven dyslexic child may not want to waive a language requirement in high school because down the road it may make admission to the college of their choice more challenging. While it may be hard to imagine considering issues like these as a freshman, it's probably smart to discuss this with your teen and their guidance counselor or any other support people on their school "team" before

obtaining a language waiver or opting out of requirements. It is at least worth a conversation to avoid regrets later.
- **Provide another round of sequencing help.** Understand that in high school, your teen may continue to struggle to organize their notes and study guides, and still require help setting up an organizational system to create order. This might include color coordinating notebooks or color-coding annotations taken when reading. Additionally, you might want to check in with them and make sure they have an organized locker and desk. The key here is that you may not be able to expect your teenager to follow through independently; it may take a much more mature and developed brain to do these things without assistance.
- **Diligence in taking breaks and staying active.** Keep your teen plugged into a physical activity (such as a sports team or a recreational activity) to provide a brain break. Exercise and physical activity in any form is crucial to get the benefits from endorphins while relieving stress and maintaining energy reserves.

If they get overwhelmed, you and your family "team" are there to coach them with a light touch. While they are likely capable, they still may need extra help, or perhaps just moral support to know that you're there if they need you.

Last but not least, remind them of how special they are and how much you love them. These are delicate times for teenagers who are busy doing the difficult work of individuating and adjusting to the growing demands of adulthood. Despite how aggressive or uncooperative they may occasionally be as adolescents, they need your love and assurance as much as ever, if not more so.

Stress Management

With a dyslexic teen, the objective in high school is to continue to support their efforts and vast accomplishments. This means a continuation of all the skills and gains they have been accruing up until now, with strategies for building upon what they've already done.

Stress can have a negative connotation—but a little bit of pressure can be a healthy motivator to increase our efficiency and energize us to do our best.[1] The question in high school becomes how to balance incentivizing your adolescent to manage a large amount of work without creating a stressed-out, anxious teen who becomes depressed or turns to unhealthy ways of coping.

Below are the essential academic and social-emotional tools and tips to best serve you and your young adult throughout the high school experience while academic demands mount. As not all learning is a straight progression up, you will note that you can expect to revisit some classic areas of struggle for your child.

Here is a (nonexhaustive) review of ideas, some of which have been recommended previously, for how you might encourage your teen to let off steam and effectively manage their work:

- **Have them make a to-do list to budget their time by giving an estimate of how long it will take to accomplish each item on the list and allocate time accordingly.** Time-management techniques can greatly alleviate anxiety and let your teen see that they have adequate time to get everything done.
- **Physical activity can be an excellent release of endorphins and decrease anxiety.**[2] Any kind of sport or physical activity that your teenager enjoys is a great way to start—whether it is just kicking a soccer ball, lifting weights, dancing, playing a quick game of basketball or catch, taking a bike ride, or walking, or an immersive activity like jumping rope that takes a lot of concentration and rhythm and can get their endorphins going quickly. If they can get out into fresh air, it can be especially energizing. Among the endless possibilities, yoga, skateboarding, and meditation can also be really effective in calming the brain.
- **Cleaning or organizing a messy bedroom or desk can bring calm to a chaotic situation.** They will likely be reluctant and

you may have to lend a hand, breaking things down one drawer or one shelf at a time, but once everything is organized, your teen is likely to experience a sense of accomplishment and reduced stress.

- **Listening to music, playing an instrument, doing an art project, or baking can be great ways to de-stress between or after more rounds of work.**
- **Sitting and talking with your teenager about new things they are learning and enjoying is a great way to reconnect.** Even a quick low-tech board game or puzzle can be a good way to touch base with your adolescent.
- **Taking a bath or shower can help them wind down and prepare for a good night's sleep.**
- **Playing a video game with a friend or joining a group game can be a quick and convenient stress reliever.** While technology may not be the ideal active break, video games tend to be very exciting and fun and offer a great mental break from work, as do video meetings with a friend or watching something on YouTube, etc. (Make sure they set a firm time limit, so that your teen knows beforehand when they will get back to work.)
- **Creative family bonding during intense weekends of work can add fun and help keep your teen connected and their energy up.** Connect over family snacks and group outings or physical exercise, or decompress and relax with a family movie or game.

In high school, I learned the benefits of the creativity of my family "team." When studying went late into the night, I needed ways to release the day's tension and reenergize. I found that being active during fifteen- or twenty-minute study breaks helped keep my energy up—my father used to take me to the garage in the basement of our building so we could roller-skate together and I could shake off long hours of studying. We would speed around the garage for twenty minutes and then I would come back upstairs ready to continue with my homework.

Baking was especially helpful to me during high school. I loved to make all kinds of breads because I enjoyed kneading the dough to break up the tedium of sitting in one place for so many hours. Other times, I baked cakes while my mother would quiz me. Part of the fun, too, was when everyone got together and shared what I made. No doubt your family will find its own unique ways to create some bonding time while simultaneously decompressing.

Emotional Support During Stressful Times in High School

If high school is a huge struggle for your teen, sitting by the sidelines and talking them through rough days may be the support you're called upon to do most. But those ordinary things may be the best way to infuse balance for a teenager in the midst of a crisis. Making time to do things together, even the simple act of eating dinner or watching a show together, can bring comfort and help thwart isolation.

Connecting in some small way during the most stressful times can provide a soothing energy at home. This type of dependable support system is huge. Just being able to kick back, listen to music with them or perhaps play their favorite games, or discuss something other than school can be a comfort. No matter how irascible they may be as teenagers and amidst all they may be confronting at school, they need to know that there is a safe place at home where they feel appreciated and loved unconditionally.

Furthermore, the fact is that your support and encouragement are key. Speaking with adult dyslexics, I have found that many believe that their success was built upon having their parents' steadfast belief in them. No matter what they experienced academically or socially with their peers, their parents' support anchored them. So, take heart when you are talking to your teens and you feel they don't hear you or are ignoring you. Keep talking—you are likely getting through to them even if they don't immediately acknowledge it or give you the satisfaction of letting you know that they're listening—and care what you're saying.

Here are some other ways to reframe the emotional challenges that your teenager may likely encounter moving forward in high school:

- **Normalizing big emotions.** Remember to allow and foster tolerance for your young adult's full range of feelings, including despair at times or even an occasional meltdown. This can be a release of pent-up emotions, particularly for teenagers going through big hormonal swings. Let them know these feelings are normal parts of life's difficult moments and that they will pass, even if it feels like they won't.
- **Resilience challenges.** Failures or frustrations can make you stronger in the long run, but some days, despite the best self-esteem practices, it's appropriate and important to acknowledge difficult feelings like sadness or frustration. Give your teen space to grieve and then shake it off. The important part is for everyone to remember that, in time, things will get better. It's essential to remind your adolescent of their vast resilience, and the times they have felt down and how they recovered. (It may also be beneficial to deliver a "mantra" again.)
- **Acting out or rebellion may be an adolescent's response to feelings of shame.**[3] Rather than being reactive to their behavior, try to remember that they may be trying to survive a painful and/or frustrating daily assault of feeling "less than" their peers. Aggression may be their way of communicating their struggle or making sure that you still care and are paying attention. Use these moments to communicate your compassion for what they may be going through and express curiosity about what is motivating their behavior. Really *hearing* what they have to say is an excellent way to encourage a teen to verbally express their needs, rather than acting out. Be sure to install limits on their behavior as guardrails to help them rein themself in. Reasonable boundaries demonstrate your love and concern, and provide reassurance that you are paying attention and care.

- **Encourage and sustain an open, nonjudgmental line of communication.** Keeping connected to your child and demonstrating your love and support and genuine interest in their concerns and hobbies can build inroads for them to open up and express what they're feeling or struggling with. Depending on the issue, get ready to keep your opinions to yourself as you may need to sit quietly as they clumsily navigate through figuring things out (as we've all had to do at times). Thinking of yourself as a sounding board may make it easier on you and allow them to *ask* for your advice if they want it.
- **Keep connected and avoid isolation.** In today's technology-filled environment, it has become more typical for both teens *and* parents to isolate themselves in their respective corners, glued to their screens. This new normal makes it that much more essential to *stay aware* that you're connecting with your child and mindful of what they're doing. During particularly rough patches in school, when the workload is legitimately heavy, it may also help to remind your dyslexic teen that they are not the only one struggling to keep up—even though it can feel that way. To thwart the feelings of isolation at home, I like to try to have family dinners whenever possible to instill the importance of family time and human connection. Having your adolescent try to find a study partner can be a big help, too.
- **Gratitude practices are especially important for teenagers.** It is easy for a struggling high schooler to get depressed and have a pity party each day. Instituting the daily practice of reviewing all they have to be thankful for helps shift anyone into a more positive frame of mind. Each night at dinner or when feasible, ask each family member the high and low point of their day and why they feel fortunate. Do not judge! Model this behavior and make sure to mention how fortunate you are for things that we can all take for granted, like food on the table, each other, our health, grandparents who are alive, a comfortable place to live, a trip you might be taking, etc. We

can all use a little reminder of how lucky we truly are rather than focusing on what we are missing.
- **If you're really having trouble getting through to your teen, they may be sending up silent smoke signals to get your attention.** Withdrawal or isolation can be precursors or symptoms of depression, so be sure to express your concern and ability to listen and be there for them. If they are still retreating, it may be time to seek professional help.

The Added Importance of Dyslexic Teens Avoiding Drugs and Alcohol

Poor self-esteem, withdrawal, and/or isolation can set a teen up for vulnerability to drug or alcohol addiction. With the pervasive drug issues and availability of substances today, dyslexic or not, parents certainly need to stay vigilant to signs of substance abuse.

Recent research has shown just how dangerous alcohol and drugs are for the adolescent brain.[4] As mentioned previously, statistics suggest that dyslexic children are more prone to anxiety and depression, possibly because of low self-esteem and higher rates of ADHD. These same factors make them more susceptible to drug and alcohol addiction as well.[5]

While I am not an advocate of drugs or alcohol for any high school kids, I believe it is important to be even more proactive about discouraging drug use and discussing the dangers of experimentation with dyslexic young adults.

For parents unfamiliar with recent findings about even casual drugs like marijuana, it may be of interest to note that marijuana is significantly more detrimental to a developing brain than an adult brain as evidenced by IQ dips in teens that were tested before and after sustained cannabis use. It's also worth mentioning that marijuana is up to seven times stronger now than it was in the 1980s and '90s, underscoring the importance of having your child tread very carefully around experimentation.[6] Even more devastating are the effects of opioid use on teenagers over the last decade. While it is outside the purview of this book to explore the symptoms and signs that a teen is using drugs or alcohol, I believe that parents should certainly keep a keen eye on their child and educate themselves about what to look out for. I also recommend sharing this information with your child and keeping an ongoing dialogue with them about the pressures they may be encountering in their peer group.

Segueing to Intrinsic Motivation

High school inevitably ramps up all the pressures of school: academic demands, more social influence, exposure to alcohol and drugs, and overall transitioning to more independence. In general, as your teenager closes in on adulthood, they are also likely increasingly aware that things "count" towards college. They are also more likely to encounter bouts of anxiety, depression, and distractibility as part of the emotional landscape while competition and social pressures ramp up in school.

If your teenager has entered high school having made big strides in building foundational skills, their good academic habits should be well established, and they are most likely taking steps towards independence. Hopefully they have cultivated a strong work ethic and continue to gain mastery over the many tools previously explored. The hope is that their drive has become more intrinsically motivated, so that they are gleaning satisfaction from the enjoyment of working hard and exploring subjects that interest them rather than focusing solely on grades and competition.

Continuing to transition to intrinsic motivation dovetails well with increasing autonomy in high school as well. Not surprisingly, research shows that children who are *extrinsically* motivated may not be as cued into their own interests, nor as clear about who they are and what gives them meaning or purpose, and may be avoiding independence.[7]

Given the high rates of anxiety, depression, and stress that teens experience today, parents are beginning to understand the real toll that focusing on grades in pursuit of "brand name" colleges can have on adolescents during formative years. When surrounded by extremely driven classmates, the desire to achieve a high GPA can easily eclipse an adolescent's discovery of their burgeoning identity and interests.

Here is where the need to objectively understand your teen's motivation level and area of interests is so key. If a rigorous and possibly competitive academic experience is what they are inclined towards and what they seem to genuinely enjoy, then by all means, I believe in encouraging and supporting that effort. But if your teen is not driven academically (and there is not a deeper issue to explore) or if their interests don't include furthering their education into college or their interests do not align with your goals for them, the best you may be able to do is to engage them in open discussions about what they want for themselves in the future.

Personally, I started to hate high school in the ninth grade when my biology teacher returned our weekly quizzes back to us in grade order in front of the whole class. As I collected my quiz last each week, the humiliation began to erode my desire to come to school. The truth was that I did not have the emotional maturity to tease out that I did not hate school in general, I just felt crushed by the weight of being repeatedly humiliated.

If you have seen a sharp change in your teen's motivation towards their studies, it could indicate some sort of embarrassment or shame they're experiencing. But if your adolescent has never been especially motivated academically, continuing to support and encourage them to find their passion elsewhere can be a wonderful option, allowing them to push through the remainder of their high school education. There are so many exciting and well-paid careers that bypass a college education, and they can be an especially great fit for a dyslexic learner who is less academically inclined.

While grades and competition will likely impact all learners to some degree in their lives, they don't necessarily guarantee happiness or success later in life. So, balancing the natural competitive instinct with the deeper, more core mission of finding meaning in work they love becomes more essential as a young adult progresses towards adulthood.

Regardless of their academic prowess, I believe that trying to find their own intrinsic motivation should be a core mission in high school. In other words, redirecting their focus towards a more meaningful experience of schooling, away from the academic rat race. Acknowledging the satisfaction gained by working hard, seeing progress, and learning new things, as opposed to chasing grades, can free up energy and enthusiasm for discovering interests and exploring curiosities.[8] Realistically, this may come down to encouraging electives that have real resonance for them—or at least piques their curiosity.

But if peer pressure or their own competitive drive is propelling them, the best you may be able to do for your teen is try to ease the strain they inflict upon themselves by offering perspective and unconditional love. Continuing to home in on their passions (possibly through extracurricular activities), while letting their choices also serve as a lesson in commitment, gives them agency and allows you to step out of the battle for control. Knowing you're there in the background for support and advice if they need it will make space for their self-discovery.

Being engaged and immersed in learning and participating in what they love are among the most important outcomes anyone can glean from their education. In the best case, by nurturing their innate interests, young adults take the courageous step towards making their dreams a reality.

Turning Lemons into Lemonade

Surely not everyone identifies that thing that profoundly excites them in high school, even with lots of exposure to a wide range of possibilities. But hopefully, with some extra focus on self-discovery, small seeds can start to sprout.

The path to uncovering my own life's passion found me in the most unexpected way—during what was one of my lowest moments in high school. I share this story of how the beginnings of my life's path revealed itself, in case your dyslexic teen is finding navigating high school especially difficult, as it was for me.

I was in eleventh grade when academic pressures had intensified and I was in the grips of chemistry, trigonometry, and Spanish 2, all while studying for the SAT. With tutors for nearly every topic, I was still failing chemistry, getting a D in trigonometry, a C- in Spanish, and barely holding my own in history and English. My days were filled with tears and feelings of helplessness and frustration as I earnestly put forth my best, despite my poor grades.

I desperately wanted to do well, but since I was not succeeding, I thought constantly about dropping out of school. There were almost nightly battles with my parents when I would cry hysterically and threaten to quit. There were also nights when I was so frustrated and angry that I would scream at the top of my lungs (not unlike "primal scream" nights in college during exam weeks). At a particularly low moment, I punched a wall so many times that I ended up with a wrist injury.

Finally, during that fateful meeting with my dean (referenced in the introduction) regarding my poor grades, the pressures culminated in academic probation and my near expulsion from school. I was told that if my grades did not improve, I would be unable to return for my senior year. I started to cry and told my dean that I was doing my best when she dryly posed the pivotal question that became a turning point in my life: "You are either not trying hard enough or you are stupid; which is it?"

Her inference was crystal clear. Her words pierced the air, verbalizing exactly what I, myself, had been fearing. Devastated, I returned home that Friday evening to relay the story to my parents and then spent the rest of the weekend exploring my options with my boyfriend, who was home from college. Everyone agreed, the decision was mine to make: either to try to ride out the rest of high school or to quit. Only I knew how much pressure I could endure. My parents would no longer force me, and even if they wanted to, I was of legal age to leave school if that was what I chose.

After agonizing about my decision that weekend, I finally came to the realization that I did not want to be a "high school dropout." In truth, I just wanted to *succeed*—and some small but strong part of me knew that I was neither stupid nor lazy.

In that same moment, I had a new vision of getting an advanced degree, and one day returning to the dean with the title of "Doctor" before my name. I knew that if I quit, I would be letting the "mean dean" win. Beneath my rage and shame, I was so hurt by her that, perversely, she became my motivation. I suddenly had clarity that what I really wanted was to try to help others so that they didn't have to go through all that I had and contend with ignorance about a disability, as well.

That Monday, I set my alarm clock and returned to school fully of my own volition. To the great relief of my parents, I had renewed purpose and determination. I voluntarily changed chemistry tutors from a handsome college student who was not a great tutor to a buttoned-up woman who knew how to explain chemistry. I reduced my social life to one night out on the weekends (and sometimes just a phone call to a friend with no plan to go out) and applied some basic communication strategies to let my teachers know how serious I was about doing the hard work to try to improve my grades. I moved to the front row in my classrooms, pushed myself to participate in class discussions as much as possible, and met regularly with the teachers whose classes I was struggling with most.

What emerged, born of necessity, was the ability to concentrate for longer periods, resulting in an expanded attention span. Mercifully, my grades gradually improved just enough so that I would not get thrown out of school.

In a remarkable shift, once my parents were at peace with the idea of me dropping out, the full responsibility and commitment to my education landed upon me. After they had sincerely told me to quit school, and I knew that they meant it, I got scared enough that my tantrums stopped and so did my other antics. While the crying continued, there was no more aggression directed at my parents, since they were not putting me into this awful situation anymore. *I* was *choosing* my plight because I really wanted to get a high school degree. There was no more misdirected anger, which allowed me to more fully enjoy and appreciate my family's support and encouragement.

Miraculously, by twelfth grade, I was getting through all of my homework independently. I was still a slow reader, which meant many nights of studying until midnight or beyond, but I managed to raise my GPA so that

I could graduate. When I finally finished high school, I was ranked near the bottom of my class. But I graduated, and for me that was a triumph.

As a teenager, despite all my emotional outbursts, I was unable to articulate my complicated feelings about what I was enduring in high school and how low my self-esteem had dipped.

This profound experience in my life still informs much of my perspective regarding children who seem to be uninterested in school. What appears as a lack of motivation may instead be depression or a serious lapse of hope. If they can no longer imagine a path forward in school, they may be giving up on themself, feeling "dumb" and defeated. Their desire to disinvest in their education may in fact be a desperate attempt to preserve their self-esteem in pursuit of success elsewhere.

Being Recognized by a Caring Adult in School

One significant difference that a dyslexic student may experience in high school is that the extra supervision that they were given with the implementation of an IEP in their earlier schooling is no longer in place. During those years when there were more "eyes on" a child, there was likely extra attention, support, and encouragement for their learning challenges. But once they enter high school, that kind of extra moral support tends to disappear.

In speaking to other parents of dyslexic learners about their child's pivotal high school experiences, the theme of having their child's abilities recognized by an adult at school emerged as significant at times when their child was really struggling. I can't stress enough how important this aspect of your child's experience can be. One grown patient of mine talked about how he had "despised" school and would often resist going. He loved playing sports and one day his gym teacher offered him an after-school job helping with one of the teams. This provided a lifeline that kept him from cutting class and gave him something to look forward to at the end of each day.

Another dyslexic child's trajectory was greatly improved when a teacher, who had seen that he was struggling, asked him to tutor a younger student. While he had previously lost interest in school and had started to act out in class, her invitation made him feel special and became a turning point for his self-esteem that reinvigorated his motivation to continue to work hard on his own schoolwork.

Another young man we'll call Edward recalled that the best day he had in high school was when a football coach screamed at his teammate who was a top student, "Why can't you play like Edward?!" Having been such a poor student, this was the first time that a skill Edward possessed was recognized by an adult in school as valuable in such a genuine way—and became a lifeline for his flagging self-worth.

Small though they may be, these morsels of recognition can be so meaningful to anyone who may feel otherwise unseen in school.

Making the Best Use of Summer Breaks

Summer breaks are another possible opportunity to boost the morale of a dyslexic teen who may be floundering during the school year. When considering how to keep your teenager engaged during their summer break, here are some things to keep in mind:

- **Support independence-building experiences as early as possible.** Have your teen pursue summer jobs, babysitting, internships, volunteer opportunities, anything they feel ready for and that can foster a positive, independent experience of taking responsibility. If it's a job, learning how to conduct themself in a work environment is an excellent way to help develop autonomy and get experience earning and handling their own money. If the work is something they're interested in, consider that a bonus. Volunteering can also be quite valuable for exploring career interests and gaining life experience. Whether it's becoming a buddy to a younger dyslexic student, working with the young or old, or serving at a soup kitchen, helping others can lift your teen's self-esteem and self-confidence.

- **Encourage reading over the summer with anything that fascinates them.** If reading is your teen's least favorite thing to do, try to find something to inspire their interest: sports, comics, movie reviews, horoscopes—even if you think it might be too easy for them. Help them find subjects and genres they enjoy. They should be encouraged to work to ramp up their reading skills during summers (or during breaks throughout the academic year) rather than during the school year. Remind them that reading for pleasure can help increase fluency.
- **To combat burnout, be sure to allow your teen some significant downtime.** Particularly during their summer break, we all need time to relax and turn off our brains from all the responsibilities and stress of the year. Let them recharge and reenergize for new challenges to come.
- **If your teen is on a college track, use extra time in summer for SAT/ACT preparation and college essays.** Use online SAT/ACT prep courses like those found at Khan Academy (www.khanacademy.org/).
- **If your teen hopes to head to college, there may be scholarship funding for higher education available for students with learning disabilities** (see page 236) that you can research online (use search terms including your country and local region with: "government grants for learning disabilities").

THE PARENTS' TOOLBOX
Thriving in High School

Help Your Teen Learn to Advocate for Themself
- At the beginning of each school year continue to have your child discuss which accommodations they have in place and why with their teachers.
- If they start to struggle with a certain topic, they should set up a teacher meeting and be prepared to ask specific questions.
- During class, they should sit in the front row and make occasional eye contact with the teacher to demonstrate that they are "actively" listening.
- Encourage your child to participate in class discussions if they are comfortable doing so to demonstrate their engagement with the material.
- Have them be mindful to turn in neat work, checked over for spelling as well as other grammatical errors.
- Make sure to instill the habit of handing in assignments on time.
- If they're struggling in certain classes, have them hand in assignments early in order to request feedback so edits can be made in advance of due dates.
- If unsatisfied with a grade, have them request ways to improve that grade with extra work.

Stress-Management Techniques
- Make a to-do list and apply it to their calendar to budget time.
- Include physical activity during times of extra stress.
- Clean and organize a messy bedroom or desk to minimize chaos.
- Take soothing, energy-changing breaks like listening to music, playing an instrument, doing an art project, baking, playing a board or video game with a friend or sibling, doing a puzzle, or taking a shower or bath.

Workload Tips
- At a particular crunch time, promote strategic prioritizing by consciously deciding what to sacrifice if necessary.
- Minimizing chaos by organizing may help your child focus.
- Utilize audiobooks and audio textbooks to save time.
- Now is the moment to lean on study skills you've learned that are especially effective for you.

Emotional Support During Stressful Times in High School
- Normalize big emotions: teens need to learn that what they feel in the moment will pass—even if it doesn't feel that way.
- Remind them that failures or frustrations are part of life for everyone and can make them stronger.
- Give your teen the space to grieve failures and then shake them off.
- Encourage an open, nonjudgmental line of communication.
- Make sure your child is keeping connected to you and their peers and avoiding isolation.
- Make family bonding a priority to instill the importance of taking intermittent breaks and relaxing during high stress times.
- Practice gratitude with them to remember the good things.

Making the Best Use of Summer Breaks
- Have your teen pursue summer jobs, internships, and/or volunteer opportunities.
- Encourage reading over the summer in areas of interest.
- Make sure they include downtime in their summer planning.
- If on a college track, use extra time in summer for SAT/ACT preparation and college essays.

CHAPTER 11

The Path to Higher Education

If your child has decided to continue with their education after high school to pursue college, it's not unusual for them to struggle with how much independence they actually feel ready for. Being fearful of big transitions, especially those moving towards adulthood and autonomy, can be terrifying—even if your teen may not be aware or want to admit it. This can be another opportunity to remind them that they are not alone, offer encouragement and validation for their feelings, and help them normalize their experiences. It may also be a good time to acknowledge the courage it takes to admit vulnerability while reminding them that you have confidence in them and how they handle themselves in challenging situations. If you are part of any parenting groups for dyslexic children, hearing from other parents about their child's college experiences may also serve to put you both at ease.

Along with all the encouragement you provide, there are also some important steps to take when your teen is a junior in high school to begin to prepare for the college application process.

Tips for SAT/ACT Prep and College Applications

Requirements for college applications seem to change frequently. Recently some schools have gone test-optional and then changed back again, so you'll want to stay current on requirements. But if your teen decides to take entrance exams, here are some time-management strategies to prepare for the college applications process:

- **Be sure to keep your adolescent's psychoeducational evaluation up-to-date.** To be able to apply for accommodations when taking college entrance exams, your teen's evaluation must be current. Check SAT/ACT websites to see how recent the evaluation needs to be.
- **If using accommodations, register early for college entrance tests (PSATs, SATs, and/or the ACT).** Students signing up to take these tests with accommodations must do so early in order to send in the required information to get approval. Because of the review process, the deadlines they post really matter—so be sure to be proactive. Colleges will not be informed of whether or not your child has taken the SAT/ACT with extended time or another accommodation.
- **Take practice tests.** Since the SAT and ACT are different, have your teen take one practice test of each (available for free online) in order to decide which is the best fit for them. Then decide on which test to pursue.
- **Budget extra time for SAT/ACT prep.** You may have to work with your child to find time in their schedule to study for their entrance exams. Use online tools like Membean, Khan Academy, and Quizlet and/or SAT/ACT websites to help with test preparation.
- **Consider test preparation classes or tutors.** There may well be a need for specific tutoring in addition to arranging accommodations. Test prep classes are also available online or in

person. Some online options include Khan Academy, Kaplan, and Princeton Review, among others.
- **Practice timing and test-taking strategies.** Since the tests are offered year round, I advise studying for college entrance exams as early as your teen feels comfortable—possibly during junior year. Early preparation affords them the option to go back and study again if they need to retake it. If your teen is still not satisfied with their scores, or they have trouble taking standardized tests, they may decide to apply to test-optional colleges instead.
- **Start early on college essays.** The summer before senior year is a great opportunity for your high schooler to use their organizational skills to budget time to write their college essays. Many universities utilize the standard essay from the Common Application (aka Common App) that is published in early August. This can give your child a leg up on crafting their essay before the demands of senior year intrude. If writing is especially challenging, it's wise to allot extra time for edits.

Selecting a College

There is value in college forethought in terms of curriculum choices and assessing your teen's ambition level long before they need to apply to schools. When they begin their search for the college that best suits their interests, you may want to consider the level of support they'll be able to access on campus for their learning differences. Here are some things to investigate as you dig into each university's resources and offerings:

- **If they're comfortable with it, encourage your teen to take the lead on navigating the college selection process.** They'll no doubt still need your support with the amount of research and the emotional weight of this major life transition but do your best to partner with them rather than lead the way.

- **Be sure to check out special resources available for learning differences while researching colleges, even if your teen thinks they may not need them.** Most colleges (including Ivy League schools) have become more sensitive to different learners and offer accommodations such as waiving or being more flexible with certain requirements (like language or science). There is great variability in the level of support colleges offer, so it's still worth taking the time to do your research with your child's potential needs in mind.
- **If you're able to visit schools, allot time to investigate facilities, schedule interviews, and take tours.**
- **If they have been granted an interview, make sure they do their homework about that college so that they can be prepared to ask the interviewer intelligent questions.**

On the Term "Learning Disabled"

Although your child (or you) may be uncomfortable with the term "learning disabled," the fact is that if your child applies for accommodations in college, they will very likely be referred to as such for legal purposes. There are many opinions on whether neurodiversity is a disability, and educational institutions continue to move away from the term "disabled" and instead recognize it as neurodiversity. I recommend discussing the terminology with your college-age child in the hopes of destigmatizing the term for them. Neither "disabled" nor "neurodiverse" are negative terms. Discussing the evolution of how dyslexia, neurodiversity, and disability were previously less understood can help you both.

Softening the Transition to College

Once your young adult is off to further their education, there are still likely to be bumps along the road, some extra neediness, and no doubt some anxiety as they adjust to a whole new life of routines, responsibilities, and a big jump in independence. Regardless if their learning challenges have kept them more dependent on you or not, the move to college can feel extremely overwhelming.

While on their way to becoming independent, here are some suggestions *for your child* that can help with their big transition:

- **As with any major transition, expect a period of discomfort and anxiety.** It is natural to fear the unknown, and there will be plenty to learn to navigate. It can be scary to be away from the watchful and helpful (and yes, sometimes annoying) eyes of your parents, particularly if you've had to lean heavily on their help throughout school. Preparation for the possible pitfalls ahead of time will help prevent you from being caught by surprise. Most importantly, remember, fear is normal and you've got the skills for this!
- **If you plan to use accommodations, notify the Office of Student Support Services (or the equivalent of a learning center) to research what documents are required to continue getting accommodations.**
- **If you are going to receive accommodations, you'll need to meet with your professor during office hours at the very beginning of the term to tell them about the accommodations you have been granted.**
- **The organizational and time-management habits that you have cultivated throughout your academic career will serve you very well and may even give you an edge in college.** Budgeting time effectively can help you manage anxieties and prevent you from getting too overwhelmed. Allotting time for parts of life outside of class, like eating, working out, doing laundry,

socializing, and doing schoolwork, is the best way to manage stress. As before, you'll want to budget time to have fun, get outside, and explore new interests and opportunities as well as take time to relax and recharge.

- **Honestly assess your own academic strengths and weaknesses to appropriately advocate for yourself.** If there are especially difficult requirements, you may want to find out if dyslexic students can take them over a summer session, if there is tutoring available, or if you can get a waiver. Each college will have its own unique policies.
- **Build confidence semester by semester to be sure you can handle your workload.** If possible, spread out especially difficult courses into separate semesters or summer sessions, particularly at the start of college, to avoid getting overwhelmed.
- **Be cognizant of how you're managing emotionally as you transition into university life.** College is a huge adjustment for everybody, and you don't have to face the challenges on your own. If you get too overwhelmed or start to falter, take advantage of the mental health resources available for support. There is no shame in reaching out for help as you try to adapt to your new environment.
- **Allow yourself the freedom to explore a course that is of interest but may be far afield from your major or that you may find intimidating.** While you may not want to do this in your first year, college is a wonderful opportunity to experiment with subjects that you may never be exposed to again.

High School Habits Paying Off

It is not unusual that after all the intense energy and time committed to getting through school that dyslexic students find their college workload relatively manageable. With their time-management and organizational skills, along with improved reading fluency, best study practices, and work-arounds for various weaknesses, your young adult will likely be well prepared to hit their stride in college.

My Own Jagged Path

As many of us know, the path to higher education and then onto finding a happy work life is not always as straightforward as one might hope. While many certainly do move onward through college and possibly on to graduate school and then a satisfying career, things don't always tie up so neatly. The reality, of course, is that even if your child is not a dyslexic learner, there are many wide-ranging and circuitous paths to success.

My own journey to my "dream career" was neither direct nor uncomplicated. Fortunately, like so many dyslexic learners, my resilience and tenacity eventually brought me through life's big challenges and made me stronger. But my parents had to spend plenty of sleepless nights as I inched my way along.

If you are going through a circuitous route with your teen, now is the time I want to impart a "mantra" to you: *Your dyslexic learner's struggles after high school (or even before) are temporary. Floundering before finding their way is not unexpected and it will not go on forever. Their road to success may wind more than yours did, but don't forget that they likely have the grit and resilience to get back up over and over again if they fail. They will figure things out with your steadfast belief in them, your good ear, and your guidance when they ask for it. You have helped them to put all the tools in place to navigate the world, including building confidence in their strengths. Even if they are not yet ready to be fully independent, they are likely set to find their way.*

Taking Slow but Steady Steps Forward
To illustrate what this can look like from one who has been there, I offer you a glimpse of how my alternative path unfolded with my own learning and confidence issues in the mix.

For my first college experience, I chose what I believed to be the university with the best reputation that accepted me from a list generated by the guidance counselor at my high school. Months after my first visit to the campus, I found myself installed in my dorm room, feeling uneasy about starting classes away from the support of my mother. Despite all I had accomplished getting through high school, I was still frightened to be so far from home and insecure about how I would manage if I needed help with my schoolwork. (At that time, there was no learning support office at the college that I was attending.)

Equally unsettling was the amount of partying going on, which had no appeal for me after having become such a dedicated student in high school. So six weeks into my freshman year, depressed and overwhelmed, I retreated home without a plan for how I would proceed.

Back in New York, alone with my parents and with my friends all away at college, I quickly started to feel like a failure and a quitter. My parents let me feel sorry for myself for a total of two days, then took me downtown to register for college courses as a nonmatriculated student. I spent the next year taking introductory classes (including psychology) that were full of mostly older, continuing education students taking courses for enjoyment while I tried to regroup and plot my course forward.

Socially, I was out of place, sad, and frightened of what it meant to have jumped ship from my original college plan. Sensing that I needed a break to regain my confidence, my mom convinced me to take fewer classes than what would be considered a normal freshman course load, to avoid creating a very stressful first semester. One of the first classes I chose was Art Therapy, which I found fascinating, and I soon went on to become a Certified Art Therapist. Then, as part of my program, I got to do an internship with autistic children. I discovered that I really enjoyed working with children, particularly those who were neurodiverse.

Acquiring these new skills felt good, and my self-esteem began to recover. Despite still needing help proofreading my big papers, I was doing well handling all of the assigned reading and work required. For the first time in my life I had no tutors, and something inside me was quietly telling me that I was starting to find my way.

Fortunately for me, my parents continued to be an important source of stability and wisdom, and their faith in me helped to build up my confidence. After a full year (along with summer school to make up credits), I felt my footing to be more solid and decided to apply to universities for the following January. I had gotten very good grades and enjoyed interesting courses besides my core academics and was starting to feel confident that I might have a shot at getting into a college that I hadn't dared apply to initially while in high school.

In my application, I explained that I had a learning disability, which was reflected in my high school grades. I went on to clarify some of the strategies that had helped me academically since high school, and that I planned to continue doing very well in college and learn more about my field of interest: psychology.

When I received the admission reply, many weeks later, no one could have been more surprised than I was to have been accepted into my college of choice. Finally, and most unexpectedly, I had the opportunity to attend the University of Pennsylvania!

I share this story to remind parents at this interval in their child's life about the necessity to avoid the temptation to design a so-called perfect path for your child. We all need the freedom to write our own unique story that may not conform to anyone else's timeline. While college ultimately worked out for me, it was hard fought and nothing like what my parents or I could have anticipated.

It turned out that an unexpected gift of being dyslexic was that my struggles ironically gave me the courage it took to derail my first game plan. Knowing that I had the resilience to try again unconsciously propelled me to follow my inner voice. Having long since abandoned the notion of academic perfection, I was liberated to sidestep its trappings. The invaluable life lesson was that I ultimately got to where I had always wanted to be.

I like to tell parents my story to prepare them for the possibilities that things may not be smooth sailing just because their child makes it to college—and to encourage them not to give up on their young adult. My experience supports my conviction that it is essential for parents to keep faith; part of championing your child means believing in them during these moments of uncertainty. I encourage you to give your child the gift of unconditional belief in them.

Self-Esteem Baggage

Despite the positive experiences I'd had taking college courses after high school and the thrill of being accepted into an Ivy League school, I continued to be riddled with insecurity. Disappointingly, things did not magically change by getting into Penn, as I had hoped they might. While finishing out my undergraduate degree, I had a constant sense that I did not belong there and that I was not as smart as the other students, despite my good GPA.

When I hear teens talk about being plagued by these kinds of self-esteem issues in school today, I always encourage them to seek out peers to share their experiences with. As I've said so many times throughout this book, if these emotional remnants persist, it might be time to speak with a counselor. Psychological services are a vital resource on campuses and can help address the often self-imposed strain and anxiety that shame can cast.

Avoiding Taking Inventory of Others

If your young adult is feeling insecure, remind them of all they've accomplished and have them take note of their academic progress. Help them recall how with effort and time, semester after semester, things fall into place, skill sets build, and milestones get easier. They may be so used to striving that your young adult has not stopped to notice how far they have come.

At the same time, getting a more intimate view of how others study, particularly conspicuous when living on campus with roommates, can lead to negative self-comparisons. While some students can party and skip class and still maintain their high GPA, most others and certainly dyslexic learners will likely need to continue to be more disciplined and dedicated.

Focusing on doing what they need to do for their own brain's wiring rather than paying attention to others' work ethics and practices will help to avoid the slippery slope towards self-attack in the form of feeling "less than." Sticking with our own knowledge of what works best for us, and having the discipline and dedication to apply those strategies, will continue to be the best plan for success. For many of us, this is a constant work in progress.

As discussed throughout this book, we all have individual talents and skills that stack the deck differently—sometimes in our favor, and sometimes not. From my experience, quieting that comparative voice gets easier with time. The more solid I have felt in my own processes, the more I've been able to avoid comparing it with that of others. Surely the most productive way to live with this basic human predicament is to focus on the things we can each control.

Keeping a Strong Work Ethic in Check

Ironically perhaps, as a big shift from years past, applying the discipline to *stop* working and trust that our academic or work lives won't suffer can be a real adjustment after so many years of furiously trying to keep up with our peers. Taking a break for physical exercise or to socialize may at times feel as challenging as it originally was to build *up* one's attention span and work ethic.

Becoming excessively focused on work is a real risk for an adult who spent most of their youth diligently grinding away. It's important to be mindful not to lean so heavily on attending to one's career that one strays from a healthy work-life balance. A strong work ethic is commendable but not at the expense of having it take over one's entire life. This is one of the adjustments any type of learner who is accustomed to putting in long hours needs to make in the transition to living independently, but it may come as a real shock to the system for a dyslexic learner.

The Complementary Values of a Strong Work Ethic and Humility

On the very positive side of a strong work ethic, the humility it takes to apply oneself with so much diligence can add a profound dimension to a dyslexic learner's character. The upside of growing up more aware of one's own deficits can be the willingness to learn from others, acknowledge one's own limitations, and embrace feedback. Knowing that you will likely need to put more effort and dedication into reaching academic goals can also make you more respectful of what it takes to achieve accomplishments in any arena. The humility your different learner has developed as a fallout from their struggles can be another unexpected gift of dyslexia—an extremely grounding point from which to meet the world, and may likely evoke cooperation from others. The humble willingness to rigorously apply oneself without any presumption of *success* might just be a crucial element for achieving it.

Positive Self-Talk While Transitioning to Independence

Away from the constant support and positive feedback from one's family, the ability to deliver affirming internal messages to oneself becomes extremely important.

Maintaining a healthy work-life balance and sustaining a positive attitude, especially if one is prone to comparing themselves negatively to others, may be a new muscle to strengthen for a dyslexic learner. Journaling to write affirmations can help override one's fears and provide a counterweight to habitual self-defeating voices. Setting up occasional rewards for *ourselves*, to reinforce and acknowledge hard work, is certainly appropriate as well. Rather than having a parent there to underscore their effort, a young adult must segue to installing their own inner system of positive reinforcement. This is a great opportunity for them to take inventory of all that has gone into their own accomplishments.

THE PARENTS' TOOLBOX
The Path to Higher Education

Tips for SAT/ACT Prep and College Applications

- Be sure your child's psychoeducational evaluation is current and up-to-date in order to be able to apply for accommodations when taking college entrance exams and possibly for college classes as well. Check college and professional exam websites to see how recent the evaluation needs to be.
- If using accommodations, register early for college entrance tests (PSATs, SATs, and/or the ACT, etc.). Students signing up to take these tests with accommodations must do so in advance and send in the required information to get approval.
- Have your child take both an SAT and ACT practice test (available for free online) to enable your child to decide which one is the best fit.
- Have your child budget extra time for SAT/ACT prep with online tools from the ACT website, the College Board website, as well as Khan Academy, Zinc, Kaplan, and Princeton Review. This will help with content as well as timing and test-taking strategies.
- Encourage your child to start early on college essays. Common App essays are posted in early August. The summer before senior year is a great time to begin.

Selecting a College

Here are some things to investigate as you dig into each university's resources and offerings with your child:

- Since there is great variability in colleges' level of support, check out the policies related to learning differences, including possible accommodations such as waiving or being more flexible with certain requirements (like language or science).
- If you're able to visit schools with your child, be sure to investigate facilities, schedule interviews, and take tours.

- If they have been granted an interview, make sure they do their homework by researching that college and being prepared to ask the interviewer intelligent questions.

Easing into the College Transition

Here are some strategic tips *for your young adult* to succeed in college:
- Know that it is natural to fear the unknown, and being away from your family can cause anxiety—but remember, you have been steadily building the skills for this!
- If using accommodations, notify the Office of Student Support Services (or the equivalent of a learning center) to research what documents are required to continue getting accommodations.
- If receiving accommodations, meet with professors during office hours at the beginning of the term to tell them about the accommodations you have been granted.
- If there are especially difficult requirements, you may want to try to take them over a summer session or research if there is tutoring available. Alternatively, you may want to find out if dyslexic students are entitled to a waiver.
- If possible, spread out especially difficult courses into separate semesters or summer sessions, particularly at the start of college, to avoid getting overwhelmed.
- Remember that the organizational and time-management habits that you have cultivated throughout your academic career will serve you very well and may even give you an edge in college.
- Be cognizant of how you're managing emotionally as you transition into university life. There is no shame in reaching out for help as you try to adapt to your new environment.
- Explore a course that is of interest but may be far afield from your major or that you may find intimidating. While you may not want to do this in your first year, college is a wonderful opportunity to discover new areas of interest.

CHAPTER 12

Life After College

When my undergraduate education was complete, somehow things felt oddly anticlimactic for me. It felt exciting and important but at the same time I was left without a straightforward path for how to move forward. Rather than what might be considered a perfect Instagram moment today launching me into the work world, the reality was that after all the years of academic structure, suddenly being thrust into the "real world" was extremely unnerving. For students who have had to exert so much time and attention to get through their academics, the shock of the school-to-work transition, whether after college or after graduate school, may indeed be more profound.

For my patients who have delayed "real life" by going on to graduate school, I have often noted that their transition into the work world was more seamless because of the specialized path of their profession. Once they graduated, they had a good sense of what was expected of them and had usually had some sort of work experience in their field (by way of internships or summer jobs) to ease their transition.

Back at home for me, after my college graduation, I felt unsure of how to proceed to become an independent adult. With the clarity of hindsight, my pattern seemed to consistently be that regardless of successes at each stage, when it was time to face the next life transition, I felt held back by a lapse in confidence. In my case, taking a temporary job for a stretch or hedging my bets by starting in a master's program, rather than applying directly to a doctoral program, felt much more manageable.

Certainly, I am very aware that not everyone can consider these options. I mention them to underscore that even with the financial support and encouragement that my parents were able to provide, the social-emotional impact of my formative struggles in school were still deeply embedded within me and showed up as nagging fears about my own abilities and intelligence. Surrounded at each stage of my education with high-functioning students, I was often acutely aware of differences in my learning processes and the extra diligence it took for me to retain information as compared with my peers.

Perhaps as a result of my deep interest in the workings of the brain and my fascination with psychology, I was more aware that my own cognitive processes were different and less streamlined than the standard learners around me, thus adding to my persistent insecurity. What I was less aware of was the grit I had acquired and how it fueled my drive to persevere and succeed regardless.

In retrospect, I can see that the only one holding me back, ultimately, was me. My parents had always tried to help me see my own intelligence and talents but I was never fully convinced that they were entirely objective.

So, even with the many effective and reliable work-arounds and habits that I had cultivated, I had to repeatedly prove to myself that I could keep up and succeed in new settings. I never assumed I would meet with success despite knowing deep down that my tenacity would not allow me to fail. Fortunately, even if I felt at one moment like I could not continue on in school (or whatever the next step was), after a little time and distance, I was able to move past my fears and continue on to the next challenge.

Just like when they were younger, your child may likely need time, space, and moral support while they gather up courage to approach their next move. Remind them of their grit and resilience. They may then be ready and willing to put themselves out there again and take on a new challenge. Don't be afraid to remind them that it is rarely too late to try again.

It's important to note that when I was growing up, children did not have the benefit of many of the effective interventions that exist today, nor was there the same level of awareness of how to address the self-esteem issues that dyslexic learners face. Experiences like those I've described hopefully illustrate why I feel so strongly about putting a full arsenal of practices in place when children are quite young, in hopes of avoiding the entrenched negative thought patterns that can develop.

Hopefully, your young adult won't have the formidable self-esteem lapses that I did. But if they do, taking those small, more manageable bites of the apple, building up gradually to larger goals, can be a good way to accrue the confidence they need for a big transition.

When it's time for your child to start to pursue work opportunities or internships, they'll need to itemize their own previous work experiences, volunteer positions, internships, clubs, and references to start to build a résumé. There are plenty of prototypes online that they can follow, but the important thing is that they be extremely diligent about avoiding formatting and grammar mistakes, misspellings, and typographical errors.

If your young adult is ready to enter the workforce, seeking guidance from a mentor or coworkers at a new job can provide valuable insights into understanding new responsibilities, timelines, and organizational protocols. If that kind of introduction is not available, it may be useful to write out or discuss specific expectations after talking to coworkers or a new boss. Consciously anticipating expectations in the form of responsibilities and productivity in a new work setting can help shorten the learning curve to adapt in a new setting and minimize anxiety.

Residual Academic Challenges and Fixes

One of the frustrations of graduate school for me had to do with test anxiety. Regardless of the many years of school under my belt, I was still unable to assess whether I knew material adequately for exams. This unsettling feeling had me perpetually bracing for failure despite my successful track record of the recent past. To address this irrational dread, I developed a ritual to comfort myself by wearing an article of clothing from college that I attributed to being "good luck." But no matter how far along I got in school, my heart was always beating rapidly and my palms were always sweaty before an exam.

Undeterred by the lapses in confidence and buoyed by successes in my graduate program, I next considered the most daunting part of a PhD program: writing a dissertation. The added complexity and length of such a research project felt intimidating. Fortunately, many of my group assignments in graduate school had inadvertently taught me to better organize and more efficiently scaffold papers. Learning from my peers, my written organizational skills began to improve and I was able to gain confidence. Ultimately, after going through the process repeatedly with others, even my dissertation became very manageable.

Hitting Their Stride

It may be reassuring to remember that if your young adult has gotten through college, they are no doubt very capable. Moving on to a higher level of education may simply be a matter of honing their skill set even further—but they may still need extended time for exams and/or possibly other accommodations. For the most part, though, they are likely set up to succeed and build upon the compensatory skills they have been amassing throughout their education.

By the time your child has completed college, they have likely seen enough success that dyslexia has evolved to be part of their "story" but not the defining aspect of who they are. Dyslexia is, no doubt, a foundational aspect of what makes them unique and possibly an important part of their life experience. It has probably also helped push them to discover their own resilience, drive, and strength along with all the skills and knowledge they have fought to acquire. Most essentially, they are hopefully well-equipped to deliver positive self-talk to get through life's tough days—and understand that, like all humans, they will continue to have to grapple with their own weaknesses as well. My hope is that they have learned to take missteps in stride, approach setbacks with a sense of humor, and have built up the confidence, inner strength, skills, and grit that make them feel like they can accomplish anything.

If there is still lingering emotional baggage related to dyslexia, they may continue to need you to champion them; their own ability to objectively recognize their inner strength should be robust by now, as well as having developed a supportive peer group. The reality that everyone has struggles in different areas of their lives has likely become clear, allowing them to feel less alone. Practicing gratitude will also go a long way to bring perspective when things get especially tough.

Tips for Your Adult to Transition to a New Work Environment at Any Age

When starting a new job, your adult will want to clarify what is required of them and take notes. They should:

- Ask questions early on before it is assumed that you know everything.
- Make lists of priorities and tasks to track what needs to be done and the timeline that is expected.
- Find a mentor at work to help you learn the ropes.
- Continue using a day planner to keep on track for small and large projects.
- Use spell check. Make sure to avoid errors, even on quick emails, to present yourself well in a professional setting.

- Keep your desk and office organized to help with day-to-day functioning and efficiency.
- Turn off all social media at work to minimize distractions.
- Set yourself up for success by over-preparing for presentations. If you're uncomfortable reading in public, print your remarks in a larger, dyslexic-friendly font and create bullet points to improve readability.
- When possible, complete your work in advance. That way you are always prepared, and people learn they can rely on you.

A YOUNG ADULT'S TOOLBOX
Tips for Transitioning to a New Work Environment at Any Age

When starting a new job,
- Ask questions early on before it is assumed that you know everything.
- Make lists of priorities and tasks to track what needs to be done and the timeline that is expected.
- Find a mentor at work to help teach you the ropes.
- Continue using a day planner to stay on track for small and large projects.
- Use spell check. Make sure to avoid errors, even on quick emails, to present yourself well in a professional setting.
- Keep your desk and office organized to help with day-to-day functioning and efficiency.
- Turn off all social media at work to minimize distractions.
- Set yourself up for success by over-preparing for presentations. If you're uncomfortable reading in public, print your remarks in a larger, dyslexic-friendly font and create bullet points to improve readability.
- When possible, complete your work in advance. That way you are always prepared, and people learn they can rely on you.

PART 4

Making Peace with Dyslexia

CHAPTER 13

A Bright Future

While familiarity with dyslexia in the educational sphere is far from universal at this point, I hope you have gained a full understanding of what your dyslexic child may need throughout their educational and emotional journey into adulthood.

As I've said all along throughout this book, reviewing practices to bolster your child's academic success are key—and go hand in hand with supporting their emotional well-being, minimizing shame, supporting the development of their self-esteem and resilience with suggestions to nurture the drive and commitment central for your child to get through their education, and beyond. It's absolutely essential to shift the perception of dyslexia's effects to help shape your child's notion of their great potential and enrich their understanding of the upside of their learning differences.

It is no doubt a legitimately confusing ask for any young person to fully comprehend the notion that they're bright and can learn well in lots of ways—but not necessarily in the ways that most of their peers do. Likewise, being regularly reminded of your gifts and great potential while knowing it may take years to catch up with your classmates in certain realms would require anyone to dig deep. But this is indeed the central message that your child will need to metabolize—with it, hopefully they develop patience and a deep respect for their own process. If we can help them do this, the hope is that they can bypass the false assumption that so very many dyslexic learners make—that they are in any way "less than."

At the same time, while your child grapples with the complexities of understanding what dyslexia means in their life, a parent must adjust along with them. Implicit in these many suggestions is your own strong work ethic and your ability to bolster your own spirits during the journey of raising a dyslexic learner. It is certainly not easy to coach a child through an alternative path and provide the extra support they may need academically and emotionally, all while assuring them that they are building strengths like grit and resilience, which they may be blissfully unaware that they'll ever need.

Your child's journey may also occasionally have *you* swimming against the tide of your own peer group, as it did for my parents at times. Others may not always understand or relate to the different style of parenting that a dyslexic child may benefit from. Thus, managing and being sensitive and compassionate to your own challenges must be part of the empathic role you hope to provide for your child. And as stated previously, depending on the academic challenges you've endured yourself, being part of your dyslexic child's journey can potentially trigger your own childhood wounds.

However, for your child, the important thing, from the start of their education, is to be alert to changes in behavior such as isolation, depression, or anxiety. They may be indications of a learning difference that, if left unaddressed, can leave self-esteem issues to take root.

In fact, throughout their schooling, you, as a parent, may need to continue to keep a keen eye on your child to be sure they are not hiding wounds that have the potential to erode their fledgling self-esteem and confidence. It will likely be your job to remind them of their many gifts, underscoring that their brain processes information differently, neither better than nor worse than others do.

As a parent of any type of learner, it's helpful to remember to be flexible and pick your fights. Sometimes seemingly small things that your child wants to do that you say "no" to may seem trivial to you, but can be devastating to them. For a dyslexic learner who may already feel like an outcast, having the latest haircut or getting to see the movie that "everyone" is seeing may mostly be an attempt to try to fit in socially, especially if they're not able to do so academically. Facing the dilemma of applying compassion or discipline is the tightrope that parents of teenagers must always straddle—and it's up to you to try to assess what your child may need at a given moment, although there is rarely a "right answer" in any case.

Fortunately, with the diagnostic tools, remediations, and technologies that exist today, dyslexia can be addressed earlier and more effectively than ever before, leaving an abundance of room for hope and optimism about your child's future. The advances that have been made are all indicative of the significant size of the dyslexia market to be served. But early diagnosis is still not where it should be. While the educational sphere addresses reading difficulties in the post-pandemic world, parents continue to need to be extra vigilant as there is still considerable disparity in the understanding of dyslexia in educational settings nationwide. Early detection continues to be the best predictor for students' success.[1]

Despite the statistics (up to 20 percent of the population has dyslexia), dyslexic learners still tend to experience isolation. So, starting your child early in cultivating the vocabulary to verbalize their feelings and then demonstrating your ability to really *hear* them can offer inroads to help them confront shame, shift their perspective, add humor, and ultimately gain the maturity they'll need to reject the notion that they are in any way inferior to more typical learners.

Knowing about other successful dyslexic learners, even if there are none in their immediate circle, can further help thwart the feeling of isolation and foster a positive mindset about their ability to learn and their bright future ahead. They can be reassured that rough patches won't last forever. And while life challenges are rarely packaged in pretty bows, and things don't always go as planned, having a dyslexic brain is its own kind of very wonderful human gift—and reminds us that life is so much more about loving imperfection at every turn.

Yet even the most supportive family with the best practices tailored precisely to a dyslexic child's needs cannot fuel a child's desire to succeed.

Eventually it will need to come from within your child. Putting a high value on education may begin at home, but ultimately it will be their choice as to how much effort they want to expend in school.

If academic pursuits become less appealing, you as a parent can help them find an escape plan, switching to investigate alternate passions and curiosities that better suit their brain's circuitry. Rather than a defeat, your child's discovery of new skill sets may result in a unique career path and/or expose them to undiscovered talents, interesting hobbies, and new ways to connect with others.

Along with all of your help and encouragement, creating an emotionally safe family space, delivering the "mantras" regularly, cooking favorite meals after a particularly hard day or week, injecting fun into their study time, or just staying up with them as they push through academic hurdles you are simultaneously providing morsels of hope while sustaining your child to dream of all they are capable of. Your example and your actions supply a constant whisper that their goals are attainable if they are willing to put in the hard work and commitment to keep trying. You play a vital role in encouraging your child to reach their full potential, walking the walk with them each day, harnessing your own resilience and tenacity, as well as by communicating your belief in their great abilities.

My favorite published lists of famous and successful people with learning differences from all arenas continues to be a wonderful reminder of the contributions and excellence that my fellow dyslexic learners have achieved. The scientists, architects, doctors, entrepreneurs, executives, writers, and journalists (among others), many of whom are relatively unknown, have huge accomplishments that have greatly benefited humanity. These individuals, each one with their own heartening story of overcoming struggles, represent optimism for children diligently working to adapt to an educational system designed for standard learners.

In their spirit, I truly hope that this accumulation of ideas and practices from my personal and professional lived experiences will engage you to champion your child. May they build the skills, confidence, and grit to succeed beyond limit to live out all their own dreams and aspirations.

AFTERWORD

More Dyslexia Confessions

One of the most common questions I hear from parents is "How long will it take for my child to catch up to their classmates and for their dyslexia to no longer be an issue?" Since dyslexia presents itself in a wide variety of ways, unfortunately there is no fully satisfying answer for how it may impact your child. But one thing is clear: Dyslexia does not disappear; rather, it is managed by devising work-arounds and compensatory skills over time. As your child perseveres, they will likely discover more and more ways to minimize its impact on their daily functioning. Better still, they may well develop effective, life-enriching alternative skills along the way, without even realizing it.

While certainly less apparent than when I was young, dyslexia still impacts me every day while doing certain tasks, but I have learned to manage and compensate for deficits in small ways that work for me. The effects range from mostly insignificant to rather inconvenient to quite embarrassing, depending on the day. For example, if I am reading something very technical or attempting to watch a film with subtitles, I will likely need extra time. Reading in front of colleagues at work, on the other hand, evokes feelings of being in the second grade all over again.

Similarly, when my children entered preschool, there was a volunteer program for reading to the class. Both my kids begged me to do this, so despite my initial resistance, I eventually agreed. This meant going to the school once or twice a year and reading to a class of approximately ten preschoolers. Regardless, I made sure to arrive at the school half an hour early and preread the books multiple times to familiarize myself with the text. No matter how well it went, it never became easier.

Residual effects also show themselves in my firmly ingrained habit of writing things well in advance of their due dates. I always want to be sure that I can continually edit what I have written to guarantee it is well put together and understandable. Fortunately, technology has saved me from the embarrassment of my atrocious spelling with the wonderful invention of spell check. My poor penmanship is something I am able to make fun of and laugh off when no one can read a word I have written. To this day, when I write out a note or shopping list for myself and do not use cursive writing, I still insert capital *B*s and *D*s in the middle of words, just as I did as a child to avoid the reversals of these letters.

When I first started my current job, I was occasionally required to take notes during a team meeting, and I would panic. There was no way to quickly check my spelling, nor hide my awful handwriting. In my anxiety that my peers might notice my deficits, I somehow manipulated these meetings so that I had a different role, and it became someone else's job to write the notes. Just like when I unscrewed the legs of the table in elementary school, I managed to have this switch go unnoticed. Eventually, technology came to the rescue and allowed us to type the notes directly into the computer with the extra benefit of spell check.

I am still not a natural at organization, so I compensate by being hyper-organized to the point that once I begin using a particular system, I never deviate. To this day, anything that I am asked to do at work, I finish the same day. I write my patient reports as they leave my office, and will not go home in the evening before they're all completed. While I am a dedicated employee, my behavior is mostly fueled by my insecurity that things will become too chaotic. These habits are burned into my brain.

Sequencing continues to be a challenge. I often have to recite the alphabet starting with "A" to figure out where a letter falls. Confusing left and right still can come into play when I conduct a neuropsychological evaluation that requires me to assess a child's knowledge of left and right on themselves and on me. I have to concentrate intently on the transference because the patient is sitting across from me.

When I do exercise classes online, I have noticed that quite frequently I end up working out one side of my body twice, unable to transition to the opposing positions because I get so confused. I laugh to myself when I realize one side of my body is sore but I feel nothing on my other side.

Needless to say, I get lost—a lot. This occurs for a few reasons. When I am driving a car and someone (or the GPS) tells me to make a left, I invariably make a right. When I drive with my children, they have learned to use their hands to motion which way to make the turn so that I see which direction we want to go. If I travel somewhere that is unfamiliar to me, I get lost because I can't always read the road signs fast enough and even with the map on the GPS showing me where to go, somehow I get confused. I've learned that if I have to go to a new place by car, I need to leave extra time so I don't panic when I get lost.

Similarly, my perceptual problem with eye-hand coordination has not gone away. Little annoying things like constantly misperceiving a shelf's distance and then knocking over a glass are things that I've never outgrown. On the plus side, this has brought endless joy to my children, particularly when they were toddlers. They even came up with a little song called "Mommy Is a Spiller!"

Lingering Shame

Shame is hands down the most insidious problem compounding dyslexia. The instinct to recoil because of a learning difference that initially makes someone slower at processing than their peers is a real and pernicious issue. Even if teachers and parents say all the right things, it is conceivable that a natural competitive drive in all of us leads children to constantly compare themselves to each other. The hard work for children—or even adults—is to fight the automatic surrender of their self-esteem when they see their peers surpassing them initially in school. The challenge is daunting: How can we convey to a child early on in life that what dyslexic learners bring to the party is legitimately special—and that our different wiring is an intrinsic part of our unique gifts? Particularly at the onset of troubles, when the differences present themselves, they can still feel more like barriers to success, no matter how hard we try to sell ourselves on the alternative message.

Our school system, understandably, is mostly set up to expediently support and reward how the majority of brains develop. So, it can take a huge effort of swimming upstream year after year, watching your peers move through developmental hurdles with relative ease, to continue to remind oneself that differences are not defects. Even highly successful adults, objectively accomplished in their careers, can still carry deep scars and the belief that, because they are dyslexic learners, they are somehow "stupid."

Luckily for me, my family was eventually able to corral me to laugh at myself, remind me of my strengths, and help me understand that my grit and determination could lead to success. Their effort did help to dislodge part of the shame that I had quietly taken on.

To my mother, it never mattered how much time it took other kids to pick up a skill; she was willing to work with me until I got it. Her patience certainly removed some of the sting that I was feeling in school. To my sister's credit, she never made me feel bad about all the time she spent diligently working to help me memorize Spanish vocabulary words or explain math concepts. My father, who was likely dyslexic himself, was endlessly proud of my accomplishments and made it clear that he had my back unconditionally. I was lucky enough to have a team, but research has shown, regardless of the obstacles, being championed by even just one adult who believes in your child (whether a parent or someone else) is key to a child's success.[1]

But for me, more than anything, it has been the accomplishments of getting through the different levels of my education and the privilege of working with my fellow dyslexics and other different learners that has helped me keep a steady perspective as an adult. Knowing that I am helping others confront the idiosyncrasies of their own brain's processes is a constant reminder that I am not alone. Helping them recognize their own intellect, despite their early challenges, continues to be deeply emotionally satisfying.

Yet even with all of the support I was given by my family, it was still not enough to counter the impact of some of the cruelty I encountered. Fortunately, with the many practices and resources available today and explored in this book, dyslexic learners have a better chance to achieve their goals and avoid the heavy burden of shame. I believe we can prevent some of the suffering, anxiety, and depression that dyslexia can cause.

In the meantime, I truly believe that the family is the cornerstone from which to begin mitigating the damage to a child's self-confidence. Good self-esteem practices and a strong family culture of support can help shore up the daily assault from frustrations and differences while the educational system chugs along.

In the absence of school support, the fact that my family hung in there with me, all of them in distinct and helpful ways, was key—and made me feel less alone. It also encouraged the formation of my own determination and willpower to succeed.

When I was quite young, before I could name the emotion, I was ashamed that I could not read or spell like my sister or peers. I could not kick a ball, throw, or catch with any precision, and I spent a lot of time trying to hide and avoid those activities. These feelings lingered for so long that I did not want to return to my high school reunion for fear of what everyone thought of me. But when I decided to host a small reunion at my home, no one seemed to recall my severe challenges back in school. Like most kids, what I was unaware of was that everyone else had their own issues and insecurities. They were not as focused on me as I had imagined. It's a good lesson for us all.

Afterword

I wish it were not the case, but I have consistently observed that there is some degree of shame that comes with any learning difference in our culture. One poignant example was when I heard an interview with Bobbi Brown, the makeup artist and very successful entrepreneur. Despite all of her many accomplishments, including starting companies and writing numerous books, she revealed that she is dyslexic and casually called her husband the brains in the family. I could not believe that this business mogul had just implied publicly that she regards her husband as the "smart one" because she is dyslexic. I can relate to that story, but I truly hope that this perception changes for the next generation of dyslexics.

What has given me some real hope in this regard is talking with the many dyslexic learners in recent years. I have observed that with more information available and better recognition of what dyslexia is, each generation seems better poised to emerge from school relatively unscathed.

One grandfather I spoke with recalled the terrible years he had spent in school. Although he was never formally diagnosed as dyslexic, after attempting programs at a few different colleges, he realized he had a significant learning difference—and dropped out. Dejected, he joined his family's business while his boyhood friends went on to get professional degrees. Eventually he saved enough money working for his parents that he started his own company that became very successful. Later, one of his sons was diagnosed and received good remediation for dyslexia early in elementary school. By being strategic in the classes he took in high school and working harder than his peers, his son developed what he referred to as "a high pain tolerance, excellent work ethic and grit." While he didn't always get the same results as his peers in terms of grades in high school, he was able to successfully get through medical school. He now has two sons of his own (not yet in college) who are both dyslexic but going through school successfully due to early interventions and accommodations. Having a father and grandfather who have done so well professionally has helped them understand that although they have to work harder than their peers for grades, they both feel confident that they can pursue whatever interests them.

For myself, I hid my dyslexia at work for over twenty years having been reluctant to risk being treated differently or disrespected by my colleagues. This is because I still reflexively felt insecure and was self-conscious when certain weaknesses were exposed. Fortunately, with time and experience, I have come to believe more fully in myself.

The Upside of Dyslexia

As I've gotten older and more confident, I realize more readily that absolutely everyone goes through real struggles at some point in their lives, and I can see that there are legitimate strengths that come with having to overcome any type of hardship. From this vantage point, I think it may be better to have those challenges come earlier in life because once you survive them, the confidence you gain allows you to try things that are further from your comfort zone, helping to make you more adept at handling adversity.

Getting through a rigorous education and having to try harder than those around you makes you realize that with dedication and commitment you can overcome obstacles and accomplish anything. The unusual aspect of developing that grit is that after having been so deeply humbled early in life, your ego is held in check. You become accustomed to chipping away at goals, doggedly trying different tacks until you accomplish what you set out to do. Even if you might momentarily want to give up, your brain continues to process the problem from another angle, and then another, until you find a solution.

If you have the benefit of a family reminding you to keep a sense of humor about yourself, you may also be able to better ride out the many frequent comic moments that can be a by-product of being dyslexic. Easing up and laughing off mistakes can help you to handle anything.

A few years ago, I was on a panel for SmartKids with Learning Disabilities, and we were asked to discuss the "gift of dyslexia." I found myself in a panic. Up until that point I genuinely had not felt that dyslexia was a gift. But writing this book has helped me see that the experience of growing up with dyslexia had pushed me to expand myself in so many ways that I had never fully taken stock of before. I had no idea that when I was a young kid and refused to change to an easier school (not wanting to admit defeat) that I was actually learning grit and perseverance.

Once I was admitted into college, I knew I would be able to graduate because by then I had the dedication to put in the hours to accomplish whatever was in front of me. Even if it meant going to summer school to take more difficult requirements, easing off of my social life, staying up long hours, or whatever it might be, I knew I would.

Thankfully, that deep belief in myself persists. I learned from my experiences that life is not always a direct route to your goals and that if you don't give up, you can find a way. I see now that tenacity is not a skill one sets out to acquire. Similarly, humor often grows out of life's absurdities, and with it a quiet resilience emerges that can help us navigate challenges with lightness, even when we aren't seeking it directly. Once you find that strength, you realize how useful it can be in the midst of many of life's difficult moments. These unplanned skill sets are among the most useful tools and can be a direct outgrowth of overcoming repeated setbacks.

Thanks to my family and their ability to consistently find humor, somehow things became less embarrassing, and I did not need to be so defensive if I was not perfect. I encourage my children that whatever their "imperfection" is, "own it." Life is better that way!

Resources

Links to Accomplished Dyslexics

Here are just two links of many lists of these varied and accomplished dyslexics:

www.dyslexia.com/about-dyslexia/dyslexic-achievers
/all-achievers/
https://dyslexia.yale.edu/success-stories

Organizations Devoted to Dyslexia

American Dyslexia Association:
www.american-dyslexia-association.org/
The American Speech-Language Hearing Association:
www.asha.org
Everyone Reading:
https://everyonereading.org/
International Dyslexia Association:
https://dyslexiaida.org/
Learning Disabilities Association of America:
www.ldaamerica.org

National Center for Learning Disabilities:
    www.ncld.org
Smart Kids with Learning Disabilities:
    www.smartkidswithld.org/
The Yale Center for Dyslexia & Creativity:
    https://dyslexia.yale.edu/
Winward Academy:
    www.winwardacademy.com/blog/

Governmental Agency for Learning Disabilities

Office of Special Education and Rehabilitative Services Blog
US Department of Education/US Governmental Agency with Funding for Learning Disabled Children (ages one to twenty-one): https://sites.ed.gov/osers/category/grants/osep-grants/

Online Information on ACT/SAT Accommodations

https://accommodations.collegeboard.org/request-accommodations/request/through-the-school
www.act.org/content/act/en/products-and-services/the-act/registration/accommodations.html

Educational Resources and Tools

This is a small sampling of resources as a suggested starting point in your search for the best fit for your child's needs. As with anything, and because things change so quickly on the internet, please be sure to do your own research as well. Most resources listed below are subscription (for a fee) services (except Khan Academy, YouTube, and PhET) but some schools may be able to offer free access or discounts. I recommend making the most out of each app's free trial period to see how effective they are for your child and to test how well they operate on the device your child will be using them on.

Website and App Audio Resources

- **Livescribe smartpens** transform both handwritten notes and audio into a fully synced digital format for convenient playback. The smartpens have an embedded camera to capture written content and a microphone to record spoken words. It's ideal for real-time note-taking and recording audio simultaneously.
- **Audiobooks** is a pay per month app that offers more than two hundred thousand voice recordings of books across all genres (with some free options), with tools that allow the listener to adjust the narration speed. The app is user friendly and easily returnable and books are often narrated by authors or professional actors. While a convenient option for auditory learners, not all books are available in this format.
- **LibriVox** is a volunteer-run service that provides a diverse range of free audiobooks to the public. Users can listen to these volunteer-narrated audiobooks online or download them for offline listening.
- **Speechify** is a text-to-speech app that converts written content into spoken words. Transforms text-based content such as articles, documents, or web pages into audio and allows the user to select the voice they want to hear. Some features may require a subscription.
- **Learning Ally** provides audiobooks and other accessible educational materials to individuals with visual or learning disabilities by offering alternatives to traditional print-based learning. It requires a subscription fee and may have limited content.
- **Amazon eTextbooks** offer digital versions of a wide range of textbooks and are available for purchase or rent but require

Amazon devices such as the Kindle. These electronic textbooks can be used for note-taking, highlighting, text-to-speech audio, and search capabilities (although not all textbooks offer these features).

Language and Learning Platform Apps

- **Duolingo** uses a gamelike approach to help users converse and build vocabulary in a wide variety of languages.
- **Quizlet** is designed to enable users to create and share digital flash cards. The flash cards utilize text, images, and audio to help users memorize information. The content is user-generated and tracks the user's progress.
- **Rosetta Stone** focuses on using visual and auditory strategies and focuses on pronunciation. Offers a lifetime option and thirty-day money-back guarantee.
- **IXL** has a comprehensive curriculum that helps users build math, language, science, and social studies skills. The site offers diagnostic tests to assess the user's proficiency and skill set and then builds from and tracks the results over time.
- **ST Math or JiJi** is a customized educational tool to help students in kindergarten through eighth grade focus on foundational concepts in math using visual learning tools. With the use of a penguin named JiJi, users are asked to help the penguin navigate obstacles by solving math problems.
- **Khan Academy** is an educational website that offers free online courses, lessons, and instructional videos across a wide range of subjects at (mostly) an introductory level for math, arts and humanities, economics, reading, life skills, science, computing, and test prep and practice exercises. The site offers adaptive learning features as well as progress tracking.
- **YouTube** provides a way to search for free specific help on an endless list of skills and topics (math, science, general education, literature, etc.) uploaded by users. Since there s no

standardization of content quality, it's best to find sources you trust and stick with them when possible. In the best case, the vast offerings can provide valuable information and tutorials. The subscription service allows you to avoid ads. Here are a few tutorials that I have found helpful:
- Haggerty Phonemic Awareness (YouTube)
- Example of Mapping or Scaffolding a Paper (YouTube): www.youtube.com/watch?v=jj-F6YVtsxI
- Crash Course (grades nine through twelve) is a YouTube channel providing a vast library of video lessons so the quality can vary.

- **PhET Interactive Simulations** offers free math and science simulations for educational purposes in a gamelike context. The site simplifies complex concepts in math, physics, chemistry, biology, and other sciences for students of all ages and learning styles. The quality and effectiveness of the simulations may vary, and there is no assessment feature to track progress or understanding, www.weareteachers.com/best-fonts-for-dyslexia/.

Literary Resources

- **SparkNotes** (grades seven through twelve) is most noted for its book, plays, and poem summaries; analysis and literary study guides; and test prep assistance. Content is meant to be used alongside, not in place of, readings. SparkNotes is extremely helpful for analyzing Shakespeare because it provides side-by-side translations of Shakespearean plays into modern English. Teacher reviews caution that the ads, limited support, and distracting content may be difficult for struggling readers, www.commonsense.org/education/reviews/sparknotes.
- **LitCharts** offers literary study guides for novels, plays, and poems. They explain quotes, offer in-depth character analysis, and explore themes and symbols, but students will still need to read the original material.

- **Project Gutenberg** is an online library of more than 70,000 free eBooks with an emphasis on out-of-copyright works.
- **Internet Archive:** digital library of free and borrowable books

Educational Tools
- **Obsidian** is a writing app that helps to consolidate, make sense of, and publish notes. It has the ability to link commonalities between your notes and create a visual map of your ideas as well as provide a place for brainstorming. Adapting to the technology may take time.
- **Typing Pal** is a web-based service to help improve touch-typing speed and accuracy for all ages. Through lessons and games, users can track their progress and utilize the user-friendly interface.
- **Membean** is a platform designed to improve vocabulary. The site is adaptive and changes depending on user performance. The quizzes and games can make learning vocabulary less tedious.

Glossary

Accessible Instructional Materials (AIM): Technology or learning supplies necessary to ensure equal educational opportunity (e.g., narrated books).

Accommodations: Special arrangements in school meant to help balance the playing field tailored to your child's diagnosis and individual learning needs.

Articulation: The ability to speak distinct sounds.

Attention Deficit Hyperactivity Disorder (ADHD): A set of behaviors that can include difficulty with sustained attention, hyperactive behavior (being in motion or not being able to sit for periods of time), and impulsivity (acting on things without thinking through consequences).

Auditory Learner: One who acquires information best by hearing and listening.

Auditory Skills: Skills related to hearing and discriminating sounds.

Automaticity: Ingrained learning that requires almost no conscious thought to recall.

Balanced Literacy: The approach that assumes that reading and writing are achieved by a child choosing reading materials based on their interests in order to promote a love of reading. It incorporates some phonics and whole-language approaches but relies heavily on context and pictures to recognize unfamiliar words.

Blending Sounds: The ability to put specific sounds together in a sequence.

Bullying: To abuse, aggressively dominate, or intimidate another with a real or perceived power imbalance.

Cognitive Assessment: Also known as intelligence testing or an IQ test. An assessment of verbal skills, visual perceptual skills, fluid reasoning, working memory, and processing speed.

Committee on Special Education (CSE): The committee that coordinates and carries out the special education processes for students in the district where a child's school is located, tasked with identifying and evaluating all school-age students (ages five to twenty-one) suspected of having special needs (or determining that no deficit exists).

Decoding: Associating symbols to sounds or groups of symbols to sounds, such as digraphs ("ch," "ph," etc.), and blending those sounds together to read a word.

Developmental History: A detailed review of a child's developmental educational, medical, and social-emotional history as part of a psychoeducational or neuropsychological evaluation to rule out things that could potentially cause learning failure, such as a hearing deficit, medical illness, excessive school absences, etc.

Digraphs: Two letters representing one sound (e.g., "th," "sh," "ch").

Directionality: The conceptual direction of things such as clockwise/counter-clockwise; north, south, east, and west; and right and left.

Glossary

DSM-5: The diagnostic tool published by the American Psychiatric Association to be used as a reference for mental health and brain-related conditions and disorders.

Dyslexia: A language processing disorder that can affect spoken or written language comprehension usually in stark contrast to an individual's other abilities, and without affecting intelligence. It may appear as a struggle to listen, speak, read, write, spell, or do mathematical calculations that is not primarily due to any developmental disability, emotional disturbance, or environmental, cultural, or economic disadvantage. Dyslexia can inhibit reading fluency and reading comprehension as well as writing and math. Perceptual, spatial, and sequencing skills can also be hindered. The condition varies with individuals and affects people on a spectrum from mild to moderate to severe.

Executive Functioning: Cognitive skills related to decision making, time management, attention span, and/or organization skills.

Experiential Learning: A learn by doing approach that allows learners to engage in hands-on experiences in order to deepen their understanding of a topic.

Extrinsic Motivation: Being driven by external accolades such as grades, rewards, or praise rather than an internal feeling of accomplishment or to satisfy one's own curiosity.

Family: For the purposes of this book, whatever group is part of your daily or weekly support team, whether related by blood or not; those in your child's orbit that you can depend upon and trust to be part of your family's culture and support circle.

fMRI (Functional Magnetic Resonance Imaging): Imaging technology that helps researchers see the brain perform functions in real time and watch the location of blood flow associated with different tasks. fMRIs actually highlight the less direct path that dyslexic brains utilize when reading.

Free Appropriate Public Education (FAPE): The education that every child is entitled to under the law. The three components of FAPE are (F) free—a child has the right to an education at no cost to the parent; (A) appropriate—an individualized program to meet the child's specific needs as outlined in the IEP; and (PE) public education—a child has the right to attend public school even if there are special needs.

Growth Mindset: Carol Dweck's concept that a failure is a stumbling block that can be overcome; the notion that a lack of ability or struggle is not permanent.

ICT Classroom: Integrated co-teaching classrooms use a combination of a general education and a special education teacher to provide instruction to a class with a mix of regular education children and children with IEPs.

Inclusion: A law giving all students access to the general education classroom with appropriate support to the greatest extent possible; allowing a child's educational needs to be met along with those of nondisabled student peers.

Individualized Education Plan (IEP): The educational plan required after a child is tested and meets the standards for special educational needs. The plan must assess a student's current level of performance in school, what yearly goals they should aspire to, and the services planned to help them attain their benchmarks.

Individuals with Disabilities Education Act (IDEA): The federal law protecting every student's right to an education. It addresses special needs and entitlements and related services to accommodate every child's unique needs to prepare them for their future success. Each state writes its own regulations.

Glossary

Informed Consent: A component of IDEA (see above), school districts are legally required to inform parents about specifics regarding any and all evaluations that are to be conducted, allowing parents to dispute the process.

Intrinsic Motivation: Being driven to do something in pursuit of a positive feeling of accomplishment, as opposed to for grades, rewards, or acknowledgment.

Laterality: Distinguishing between the right and left sides.

Least Restrictive Environment (LRE): The concept that a child should, whenever possible and appropriate, be educated in as close to a general education setting as possible.

Manipulatives: Tangible learning aids students can see and touch that help them acquire information more readily.

Mapping: An organizational tool that puts information into a conceptual grid to order topics and subtopics logically for constructing a written paper.

Mnemonics: Learning methods to aid in memorization, using tricks or devices like songs, rhymes, or acronyms.

Multisensory Learning: A teaching method that combines stimulating different senses while trying to present information; this includes visual, auditory, and physical input.

Neuroplasticity: The adaptive ability of the brain to change in response to life's demands.

Neuropsychological Assessment: An in-depth assessment of skills including attention, problem-solving, memory, language, IQ, visual-spatial skills, academic skills, and social-emotional functioning.

Neurotypical: Someone who processes information, learns skills, and reaches developmental milestones around the same time as their peers.

Organizational Skills: The ability to group things together in a way to minimize chaos, save time, prioritize, and use resources efficiently.

Orton-Gillingham Approach: A multisensory, phonics-based method to teach children to read (very effective for children with dyslexia, among others).

Overlearning: Reviewing or practicing information or a skill repeatedly until it can be retrieved quickly.

Phoneme: The smallest unit of sound in language that distinguishes words from one another. For example, the "b" sound in the word "bat" or the "ch" sound in the word "chunk."

Phonemic Awareness: The ability to distinguish, hear, identify, and manipulate individual sounds in spoken words. Developing phonemic awareness is considered a "prereading skill" and also helps with articulation (the ability to pronounce words correctly).

Phonetics: The study of speech sounds connecting sounds to letters and words, eventually leading a child to blend the sounds together.

Phonics: A method of reading instruction most recommended for dyslexic learners, associating letters or groups of letters with sounds that can eventually be blended into words.

Prereading Skills: Various language skills, including phonemic awareness, language immersion, articulating and parsing spoken language into phonemes, and rhyming, that help to make the process of learning to read easier.

Prior Written Notice (PWN): Any changes to a child's IEP or requests to evaluate a student require a PWN so that parents are informed of what is happening with their child's educational plan.

Reading Fluency: Reading at an acceptable pace with accuracy and expression.

Receptive Language: The ability to understand spoken or written language.

Reframing: A perspective shift to help view a situation from a different frame of reference.

Scaffolding: A method used to help a student learn new information or develop a new skill by presenting background information.

Science of Reading Approach: An interdisciplinary body of data, based on extensive studies done in many languages, to best teach reading to students.

Section 504: A federal civil rights law prohibiting discrimination against persons with disabilities and guaranteeing that their special needs will be met in public school in as close to a typical setting as possible.

Section 504 Plan: A plan generated by a CSE after a child has been tested that specifically addresses the special services, class placement, and/or accommodations that they are legally entitled to in school.

Self-Efficacy: Albert Bandura's idea regarding a child's belief in their own competency to learn. One's locus of control is internal rather than external, which in turn can increase self-motivation.

Sequencing Skills: The ability to put things in order from beginning to end, whether it is alphabetical, temporal, numerical, or in a logical progression.

SETSS (Special Education Teacher Support Services): A special education teacher placed in a regular education classroom to offer supplemental instruction and support to any children who are identified as requiring extra support through an IEP.

Shame: A painful feeling of humiliation or embarrassment.

Sight Words: Words that children are customarily taught to recall instantly without sounding them out. Examples of sight words that cannot be decoded include "the," "she," "would," "around," and "segue"—to name a few.

Social-Emotional Functioning: A child's interpersonal skills, including the ability to be self-aware, have self-control, manage emotions, and get along with others.

Soft Signs (of Dyslexia): Indicators of a developmental lag but not yet clear markers of an issue. Examples of early soft signs can include struggles with pronunciation of words, difficulty learning to write their name, and lack of interest in learning how to read.

Specific Learning Disorder: Neurodevelopmental disorder whose essential feature is persistent difficulties learning key academic skills, including reading of single words accurately and fluently, reading comprehension, written expression, arithmetic calculation, and mathematical reasoning (based on the DSM-5 definition).

Temporal Sequencing: The ability to put events in chronological order.

Typical Learner: For the purposes of this book, referring to nondyslexic learners who are able to learn to read with ease.

Visual Learner: One who acquires information best by reading, using visual images, graphics, colors, and/or maps so they can visualize the material in their mind's eye.

Notes

Introduction
1. Brock L. Eide and Fernette F. Eide, *The Dyslexic Advantage: Unlocking the Hidden Potential of the Dyslexic Brain*, revised and updated (New York: Penguin, 2023), 171.
2. Ibid., 87.

Chapter 1: Understanding Dyslexia
1. Elise de Bree et al., "A Stitch in Time…: Comparing Late-Identified, Late-Emerging and Early-Identified," *Dyslexia* 28, no. 3 (May 2022): 288.
2. Benjamin Spock and Robert Needleman, *Baby and Child Care, Ninth Edition: A Handbook for Parents of Developing Children from Birth to Adolescence* (New York: Gallery Books, 1998), 1.
3. Sally Shaywitz, *Overcoming Dyslexia*, 2nd ed. (New York: Random House, 2020), 426.
4. Eide and Eide, *The Dyslexic Advantage*, 86.

Chapter 6: Promoting the Best Study Skills and Habits
1. Colette Gray, "Understanding Cognitive Development: Automaticity and Early Years Child," *Child Care in Practice* 10, no.1 (January 2004): 40.
2. Susan Magsamen and Ivy Ross, *Your Brain on Art: How the Arts Transform Us* (New York: Random House, 2023), 159–161.
3. Pam A. Mueller and Daniel M. Oppenheimer, "The Pen Is Mightier Than the Keyboard: Advantages of Longhand over Laptop Note Taking," *Psychological Science* 25, no. 6 (2014): 1166.
4. Frances E. Jensen, with Amy Ellis Nutt, *The Teenage Brain: A Neuroscientist's Survival Guide to Raising Adolescents and Young Adults* (New York: HarperCollins, 2015), 206.

5. Rachel Barr et al., "Beyond Screen Time: A Synergistic Approach to a More Comprehensive Assessment of Family Media Exposure During Early Childhood," *Frontiers in Psychology* 41, no. 3 (2020): 1283.

6. Ibid.

7. Jensen, *The Teenage Brain*, 89.

8. Ibid., 100.

9. Rochelle M. Eime et al., "A Systematic Review of Psychological and Social Benefits of Participation in Sports for Children and Adolescents: Informing Development of a Conceptual Model of Health Through Sport," *International Journal of Behavior and Physical Activity* 10, no. 1 (2013): 13.

10. Brandon M. Savage et al., "Humor, Laughter, Learning, and Health!: A Brief Review," *Advances in Physiology Education* (2017): 1152.

11. Magsamen and Ross, *Your Brain on Art*, 148–149.

12. Elizabeth L. Bjork and Robert A. Bjork, *Memory; A Handbook of Perception and Cognition*, 2nd ed. (New York: Academic Press, 1996), 270.

13. Magsamen and Ross, *Your Brain on Art*, 18, 24.

14. Ibid., 108.

15. Ibid., 3.

16. Lisa Damour, *Under Pressure: Confronting the Epidemic of Stress and Anxiety in Girls* (New York: Ballantine Books, 2019), 25.

Chapter 7: Practices to Bolster Self-Esteem

1. Aliza Pressman, *The Five Principles of Parenting: Your Essential Guide to Raising Good Humans* (New York: Simon and Schuster, 2024), 231.

2. Ibid., 146.

3. Julia Lythcott-Haims, *How to Raise an Adult* (New York: Holt Paperbacks, 2015), 145.

4. Jonathan McKee, *The Bullying Breakthrough: Real Help for Parents and Teachers of the Bullied, Bystanders, and Bullies* (Ohio: Shiloh Run Press, 2018), 123.

Chapter 8: Skill Building in Elementary School

1. Eide and Eide, *The Dyslexia Advantage*, 203.

2. Sally Shaywitz, *Overcoming Dyslexia* (New York: Random House, 2003), 78.

Chapter 9: Adapting to Middle School

1. William Stixrud and Ned Johnson, *The Self-Driven Child: The Science and Sense of Giving Your Kids More Control over Their Lives* (New York: Penguin Books, 2018), 2.

2. Ibid., 110.

3. Damour, *Under Pressure*, 25.

4. American Psychiatric Association, *Desk Reference to the Diagnostic Criteria from DSM-5 (R)* (Arlington, TX: American Psychiatric Association Publishing, 2013), 222.

5. Ibid., 160–161.

6. Stixrud and Johnson, *The Self Driven Child*, 61.

7. Ibid., 50.

8. Carol Dweck and David Yeager, "A Growth Mindset About Intelligence" in *Handbook of Wise Interventions: How Social Psychology Can Help People Change*, eds. Gregory M. Walton and Alia J. Crum (New York: Guilford Press, 2020): 11.

9. Ibid., 10.

Chapter 10: Thriving in High School

1. Damour, *Under Pressure*, 4.

2. Peter Salmon, "Effects of Physical Exercise on Anxiety, Depression, and Sensitivity to Stress: A Unifying Theory," *Clinical Psychology Review* 21, no. 1 (2001): 51.

3. Brené Brown, *The Gifts of Imperfection: Let Go of Who You Think You're Supposed to Be and Embrace Who You Are* (New York: Simon and Schuster, 2022), PDF.

4. Jensen, *The Teenage Brain*, 130.

5. Sonali Jhanjee, "Dyslexia and Substance Abuse: The Under-Recognized Link," *Indian Journal of Psychological Medicine* 37, no. 3 (2015): 374–375.

6. Lisa Damour, *Untangled: Guiding Teenage Girls Through the Seven Transitions into Adulthood* (New York: Ballantine Books, 2016), 263.

7. Reed Larson and Natalie Rusk, "Intrinsic Motivation and Positive Development," *Advances in Child Development and Behavior* 41 (2011): 89–130, PDF.

8. Richard M. Ryan and Edward L. Deci, "Intrinsic and Extrinsic Motivation from a Self-Determination Theory Perspective: Definitions, Theory, Practices, and Future Directions," *Contemporary Educational Psychology* 61 (2020): 101860, PDF.

Chapter 13: A Bright Future

1. de Bree et al., "A Stitch in Time...," 277.

Afterword

1. Pressman, *The Five Principles of Parenting*, 26.

Bibliography

American Dyslexia Association website, 2023. www.american-dyslexia-association.org/.

Bandura, Albert. "Self-Efficacy: Toward a Unifying Theory of Behavioral Change," *Psychological Review* 84 (1977): 191–215.

Bandura, Albert, and Dale H. Schunk. "Cultivating Competence, Self-Efficacy, and Intrinsic Interest Through Proximal Self-Motivation." *Journal of Personality and Social Psychology* 41, no. 3 (1981): 586.

Barr, Rachel, Heather Kirkorian, Jenny Radesky, Sarah Coyne, Deborah Nichols, Olivia Blanchfield, Sylvia Rusnak, et al. "Beyond Screen Time: A Synergistic Approach to a More Comprehensive Assessment of Family Media Exposure During Early Childhood." *Frontiers in Psychology* 11 (2020): 1283.

Bjork, E. L., and R. A. Bjork. *Memory: Handbook of Perception and Cognition, 2nd ed.* New York: Academic Press, 1996.

Brown, Brené. *The Gifts of Imperfection: Let Go of Who You Think You're Supposed to Be and Embrace Who You Are.* New York: Simon and Schuster, 2022, PDF.

Damour, Lisa. *Untangled: Guiding Teenage Girls Through the Seven Transitions into Adulthood.* New York: Ballantine Books, 2016.

Damour, Lisa. *Under Pressure: Confronting the Epidemic of Stress and Anxiety in Girls*. New York: Ballantine Books, 2019.

de Bree, Elise H., Madelon van den Boer, Boukje M. Toering, and Peter F. de Jong. "A Stitch in Time...: Comparing Late–Identified, Late–Emerging and Early–Identified Dyslexia." *Dyslexia* 28, no. 3 (2022): 276–292.

Diagnostic and Statistical Manual of Mental Disorders, 5th ed. Washington, DC: American Psychiatric Association Publishing, 2013.

Dweck, Carol S. *Mindset: The New Psychology of Success*. New York: Random House, 2006.

Dweck, Carol, and David Yeager. "A Growth Mindset About Intelligence." In *Handbook of Wise Interventions: How Social Psychology Can Help People Change*, edited by Gregory M. Walton and Alia J. Crum, 9–35. New York: Guilford Press, 2020.

Eide, Brock L., and Fernette F. Eide. *The Dyslexic Advantage (Revised and Updated): Unlocking the Hidden Potential of the Dyslexic Brain*. Penguin, 2023.

Eime, Rochelle M., Janet A. Young, Jack T. Harvey, Melanie J. Charity and Warren R. Payne. "A Systematic Review of the Psychological and Social Benefits of Participation in Sport for Children and Adolescents: Informing Development of a Conceptual Model of Health Through Sport." *International Journal of Behavioral Nutrition and Physical Activity* 10, no. 1 (2013): 1–21.

Gray, Colette. "Understanding Cognitive Development: Automaticity and the Early Years Child." *Child Care in Practice* 10, no. 1 (2004): 39–47.

International Dyslexia Association website, 2023. https://dyslexiaida.org.

Jensen, Frances E., and Amy E. Nutt. *The Teenage Brain: A Neuroscientist's Survival Guide to Raising Adolescents and Young Adults*. New York: HarperCollins Press, 2015.

Jhanjee, Sonali. "Dyslexia and Substance Abuse: The Under-Recognized Link." *Indian Journal of Psychological Medicine* 37, no. 3 (2015): 374–375. https://journals.sagepub.com/doi/pdf/10.4103/0253-7176.162905.

Larson, Reed, and Natalie Rusk. "Intrinsic Motivation and Positive Development." *Advances in Child Development and Behavior* 41 (2011): 89–130. PDF.

Lythcott-Haims, Julie. *How to Raise an Adult: Break Free of the Overparenting Trap and Prepare Your Kid for Success.* New York: Henry Holt, 2015.

Magsamen, Susan, and Ivy Ross. *Your Brain on Art: How the Arts Transform Us.* New York: Random House, 2023.

McKee, Jonathan. *The Bullying Breakthrough: Real Help for Parents and Teachers of the Bullied, Bystanders, and Bullies.* Ohio: Shiloh Press, 2018.

Mueller, Pam A., and Daniel M. Oppenheimer. "The Pen Is Mightier Than the Keyboard: Advantages of Longhand Over Laptop Note Taking." *Psychological Science* 25, no. 6 (2014): 1159–1168.

Pressman, Aliza. *The Five Principles of Parenting: Your Essential Guide to Raising Good Humans.* New York: Simon and Schuster, 2024.

Salmon, Peter. "Effects of Physical Exercise on Anxiety, Depression, and Sensitivity to Stress: A Unifying Theory." *Clinical Psychology Review* 21, no. 1 (2001): 33–61.

Savage, Brandon M., Heidi L. Lujan, Raghavendar R. Thipparthi, and Stephen E. DiCarlo. "Humor, Laughter, Learning, and Health! A Brief Review." *Advances in Physiology Education* (2017). PDF.

Shaywitz, Bennett A., and Sally E. Shaywitz. "The American Experience: Towards a 21st Century Definition of Dyslexia." *Oxford Review of Education* 46, no. 4 (2020): 454–471.

Shaywitz, Sally. *Overcoming Dyslexia.* New York: Random House, 2003.

Bibliography

Shaywitz, Sally, MD, Jonathan Shaywitz, MD. *Overcoming Dyslexia*, 2nd ed. New York: Vintage Books, Penguin Random House, 2020.

Spock, Dr. Benjamin, and Robert Needleman. *Baby and Child Care, Ninth Edition: A Handbook for Parents of Developing Children from Birth to Adolescence*. New York: Gallery Books, 1998.

Stixrud, William, and Ned Johnson. *The Self-Driven Child: The Science and Sense of Giving Your Kids More Control over Their Lives*. New York: Penguin Books, 2018.

We Are Teachers. "Best Fonts for Dyslexia and Why They Work." www.weareteachers.com/best-fonts-for-dyslexia.

"Yale Dyslexia." *Yale Dyslexia*, 2022. https://dyslexia.yale.edu/resources/dyslexic-kids-adults/stories-from-dyslexics/one-dyslexics-experience-with-learning-american-sign-language/.

Acknowledgments

From Lisa and Jody

During the pandemic of 2020, Lisa dug up a draft of a memoir that she had written after graduate school about her travails growing up dyslexic, hoping to have the time one day to develop it further. From those original kernels, written decades prior, grew this project. Amidst an uncertain time, during what became recognized as a national reading crisis as a result of the pandemic, we began work on what we realized could be an important resource for parents. Our partnership sprang up organically, built upon a long friendship, with hopes to be a voice of encouragement and support for families struggling to adapt to a young dyslexic learner's needs.

Along the way, we have been so fortunate to have gotten the support of both our agent, Gary Krebs, for believing in us and our project, and our wonderful editor and publisher, Renée Sedliar. Thank you, Renée, for the privilege of working with you and for your consistent enthusiasm and partnership, your essential contributions, and the patience to clearly see through to the core message of our book. You made what might have been a daunting project a true pleasure. We can never thank you enough for taking us on. Big thanks to the team at Hachette Go including Nzinga Temu and Fred Francis from Balance. Your input has significantly enriched these pages, and your patience has been invaluable.

This book did indeed "take a village!" Special thanks to Meg Sheedy for championing this project early on and going above and beyond with your support and encouragement. Our heartfelt gratitude to her and the many friends, family, and colleagues who contributed so generously of their time and enthusiasm: Lauren Brody, David Brody, Ben Brody, Will Brody, Teddy Brody, Jocelyn Cheng, Dawn Davis, Julia D'Amico, Anne Devine, Sandi Farkas, Renee Frankel, Swati Grayson, Aaron Harnick, Angela Karcz, Brian Karcz, Diane Karcz, Lora Karcz, Aislinn Kimbrough, Jill Krata, Bailey Link, Briana Link, Zibby Owens, Tammy Richardson, Jane Ross, Guan-Ling Wang, Mariko Shimbori, Alyson Tockstein, and Melissa Triedman. You have all made valuable contributions of your time and/or experience to what we hope will be an infinitely useful resource for parents and educators.

To Jenn Witz, your advocacy and support of this book was an incredible act of friendship. Our heartfelt thanks to you and Scott Greenstein for your belief in our message and for your efforts to extend its reach.

From Lisa

To my amazing parents, Judy and Bob Rappaport, and my sister, Gail Rappaport Eilers, I am forever grateful for your unrelenting support and constant dedication. Your ability to reframe my failures when I couldn't and to find humor during the tough moments has anchored me throughout my life and made me a better parent. There are no words to express my love and gratitude for all you've given me.

To my husband and biggest champion, Darren, who is the reason I finally felt brave enough to share my story; you not only stepped in and put aside your own crazy schedule to help me, you have never wavered in your respect and belief in me. I can't believe how lucky I am to have you in my life. I love being a mother and wife more than anything in this world and I feel grateful for you every day.

To my children, Drew and Brooke, you never complained and always encouraged me to work on this book at the expense of time spent together. You pushed me to persevere when I experienced setbacks and were always there to offer advice from your teenage perspective. My biggest gift in life

Acknowledgments

is being your mother. I love you both more than I could have imagined possible.

To David Grayson, I would not have made it through high school without you and we have been together through thick and thin ever since. I will always be grateful for your profound and steadfast support and friendship.

To Barbara Haber, my mentor, teacher, and most trusted resource; your knowledge, wisdom, professionalism, and thorough approach to everything you do never ceases to amaze me. Thank you for your guidance and decades of mentoring. I so appreciate all of your reliable support. I loved the opportunity to get to work with you again.

To Alice Alderman, you are the original inspiration that motivated me to transform my notes into a book that I want to share with parents. Your unending support and ability to make me feel intelligent and worthy started the process. You highlighted the gifts that my dyslexia afforded me that I never recognized, all while offering a newfound friendship with a lot of laughter and fun.

To Gary Gallagher, thank you for your valuable feedback, patience, time, and computer expertise every step of the way. Your big heart and kindness throughout this process is so appreciated.

Special thanks to Lisa Damour. Beyond being an incredibly valued resource of expertise and inspiration, your extreme graciousness in offering to help support this project cannot be overstated. Thank you for the incredible work you put out into the world and for your tremendous contribution to our book. We are beyond grateful to you.

To Jody, my writing partner and dear friend, your generosity of spirit, belief in and dedication to this project was what drove it and shaped it into the book that we have written today. You magnanimously offered hours of your time helping me before I had even considered sharing my story with anyone. You reinforced what I now understand are my gifts from being dyslexic and consistently bolstered my self-esteem. You demonstrated extreme patience when working with me, especially when I read out loud to you. I owe you a wig for all the hair you must have pulled out. We have spent years laughing while working together, and that is priceless. Our

Acknowledgments

unexpected and unique journey has been made so much more fun by working together and continues to build our deep friendship, for which I will be forever grateful.

From Jody

To my wonderful husband, Gary Gallagher, thank you for your endless patience, love, friendship, moral and technological support and belief in me throughout the years of work to realize this project. I could never have done this without you. I love you so much and am so grateful for you every day.

To my mother, Judith Schneider Subotky, thank you for your unflagging moral support, friendship, unconditional love, and openness to personal growth, which has inspired me throughout my life. I love you always.

Gratitude and love to my father, Allan Lyons, who introduced me to the joys and frustrations of the puzzle of writing.

Heartfelt love and thanks to my sister, Wendy Lyons Sunshine, for her genuine encouragement, inspiration, input, and good ear throughout this project.

Love and gratitude to my abundantly wise aunt, Alice Shafran, who continues to inspire me with her amazing gift with words and for having so kindly offered her vast talents to this project.

To Lisa: For me, the informal research for this book began unwittingly decades ago when I first had the pleasure of getting to know you and learning the extraordinary ways in which your family works. I was in awe from my earliest introduction, and as our friendship grew, so did my amazement. I could never have imagined that years later I would come to understand so much more profoundly the deep underpinnings of your family bond by embarking upon this amazing project with you.

I want to express my earnest gratitude for your generous spirit throughout our friendship and for the opportunity to take this ride with you. Your encouragement, grit, resilience, and ability to laugh during the

Acknowledgments

many ups and downs of writing has made it a joy to be a part of. Thanks, too, to your family for allowing me to take license in writing this shared family experience.

Lisa, I continue to be inspired by your willingness to vulnerably expose the personal and professional parts of your journey as a dyslexic learner for the benefit of so many. Thank you for your patience and embracing my input to contribute to your lived experience through my more typical learner lens. It is truly a gift of a lifetime.

Index

academic achievement, evaluation of, 37
academic clues of dyslexia, 11–12
academic success
 celebrating, 91–93
 delayed, 4
 desire for, 227–228
 mantras about, 125–126
 reframing, 54
 tips for (see study skills/habits)
 in young adults, 220–221
Academy of Pediatrics, 112
accommodations, 49–51, 148, 207
acting out, 14, 84, 132, 157, 189
adults. See dyslexic adults
advocating for children, 27–29, 52–53
affirmations, 59, 214
aggressive behavior, 132–133, 189
alcohol, avoiding, 191–192
alphabet, sequencing, 71
American Dyslexia Association, 112
American Psychiatric Association, 6
analog clocks, 68, 69, 153
Annual Review, 30–31
anxiety
 bullying and, 139
 in dyslexia, 11, 14, 164
 in high school, 183–184, 186, 191, 192
 in middle school, 164–165, 175
 symptoms of, 165
 test, 104, 220
appearance, 168–169
apps
 and dopamine, 111
 for dyslexic learners, 17, 50, 53
 for math, 109–110
art, creating, 115–116, 187
articulation, 63
attention
 focused, 13
 increasing, 114–115, 154
 problems with, 11

Index

attention deficit hyperactivity
    disorder (ADHD), 13, 103, 154
audiobooks, 17, 50, 105–106, 110,
    117, 184, 239
auditory learning, 105–106
automaticity of recall,
    103–105, 108
autonomy
    importance of, 120–121
    in teenagers, 121–122, 158–160,
        168–170, 182
    See also independence

Baby and Child Care (Spock), 9
baking, 188
balance
    study habits and, 110–113
    work and, 214
Balanced Literacy, 49
beginning sounds, 63–64
behavioral clues of dyslexia, 11
blending sounds, 64–65, 107
books
    reading for pleasure, 151
    types of, 110
    See also audiobooks; reading
boundaries
    and self-esteem, 132
    setting, 111–112, 132–133,
        169, 189
brain
    creating art and, 115
    dyslexic, 4, 154
    educating children about
        workings of, 45
    sleep and, 113

brain imaging, 4, 154
brainstorming, 172
breaks
    in college, 213
    and humor, 88
    increasing attention with,
        114–115, 154
    "low-tech," 115–116
    needs for, 14, 185
    as stress relief, 175, 187–188
    in the summer, 198–199
bullying
    confronting, 138–140
    symptoms of, 139
The Bullying Breakthrough
    (McKee), 139

calculators, 50
categorizing exercises, 71–72
children. See dyslexic children
Child Study Team (CST), 28–29
choice. See independence
chores, 89
chunking (mnemonic
    technique), 108
classmates
    catching up to, 4, 225
    explaining accommodations
        to, 50
    feeling isolated from, 124
    keeping pace with, 9, 45
classroom(s)
    discomfort in, 130
    frustration in, 148
    settings in, 47–48
    See also school(s)

Index

clocks, 68, 69, 153. *See also* telling time
clustering (mnemonic technique), 109
cognitive assessment, 37
college essays, 199, 205
college/university, 203–216
   life after, 217–222
   preparation for, 199, 204–205
   scholarships for, 199
   selecting, 205–206
   self-comparison in, 212–213
   self-esteem in, 212
   study skills in, 207, 208–209
   support available in, 206
   transition to, 207–208
   work ethic in, 213–214
   work-life balance in, 214
color-coordinated notes, 185
comic books, 110
Committee on Special Education (CSE), 28–29, 30
communication
   about bullying, 139
   and self-advocacy, 122–123, 182–183
   with teenagers, 157–158, 181, 188, 190
compassion, 81
compensatory skills, 4, 8, 25
competition
   avoiding, among siblings, 82
   and motivation, 193, 194
conceptual language exercises, 71–73
conflict
   family, 85
   in middle school, 169
consent, informed, 29
consequences, 131, 132, 133–134, 160, 168
cortisol, 115
cost-benefit analysis, 159
creativity, 20, 115–116
critical building blocks of language, 60–66
crying
   empathy for, 81
   exercises and, 58
   frustration and, 131

Damour, Lisa, 164
days of the week, 70
deadlines, 99–102, 184
decision-making
   about education, 161, 195
   in college selection, 205–206
   encouraging, 120
   questions for, 159, 168
   talking children through, 159
decoding, 62
depression
   bullying and, 139
   in dyslexia, 11, 14, 164
   in high school, 186, 190, 191, 192
   in middle school, 164–165
   symptoms of, 165, 197
desks, organizing, 103, 171, 185, 186–187
developmental history, 37

Index

diagnosis, 23–39
  accepting, 24, 47
  delayed, 8
  hiding from child, 24–25
  honesty about, 42–45
  in older children, 25–26
  processing, 47, 54
  providing context for, 45–47
  as relief, 26, 47
  See also evaluation
Diagnostic and Statistical Manual of Mental Disorders, Fifth Edition (DSM-5), 6
diet, healthy, 112–113
different learners, 7
digital clocks, 68
digraphs, 63
directional/spatial concepts, exercises for, 66–68
discrimination, 28
dissertation, 220
distractibility, 11, 111–112
dominant side, 66
dopamine, 111, 115
driving, 231
drugs, avoiding, 191–192
Dweck, Carol, 170
dyscalculia, 6, 68
dysgraphia, 6, 107, 172–173
dyslexia
  and ADHD, 13, 154
  brain imaging in, 4, 154
  common signs of, 11–12
  controversy over subgroups of, 5–7
  defining, 4–5
  diagnosis of (*see* diagnosis; evaluation)
  and drug and alcohol use, 191–192
  early signs of, 8–9
  genetic component for, 9
  gifts of, 19–21, 235–236
  importance of terminology of, 7
  in parents, 87
  prevalence of, 3, 19, 46
  soft signs of, 9–10, 66, 147
  success stories, 15, 25, 45, 234–235
  understanding, 3–22
dyslexia community
  finding tutors in, 53
  growth of, 14–15
  phonetic approach resources from, 150–151
  technology and, 17–18
dyslexic adults
  daily functioning in, 229–231
  life after college, 217–222
  parents as, 87
  self-comparison by, 212–213
  self-esteem in, 212, 232
  shame in, 231–235
  successful, 220–221
  transitioning to college, 207–208
  transitioning to independence, 214
  transitioning to work, 217, 219, 221–222
  using habits learned in school, 208–209

work ethic of, 213–214
work-life balance of, 214
dyslexic children
  accommodations for, 49–51, 148
  advocating for, 27–29, 52–53
  classroom settings for, 47–48
  diagnosis in (see diagnosis; evaluation)
  in elementary school (see elementary school)
  exercises for (see exercises/games)
  explaining accommodations to, 50
  explaining accommodations to classmates, 50
  hiding learning issues, 4, 8, 25, 147, 149
  interests of, 163–164
  IQ testing in, 44–45
  reading methods for, 48–49, 150–151
  rights of, 27–29
  self-advocacy in, 122–123
  self-esteem in (see self-esteem)
  strengths of, 18, 46
  study skills for (see study skills/habits)
  as victims of bullying, 138–140
  weaknesses of, 46
dyslexic teenagers
  anxiety and depression in, 164–165, 186, 191, 192
  autonomy in, 121–122, 158–160, 168–170, 182
  avoiding drugs and alcohol, 191–192
  being recognized by adults in, 197–198
  bonding with, 175–176, 187, 188, 190
  college selection by, 205–206
  decision-making in, 159
  emotional support for, 188–191
  feelings in, 121, 164–165, 181, 189
  finding life's purpose, 192, 193, 194–197
  growth mindset in, 170
  in high school (see high school)
  hormonal swings in, 158, 189
  in middle school (see middle school)
  motivation in, 160–164, 192–194
  opening up to parents, 157–158, 181
  preparing for college, 199, 204–205
  resisting gratitude practices, 135–136
  self-advocacy in, 182–183, 208
  self-efficacy in, 165–168
  stress relief for, 175–177, 185–188
  study skills for (see study skills/habits)
  on summer breaks, 198–199
  transitioning to college, 207–208

education. *See* school(s)
educational resources
　availability of, 15–16
　technological, 17–18
educational testing, 37
effort
　children validating own, 125
　emphasizing over grades, 54, 92–93, 127–128, 166
　rewarding, 91–92, 128, 167
elaboration (mnemonic technique), 109
elementary school
　building attention span in, 154
　classroom frustration in, 148
　homework help in, 153–154
　multisensory learning in, 152
　parents checking homework in, 134
　reading out loud in, 148–149
　sequencing skills in, 152–153
　skill building in, 147–156
　teaching methods for reading in, 48–49, 150–151
　time management for, 100–101
emotion(s)
　big, normalizing, 189
　in college transition, 208
　parents supporting, 188–191
　in teenagers, 121, 164–165
　See also feelings
emotional awareness exercises, 72–73
emotional safety
　family team and, 81, 228
　for teenagers, 188

empathy, 81, 125, 132, 139, 171
enabling, 132
ending sounds, 64
endorphins, 113, 115
evaluation
　before college application, 204
　components of, 37–38
　explaining to children, 38–39, 42–43
　goals of, 26
　informed consent, 29
　for older children, 25–26
　parents requesting, 23, 26, 30–31, 73–74
　private, 32–36, 38, 39, 42
　process of, 30–32
　reasons for, 23–24
　school, 26–27, 30–32, 39, 42
　supplemental, 31
　See also diagnosis
Everyone Reading, 16
exams
　accommodations for, 49–50
　quizzes as preparation for, 107–108
　See also test(s)
executive functioning skills, 13, 37
exercise (physical activity)
　benefits of, 113
　in college, 213
　in high school, 185, 186
exercises/games, 55–76
　approaches to, 56–57
　for developing conceptual language, 71–73

for developing directional/spatial concepts, 66–68
for developing phonemic awareness, 60–66, 150–151
for developing time concepts, 68–71, 153
pace of, 56, 57
professional help with, 73–74
progressing through, 61
resistance to, 56, 57–58, 73
as study method, 107–108
tips for, 58–60
year, months of, 70
expanding file folders, 100, 102
experiential learning, 106–107
expressive language, 4, 37
extracurricular activities, 101, 136–137, 143, 155, 156, 161, 194
extrinsic motivation, 162, 192
eye-hand coordination, 231

failures
allowing time to heal after, 130
consequences of, 168
and developing self-efficacy, 165–168
and finding life's purpose, 194–197
and frustration, 189
mantras about, 125–126
reframing as opportunity, 128–129, 167
See also mistakes
family/family team, 79–98

acknowledging impact of dyslexia on, 82–84
bonding, 187
conflict in, 85
different opinions in, 93–95
diversity of, 79–80
and emotional safety, 81, 228
finding extra support, 95–96
humor used by, 87–89, 94–95, 137–138
importance of, 80
inclusion in, 89, 90–91
isolation in, 190
managing expectations in, 91–93
managing inequities in, 84–85
power struggles in, 87
rules of, 81
supporting dyslexic adults, 232
See also parents; siblings
feelings
"at ease," 130
big, normalizing, 189
bullying and, 139
delivering mantras and, 124–127
empathy for, 81, 125, 132
exercises for, 72–73
"hating school," 181, 193
"less than," 127, 140, 161, 189, 213
reframing, 125
in teenagers, 121, 164–165, 181, 189
See also emotion(s)
file folders, 100, 102
financial assistance, 16
flash cards, 17, 109

fonts, and reading, 148–149
food, healthy, 112–113
foreign language
  in middle school, 173–174
  opting out of, 50, 174, 184–185
Free Appropriate Public Education (FAPE), 27
frustration
  in classroom, 148
  exercises and, 58
  expressing, 125, 131, 132
  in high school, 181, 189, 195
  in middle school, 158, 160–161, 171
  minimizing, 148
  pent-up, 14, 131
frustration tolerance, 129, 130–131
functional magnetic resonance imaging (fMRI), 4, 154

generalizations, negative, 170
genetics, 9
Google Keep, 100–101, 171
grades
  emphasizing effort over, 54, 92–93, 127–128, 166
  mantras about, 126, 166
  in middle school, 162, 166–167, 176
  and motivation, 162, 192
  of siblings, 92
graduate school, 217
grammar apps, 17
Grammarly, 172
graphic novels, 110

gratitude practices, 135–136, 190–191
grit
  developing, 129, 166
  as gift of dyslexia, 236
  mantras about, 125–126, 209
  in young adults, 219
grouping objects, exercises for, 71–72
growth mindset, 170
guided questions, 168

handwriting notes, 108
"hating school" feeling, 181, 193
healthy food, 112–113
hearing. See receptive language
helicopter parents, 129
helping others, 135–136
high school, 181–201
  avoiding drugs and alcohol in, 191–192
  being recognized by adults in, 197–198
  challenges of, 181
  dropping out of, 195, 196
  emotional support in, 188–191
  finding life's purpose in, 192, 193, 194–197
  frustration in, 181, 189, 195
  motivation in, 192–194, 196
  stress relief in, 185–188
  study skills in, 183–185, 186–187
  summer breaks in, 198–199

Index

time management for, 101, 183–184, 186
high school degree, 18–19
homework
  avoidance of, 11
  in college, 208
  and frustration, 131
  in high school, 183–185
  in middle school, 158, 160, 162, 174
  no devices during, 111, 112
  parents checking, 134
  parents helping with, 153–154
  time-management skills for, 100–101, 182–183
hormonal swings, 158, 189
hospital-based clinic, 33
humiliation, 149, 193
humility, 4, 214
humor
  benefits of, 113
  family using, 87–89, 94–95, 137–138
  as gift of dyslexia, 236
  in middle school, 176–177
  owning strengths and weaknesses with, 137–138
  resilience, 113
  self-deprecating, 88
hyperactivity, 13

imagery (mnemonic technique), 109
immersion, total, 163
impulsivity, 13
inclusion, 29

independence
  building, in summer breaks, 198–199
  in college, 214
  control and, 131
  importance of, 120–121
  and self-advocacy, 122–123
  in teenagers, 121–122, 158–160, 168–170, 182
individuality, 90
Individualized Education Plan (IEP), 27, 29, 30–31, 42
Individuals with Disabilities Education Act (IDEA), 27–28, 29
informed consent, 29
Integrated Co-Teaching (ICT) classroom, 47–48
intelligence, of dyslexic children, 3, 8, 20
intelligence testing, 37, 44–45
interactive learning, 106–107
interests
  bonding with teenagers around, 181, 190
  developing, 163–164
  in exercises, 59
International Dyslexia Association (IDA), 5, 33
intrinsic motivation
  developing, 162–164, 192–194
  rewards in, 128
IQ test, 37, 44–45
irritability, in teenagers, 121
isolating sounds, 65
isolation, 124, 190, 191, 227

jobs
   after college, 217, 219, 221–222
   in high school, 198
Johnson, Ned, 162
journaling, 214

KhanAcademy.org, 53

language
   conceptual, 71–73
   critical building blocks of, 60–66
   expressive, 4, 37
   foreign (see foreign language)
   receptive, 4, 37
language immersion, 60
language requirement, opting out of, 50, 174, 184–185
laterality
   in dyslexic adults, 231
   exercises for, 66–67
   visual cues for, 67
laughter
   benefits of, 113
   at oneself, 88, 114
   See also humor
learning
   disparity in, 3–4
   growth mindset and, 170
   lack of interest in, 160–161
   multisensory, 152
   pleasure of, 164
   resistance to, 11
   styles of, 105–107
Learning Disabilities Association of America (LDA), 5, 33

least restrictive environment (LRE), 29
lectures, recording, 50, 109, 172
left and right
   dyslexic adults and, 231
   exercises for, 66–67
   visual cues for, 67
"less than" feeling, 127, 140, 161, 189, 213
letters, identifying, 63–64
listening
   in confronting bullying, 139
   and self-esteem, 124
   See also receptive language
lists, making, 99, 116, 171, 221, 222
Livescribe smartpen, 50, 106, 172
lockers, organizing, 103, 171, 185
long-term memory, 105
"low-tech" breaks, 115–116

magazines, 110
Magsamen, Susan, 115
mantras, 124–127, 131, 141, 143, 166, 176, 179, 183, 207, 209, 228
"mapping" (brainstorming method), 172
marijuana, 191
master's program, 218
math apps, 109–110
McKee, Jonathan, 139
meetings with teachers
   children arranging, 122–123, 182–183, 196
   getting questions ready prior, 52
   parents arranging, 148

Index

memory
  long-term, 105
  mnemonics for, 67, 108–109
  working, 13
middle school, 157–179
  anxiety and depression in, 164–165
  avoiding negative generalizations in, 170
  challenges of, 157, 161
  decision-making in, 159
  foreign language in, 173–174
  freedoms given in, 168–170
  frustration in, 158, 160–161, 171
  grades in, 162, 166–167, 176
  humor in, 176–177
  late, goal for, 174
  motivation in, 160–164
  parental role changing in, 158–160
  parents checking homework, 134
  self-efficacy in, 165–168
  stress relief for, 175–177
  study skills in, 171–174
  time management for, 101, 171
mindset, growth, 170
mistakes
  consequences of, 168
  learning lessons from, 122, 128–129, 167
  mantras about, 125–126
  opportunities presented by, 127, 128–129
  See also failures
mnemonics, 67, 108–109
moderation, study habits and, 110–113

months of the year, 70
motivation
  depression and, 197
  dyslexia diagnosis and, 42
  extrinsic, 162, 192
  in high school, 192–194, 196
  intrinsic (*see* intrinsic motivation)
  in middle school, 160–164
  teachers and, 198
multisensory learning, 152
music, 155, 156, 176, 187, 188, 200

narration devices, 17. *See also* audiobooks
negative generalizations, 170
negative self-talk, 124
neurodiversity
  as disability, 206
  mainstreamed, 15
neuroplasticity, 115
neuropsychological assessment, 33, 37
"Never Eat Soggy Waffles" (mnemonic), 67
notebooks, 102
notes/note-taking
  color-coordinated, 185
  copying, 172
  dating, 102
  by dyslexic adults, 230
  organizing, 102
  reviewing, 107, 108
  smartpens for, 50, 106, 172
  tools for, 17, 172
  writing and rewriting, 108

notifications, turning off, 112
numbers
　difficulties with, 12
　processing, in dyscalculia, 6
　recognizing, exercises for, 68
nutrition, 112–113

online support groups, 17–18
opioid use, 191–192
organizing
　in college, 207, 208–209
　difficulties with, 12
　by dyslexic adults, 230
　in elementary school, 152–153
　exercises for, 71–72
　file folders for, 100, 102
　in high school, 182, 185,
　　186–187
　lockers and desks, 103, 171, 185,
　　186–187
　in middle school, 171–172
　rooms, 152–153, 186–187
　study materials, 102
　time (see time management
　　skills)
　writing projects, 103,
　　171–172, 220
Orton-Gillingham Approach,
　49, 150
outbursts
　exercises and, 58
　frustration and, 131
outline, for research papers,
　171–172
overlearning, 103–105
"over parenting," 121

parents
　as advocates for children, 27–29,
　　52–53
　autonomy supported by,
　　120–122, 158–160, 182
　bonding with teenagers,
　　175–176, 187, 188, 190
　building support team, 52
　confronting bullying, 138–140
　dealing with sibling rivalry, 82
　differing opinions of, 93–95
　dyslexia subgroups, 5, 7
　dyslexic, 87
　exercises used by (see exercises/
　　games)
　finding child's motivation,
　　160–164
　freedoms given by, 168–170,
　　226–227
　helicopter, 129
　helping with homework,
　　153–154
　helping with organizing,
　　102–103, 152–153
　helping with reading, 150–151
　hiding diagnosis, 24–25
　humor used by, 87–89, 94–95,
　　137–138
　managing family imbalances
　　84–85
　mantras by, 124–127, 166, 209
　modeling good habits, 114
　multisensory learning used
　　by, 152
　noticing soft signs of
　　dyslexia, 9–10

nurturing self-esteem (*see* self-esteem)
peers of, 226
processing diagnosis, 54
providing context for diagnosis, 45–47
reframing failures, 125–126, 128–129, 130, 165–168
requesting dyslexia evaluation, 23, 26, 30–31, 73–74
self-care for, 22, 54, 114, 117
sharing private evaluation with school, 36, 38
sharing resilience stories, 166–167
snowplow, 129
special relationship with child, 85–87
stress in, 86–87
study skills promoted by (*see* study skills/habits)
support from, 18–19, 21–22, 188–191
teenagers opening up to, 157–158, 181
well-being of, 54, 94
See also family/family team
peer pressure, 194
pen/pencil case, 102
perfection, 20–21, 80, 129
PhD program, 220
phoneme, 62
phonemic awareness exercises, 60–66, 150–151
phone numbers, memorizing, 69–70

phonetic approach, 48–49, 150–151
physical activity. *See* exercise (physical activity)
"Picnic Game," 71
planning, 99–102
    in middle school, 171–172
    for overlearning, 104
    See also organizing
pleasure books, 151
pleasure of learning, 164
positive self-talk, 214, 221
positive stress, 186
preferential seating, 50
prioritizing
    in high school, 184
    homework, 101
    learning concept of, 100
    in middle school, 171
Prior Written Notice (PWN), 29
processing issues
    evaluation of, 37
    with numbers, 6
    overlearning for, 104
    and time needs, 4
psychologists
    assisting with school lockers, 103
    choosing for evaluation, 33–36
    explaining diagnosis to children, 42–43
    questions for, 34–36
    style of, 36
punishments, 133

Index

questions
  for decision-making, 159, 168
  guided, 168
  by parents, prior to meetings, 52
  for psychologists, 34–36
Quizlet, 107–108
quizzes
  custom-generated, 17
  as study method, 107–108

reading
  along with audiobook, 106
  difficulties with, 11, 148–149
  encouraging, 110
  exercises for, 60–66
  fonts and, 148–149
  out loud, 148–149
  for pleasure, 151
  in summer breaks, 199
  teaching methods for, 48–49, 150–151
  See also books
receptive language, 4, 37
rehearsal, 108
relaxation techniques, 116
repetition, and reading, 56, 108, 151. *See also* rehearsal
resilience, 20, 51, 91, 98, 126, 142, 165, 168, 178, 211, 221, 225, 226, 228, 262
  developing, 4, 21, 128–129, 166
  as gift of dyslexia, 236
  in high school, 189
  mantras about, 125–126, 209
  sharing stories about, 166–167
  in young adults, 219

resistance
  to exercises, 56, 57–58, 73
  to gratitude practices, 135–136
  to learning, 11
  to working hard, 161
rewards
  children choosing, 128
  for effort, 91–92, 128, 167
  for exercises, 59
  in intrinsic motivation, 128
  self-rewards, 214
  social, 128
rhyming
  difficulties with, 11
  exercises for, 61, 62
  importance of, 62
ridicule, 137
right. *See* left and right
rights
  school evaluations and, 30–31
  terminology of, 27–29
room, organizing, 152–153, 186–187
Ross, Ivy, 115
Rush Hour (game), 67–68
Rush Hour Junior (game), 67–68

SAT/ACT preparation, 199, 204
scaffolding, 106, 154
scholarships, 16, 199
school(s)
  building support team in, 52
  bullying in, 138–140
  classroom settings in, 47–48
  confronting resistance in, 53
  evaluation in, 26–27, 30–32, 39, 42

Index

lack of enthusiasm for, 11
mantras about, 126
relaxing after, 100
resources of, 15–16
rights in, 27–29
rules about technology in, 109–110
sharing private evaluation with, 36, 38
teaching methods for reading, 48–49, 150–151
See also college/university; elementary school; high school; middle school
Science of Reading, 48–49, 150
screen time
  limits on, 111–112
  and sleep, 113
Section 504, 28
Section 504 Plan, 28
self-advocacy, 122–123, 182–183, 208
self-care
  for children, 110–113
  for parents, 22
  parents modeling, 114
self-comparisons, 212–213
self-consciousness, 124
self-deprecating humor, 88
self-discipline, 112
self-efficacy, 165–168
self-esteem, 119–144
  acknowledging effort and, 127–128
  autonomy in teenagers and, 121–122

  confronting bullying and, 138–140
  delivering mantras and, 124–127
  in dyslexic adults, 212, 232
  extracurricular activities and, 136–137, 155
  frustration tolerance and, 129, 130–131
  gratitude practices and helping others and, 135–136
  healing after failure and, 130
  humor and, 137–138
  interests and, 163
  nurturing independence and, 120–121
  parents listening and, 124
  preserving, 132–133
  reframing failure as opportunity and, 128–129
  self-advocacy and, 122–123
self-regulation, 131, 132–133
self-rewards, 214
self-sufficiency, 120
self-talk
  negative, 124
  positive, 214, 221
senses, and learning, 152
sequencing
  difficulties with, 12
  by dyslexic adults, 231
  in elementary school, 152–153
  exercises for, 69–71
  in high school, 185

Index

serotonin, 115
shame
   and acting out, 189
   bullying and, 139
   delayed diagnosis and, 8
   in dyslexic adults, 231–235
   exercises and, 57–58
   and motivation, 193, 196
siblings
   competition between, 82
   during exercises, 59
   grade disparities between, 92
   inclusion of, 90
   resentment in, 84
   support from, 83
sight words, 62
"Simon Says" (game), 66
sleep, 113
Smart Kids with LD, 33
smartpens, 50, 106, 172
snowplow parents, 129
social emotional functioning, evaluation of, 37–38
socializing, 116, 157, 213
social media, 111, 112
social rewards, 128
soft signs of dyslexia, 9–10, 66, 147
song, for memory, 70
sounds
   awareness of, 61
   beginning, 63–64
   blending, 64–65
   chunking, 66
   clear and distinct, 63
   ending, 64
   isolating, 65

spatial concepts, exercises for, 66–68
speaking. *See* expressive language
Specialized Education Teacher Support Services (SETSS), 30, 47
specific learning disorder, 6
spell check, 50, 172
spelling difficulties, 11
Spock, Benjamin, 9
sports. *See* exercise (physical activity)
Stixrud, William, 162
storytelling, learning by, 106
strengths
   of family members, 89
   mantras about, 125
   owning, with humor, 137–138
stress
   exercises and, 58
   in parents, 86–87
   positive, 186
stress relief. *See also* relaxation techniques
   breaks for, 14
   emotional support for, 188–191
   in high school, 185–188
   humor, 113
   in middle school, 175–177
study breaks. *See* breaks
study buddy, 107
study games, 107–108
study skills/habits, 99–118
   apps for, 17
   for balance and moderation, 110–113

Index

in college, 207, 208–209
effective study practices, 103–105, 173
in elementary school, 147–156
in high school, 183–185, 186–187
increasing attention with breaks, 114–115
learning styles, 105–107
"low-tech" breaks, 115–116
in middle school, 171–174
organizing lockers and desks, 103, 171, 185, 186–187
organizing room, 152–153, 186–187
organizing study materials, 102
organizing writing projects, 103, 171–172, 220
parents modeling, 114
study methods, 107–110
time-management practices, 99–102, 183–184
substance abuse, 191–192
success. *See* academic success
success stories, 15, 25, 45, 234–235
summer breaks, 198–199
supplemental evaluation, 31
support groups, 96, 150–151
supportive technology, 17–18
support team, 52

tantrums
  exercises and, 58
  frustration and, 131
tasks, 89
teachers
  assisting with writing projects, 103
  contacting, about bullying, 140
  dyslexia awareness of, 15
  dyslexia evaluation requested by, 30
  on dyslexia subgroups, 5, 7
  identifying early signs of dyslexia, 8
  meetings with (see meetings with teachers)
  support from, in high school, 197–198
  talking about exercises to, 58
  See also school(s)
teaching others (study method), 107
teasing, 87–89
technology
  and dysgraphia, 172
  and isolation, 190
  moderate use of, 111–112
  staying aware of, 109–110
  supportive, 17–18, 117, 173, 178, 227, 235–240
teenagers. *See* dyslexic teenagers
temporal organization
  defining, 12
  difficulties with, 12
  exercises for, 66–71, 153
  importance of, 153

Index

test(s)
  accommodations for, 49–50
  anxiety during, 104, 220
  for college application, 199, 204–205
  overlearning for, 104
  quizzes as preparation for, 107–108
test preparation apps, 17
thesis statement, 172
time
  needed for catch-up to classmates, 4, 225
  needed for homework, 101, 183–184
  needed for processing, 4, 154
  needed to heal, after failure, 130
  telling, 68
  during tests, 104
time and a half (accommodation), 49–50
time concepts
  exercises for, 68–71, 153
  importance of, 68–71, 153
  See also temporal organization
time management skills
  for college, 204–205, 207, 208–209
  for elementary school, 100–101
  for high school, 101, 183–184, 186
  learning, 99–102
  for middle school, 101, 171
  for weekends, 101

"time out," 133
to-do lists, 186
total immersion, 163
transcription devices, 17
tutor(s)
  for college preparation, 204–205
  finding, 53–54
  phonetic approach used by, 150
tutorials, 17
Twister (game), 66–67
two-syllable words, 66
typing notes, 108

understood.org, 29

video games, 187
visual cues
  for blending, 65, 107
  for laterality, 67
visual learning, 105
vocabulary, expanding, 60
volunteering, 198–199

weaknesses
  mantras about, 125
  owning, with humor, 137–138
week, days of, 70
weekends
  family bonding during, 187
  time management for, 101
well-being
  of dyslexic children, 72, 225
  exercise and, 113
  of parents, 54, 94

withdrawal
  exercises and, 58
  in teenagers, 191
words
  sight, 62
  two-syllable, 66
work
  in high school, 198
  transitioning to, 217, 219, 221–222
working memory, 13
work-life balance, 214

writing
  difficulties with, 11
  dysgraphia, 6, 172–173
  by dyslexic adults, 230
  notes, 108
  tips for, 172–173
writing projects, organizing, 103, 171–172, 220

Yale Center for Dyslexia & Creativity, 15
Your Brain on Art (Ross and Magsamen), 115